STRUCK

STRUCK
A Season on a Fire Lookout

Nancy Canyon

Sidekick Press
Bellingham, Washington

This memoir represents the author's recollection of her past. These true stories are faithfully composed based on memory, photographs, diary entries, and other supporting documents. Conversations between individuals are meant to reflect the essence, meaning, and spirit of the events described.

Published 2024
Printed in the United States of America
ISBN: 978-1-958808-31-3
LCCN: 2024906797

Sidekick Press
2950 Newmarket Street, Suite 101-329
Bellingham, Washington 98226
sidekickpress.com

Struck: A Season on a Fire Lookout

Cover design by Andrea Gabriel
Cover artwork by Nancy Canyon

Portions of this memoir have been previously published:
"Terrible Storm," *Able Muse*, 2012
"Anvil Cloud," *Adanna Literary Journal*, Issue #5, 2015
"Heat," *Labyrinth*, 2015
"Losing My Virginity," *Memory into Memoir*, 2017
"My Brother Visits," True Stories, Vol. II, 2019
"A Terrible Storm," True Stories, Vol. III, 2020

Dedicated to all those who help keep our forests safe.

Nature is always lovely, invincible, glad, whatever is done and suffered by her creatures. All scars she heals, whether in rocks or water or sky or hearts.
—*John of the Mountains: The Unpublished Journals of John Muir* (1938)

prologue

A wooden match ignites. Jack touches the flame to the joint he has finished rolling. He takes a deep drag, holding in the smoke until he can hold no longer. He releases it and hands the doobie to New York Tom. Tom caught a ride up to Corral Hill with a hunter earlier this morning. He is relieved to be away from his roommates, a couple from New York City who think they can make it in the backwoods as artists. Tom takes a drag and hands the joint to me.

"No," I say, waving it away. "We're on the clock."

He shrugs, looking replete as he hands the joint back to Jack. Beyond the two men, a small black cloud stains the otherwise cloudless sky of midday.

I ignore their stoned banter and step around Tom, raising high-powered binoculars to the single distant cloud. Magnified, there's no mistaking the small cumulus speeding toward us as anything but a thunderhead. Abruptly it arcs a blinding bolt to the ground.

I shout over the thunderclap, "We're gonna get hit," and make a dash for the bed.

Jack sprints after me, pointing to the green chair. "Sit there, Tom," he shouts, leaping onto the bed beside me.

Tom jumps into the Naugahyde chair with the glass insulators cupping each of the four wooden legs. And just like that, a blazing flash of light arcs to the lightning rod with a sonic-like boom. Struck!

"Fuck, fuck, fuck," Jack shouts.

"Shit," I say, falling back on the bed, heart pounding, eyes watering. I turn to look at Tom. A sheet of white, and mouth agape, he begins to laugh hysterically. I turn and look in the other direction, watching the little cloud barreling on, the forest quiet in its wake.

By now, the thunderhead is far past the tower, beyond the adjacent clear-cut to the north. No other clouds are in sight. I pull myself off the bed and stumble outside to check the grounding wire. The air is weighted with ozone. Prickling static tingles my scalp. On the west side of the tower, the copper wire—polished new-penny bright—buzzes like a yellow jacket. I turn on my heels and dash back inside, slamming the door behind me. "Crap, the wire's buzzing. It could have arced."

"Just harmless static," Jack says. "It'll dissipate soon."

"You sure?"

"Positive," he says and relights the joint, takes a hit, and hands it to Tom.

Tom continues to laugh. His tall frame remains folded into the green chair, knees to chin. He reaches a shaking hand toward Jack. He takes a long drag off the joint and noticeably relaxes.

Jack seems to know everything about electricity, so I decide, static it is. Still, I'm shaky, my heart pounding fast. I move weak-legged to the stove to put on a kettle of water. *When in doubt*, I think, *make a cup of tea!* I strike a match and light the propane burner, noticing beyond the blue propane flame, a thin curl of smoke rising between the evergreens down by the road. Pointing, I shout, "Fire!"

Things We Packed

Polarized sunglasses

Suntan lotion

Dr. Bronner's Pure-Castile soap

Deodorant: Secret, Right Guard

Cutoffs, halter tops, jeans, undies, jacket, Jack's cutoffs, T-shirts, underwear, socks, flip-flops, jacket

Bag balm for Jack's dry skin

Good books

Marijuana, rolling papers, pipe, matches

Beer-making supplies

Stone-ground whole-wheat flour

Fannie Farmer cookbook

Mixing bowl for bread dough

Sourdough starter from Mrs. Bard

Paper plates & paper towels

Guitar & music

.22 pistol & ammo, hunting knife

Dr. Scholl's sandals

SLR Minolta & film

Pillows & sleeping bags

Handmade boots

Sweater patterns, yarn, knitting needles, ruler

Sketch pad, pencils, kneaded eraser, ink pens, watercolors

Lip gloss, mirror, comb, brush, shears, contacts & solution

A bit of money

one

Arizona Vandervort grabs my hand with his big mitt and shakes it exuberantly. His smile is nearly as wide as the brim of his white cowboy hat, his snap shirt secure over a big belly, his fancy boots shuffling beneath his massive frame.

"Hi, I'm Nancy Nelson," I say in a quiet voice. I pull my hand away quickly and step backward.

Jack steps in front of me, beaming as he reaches out his right hand. "Jack Nelson. How's it going?" He draws in a breath and shakes Arizona's hand, grinning.

"Peachy!" our new fire-control boss says. "Just peachy!"

Arizona stands next to the information counter in the Clearwater Ranger District office. Behind him, a forest-green wall covered in shelving is alive with buzzing and blinking two-way radios. I hear a man's voice break with static. Arizona turns to listen. "You'll get used it," he says, swinging back toward us. He pushes paperwork across the counter to Jack. "It's Corral Hill Lookout Attendant," he says, pointing to a line asking for a job title. "Fill 'em out, then we'll get going."

I step up to the counter and take over, scribbling down the job title and our names while Arizona picks up the radio handset.

His voice is loud, making it hard for me to concentrate. Jack worries his mustache. I'm afraid he'll start nervous-sweating, so I work quickly, filling out his form as well as mine.

Arizona leaves the room and returns with a steaming cup of burnt coffee. He sips the hot liquid as he studies the map papering the back wall. "Your tower's here," he says, pointing. "Smack dab in the middle of the district." He guffaws. "Hell of a lot of territory to keep an eye on." He ambles over to the counter and jots something on a scrap of paper. "Directions to the tower in case we get separated. Some don't have a good sense of direction, ya know."

Jack and I smile at each other. We'd been all over the mountains above Priest Lake, picking huckleberries and exploring, sometimes camping in an abandoned hunter's cabin or in Jack's pup tent he'd thought to strap to the back of the motorcycle. Jack reads over the directions and nods slowly, his lips pressed in a straight line. "Isn't too far, then?"

"Not as the crow flies," Arizona says. "The snow went long this year." He grabs keys from a wall hook and flings open the door. "So, the roads ain't too good. Won't be no time before you're up there," he says, grinning, "and wishing you weren't, I 'spect." He waves a hand for us to follow. "Shutters just got bolted open, propane tank filled, and outhouse prepped, you'll be okay with the rest of the stuff that ain't done." He salutes us and is about to stride off across the parking lot when an International Scout pulls in, its engine shuts off, and a couple steps out.

"Arizona, sir," the man says.

"Well, hell's bells. If it ain't Jim and the little woman . . ."

"Hey," Nan says, her New York accent obvious. She gives Arizona a hug, steps back, and rests her hand on her pregnant belly, smiling.

"Well, would you look at that. Must be the water," Arizona quips. "Congratulations."

"Thanks!"

"Here, I want you to meet some folks. Jack and Nancy Nelson, our new Corral Hill lookout attendants."

We step forward and say hello to the couple. Jim extends his hand to Jack and Nan pulls me into a hug. I giggle, stepping back. "When are you expecting?" I say.

"October," she says. "Hey, good luck up there. We'll come visit."

"Sounds good," I say, turning to see Arizona heading for his truck. "We gotta run."

"Have fun," she calls after us. "We manned the tower last year. It's a blast."

Arizona hurries across the lot and climbs into a green USFS truck. Waving an arm out the driver's window, he signals for us to follow.

I settle into the passenger seat; Jude, our cat, is tucked under the bed covers in the back. Jack manhandles our bread truck camper—his Bridgestone strapped on back—out of the parking lot and onto the road. The caravan east is short, and just like that, we're leaving town.

"Not much to Grangeville," I say. "Hope Jim and Nan come for a visit. They seem nice."

"Why not?" Jack says, rounding the corner onto the highway.

Grangeville is thirty miles east of Lewiston on ID-13, and fifty miles south of I-90—the highway to home—and a little over fourteen miles to the turnoff to Corral Hill Lookout. The truck is used to negotiating rutted roads, but I worry that the old Ford will get stuck again, like it did on the way to Lost Lake on one of our overnight camping expeditions.

After we got married in May 1970, we worked the summer at Hill's Resort. That fall, we took off on our honeymoon road trip around the country in the bread truck camper. While on our road trip, we visited relatives in Illinois and Pennsylvania and ended up staying the winter in Boone, North Carolina, where our astrologer friend and her family lived. On our way home in the early spring of 1971, Jack's mother died suddenly from a brain aneurysm. We were in Texas when the state patrol pulled us over and told us to call home. We drove directly to the airport and flew home to Spokane, Washington.

When we arrived back in Spokane, Jack's father blamed us for his wife's death. She wouldn't have died if we'd been there. The pall of grief in the house was frightening. I wanted to be back on the road, but the funeral was the next day. And we needed to stay with Jack Sr. and Jack's little sister for a while before returning to Texas and resuming our road trip around the United States.

At the funeral, I spotted my stepdad across the cemetery. We hadn't seen each other since we left for our road trip the previous fall. Jack and I had married in the spring against his wishes. In fact, Mom told me later that he almost didn't come to our wedding. But he bought us our bread truck camper and seemingly had come to terms with my new status.

When I saw him across the lawn that day, I quickly turned away. He approached me from behind, calling out, "Nance!" I turned around. "I'm sorry for your loss," he said and leaned in to hug me. I remained unresponsive as he wrapped his arms around me, then stepped back, feeling uncomfortable.

"We gotta go," I said, and turned away.

After years of his sexual abuse, I realize that my ability to read my gut and react is diminished. I want to feel normal again. I want my power back. I want to feel comfortable being me.

I watch out the truck window, seeing the turnoff to the South Fork of the Clearwater and a sign marking the firefighters' camp. Arizona speeds past the turnoff, heading east on the highway, ditching our aged truck. A governor keeps our truck steady at forty miles per hour, except on a steep grade when Jack's foot hovers above the brake pedal, ready to rein her in if she begins to shake while picking up speed. But the trip to the tower is mostly uphill. The trek to Corral Hill will be slow going.

Jack wipes his forehead with the hem of his shirt. He is wearing flip-flops with socks as usual, his standard attire, along with blue jeans and a white T-shirt. I'm comfortable in an extra pair of his jeans and his mother's blue-green blouse that I confiscated after the funeral, per my new father-in-law's suggestion. I loved seeing Gladys in the green-flowered blouse. I run my hand down my sleeve as I watch the dry Idaho terrain careen past. I know we both miss her terribly, although Jack refuses to talk about it. He keeps his pain close, or maybe he just numbs it with beer and pot.

Just past a lush field of blue-violet flowers that Arizona later informs us are camas plants—one of the Native American staples—we turn south onto Lightning Creek Road, a level-though-potholed dirt road. The truck is doing fine until we hit washboard, which shakes the Ford so violently it nearly bounces off the grade onto a sloped shoulder. Powdery dust filters through cracks around the door and the partially open window. My eyes water and my contacts hurt so bad I can barely open my eyes.

"Crap!" I shout, hanging onto my seat. "The truck's coming apart."

"She's fine," Jack hollers, double-clutching down to granny gear, slowing the truck to a crawl. Arizona draws ahead and the snake of dust smothering us eases up a bit.

Nose covered with a hand and eyes tearing, I turn to Jack, whose face glistens with sweat. His fingers white-knuckle the oversized steering wheel, pull at his beard on a straightaway, grip the steering wheel again with both hands at the next tight corner.

In the distance, I spot the turnoff to Elk City Wagon Road and call out over the engine's rumble for Jack to follow. He takes my navigational advice and swings onto a country road dotted with range cattle. Just past a grassy field, a farm lazes in the sun. The farmer stops hoeing his vegetable garden and stands at attention, watching our green bread truck approach. He waves as we pass. We raise our hands, waving back through the dusty windshield.

Just beyond the farmer's place, the road narrows to a single-lane logging road. A few more switchbacks and we round a blind corner. Jack wrenches the wheel to the right, yanking the truck onto the shoulder just in time to avoid a heavily loaded logging truck barreling toward us. I gasp as it passes, jamming my feet into the floorboards. A cloud of dust envelops us. We wait for the fine powder and our hearts to settle before proceeding. Once we're moving again, Jack turns on the single-blade wiper. With each swipe, beige granules tumble down the glass in tiny rivulets.

Soon we catch sight of Arizona's green USFS truck not far ahead of us on the winding road. I recall him referring to the area as *the territory*. Beyond *the territory*, a rocky peak reaches hard into the cloudless blue sky: *Pilot Knob*, we heard our boss call it, *the tallest peak in the surrounding area*. The remote lookout sits on a pinnacle of stone.

Eventually, I catch a glimpse of our tower between the trees. Our home away from home: Corral Hill Lookout looming forty-five feet above the six-thousand-foot mountain. We turn left onto the final stretch of road, lumbering up the last steep approach to the tower. The truck rounds the corner and Jack parks next to Arizona's rig at the base of Corral Hill Lookout.

I sit there for a few minutes, basking in the surrealism of it all. We're on top of a mountain, ready to spend the summer as lookout attendants. I turn to Jack and laugh. "Far out!" I say.

"Fucking-A!" he says.

Laughing, I open the door to let Jude out. She leaps to the ground and runs for the brush.

Fire Tower Equipment

Osborne Firefinder
Strike log
Ridge graph
High-powered binoculars
Two-way radio
Lightning rod
Glass insulators
Outhouse
Lye
Shovel
Bucket
Pulaski
Hard hat
Work gloves
Water bladder
Igloo cooler
Telephone
Gas light, stove & fridge
Propane tank
Single bed
Picnic table
Green chair
Weather station
US flag

two

Winded, we greet Arizona inside the sixteen-by-sixteen-foot cabin perched forty-five feet in the air. Our new boss looks even larger standing inside the small space. His white cowboy hat is sweat-stained, his snap shirt threadbare, and his jeans and boots dusty. I'm surprised I didn't notice it earlier at the ranger station: his large silver belt buckle sporting his name, Arizona.

I walk around the cabin, touching the counters and heater, the picnic table and little gas stove. It's the same layout as the tower overlooking Priest Lake. The one we visited last summer. The one that inspired us to apply for this adventurous job.

Arizona launches into our duties. "This here is the Osborne Firefinder," he says. "You'll sight smokes and report the coordinates to Clearwater Ranger District." He shuffles around the firefinder, the central feature of the room, explaining how to determine the coordinates of a fire by calculating the distance of a fixed object and the degrees that the crosshairs line up with the object on the horizon.

I touch the metal ring circling a topographical map. It's etched with tiny lines marking 360 degrees, just like the degrees marking the outside edge of an astrology chart. A wire stretches across the center of the map, from the notch on one side to crosshairs on the other. On the north side of the firefinder cabinet is a two-way radio, on the west side, a couple of bookshelves. Opposite the bookshelves is a large black telephone mounted inside a nook. I lift the receiver and hold it to my ear. Nothing.

"Before two-way radios, fires got reported by phone," Arizona explains. "Phone wires are strung from limb to limb to town. Before that, homing pigeons delivered the bad news." Arizona wipes his forehead with a neckerchief and laughs.

I raise my eyebrows, perhaps looking worried, because the next thing Arizona says is, "Don't worry; you'll catch on."

He picks up the radio receiver. "Once the smoke is lined up, call in the coordinates. Give it a try." He waggles a finger at the firefinder, a teasing look in his eyes. "Go on!"

Holding my breath, I look through the peephole, spotting beyond the crosshairs a plume of industrial smoke rising above the prairie near the horizon. I study the wheel and say, "Ninety-three degrees and thirty minutes."

"Good. Now call it in." He picks up the handset and demonstrates in a booming voice, "Clearwater Ranger Station, this is Corral Hill Lookout, over."

Coming back, we hear: "Corral Hill, this is Clearwater Ranger Station, come in."

Arizona says, "Testing, one, two, three, over and out." Grinning, he hands me the receiver.

Heart pounding, I raise the handset to my mouth and in a tentative voice say, "Clearwater . . ."

"Ranger Station," Arizona mouths.

". . . Ranger Station . . ."

A woman answers. I open my mouth to relay coordinates but am suddenly tongue-tied. I feel my face flushing, sweat blooming across my upper lip. I wipe it away with the back of my hand.

Arizona prompts: "This is Corral Hill Lookout calling, come in."

I repeat his words, keeping my eyes lowered, pretending to study the map.

He laughs heartily, grabbing the handset away from me to sign off. Next, he flips open the logbook where we are to record the daily weather. "Listen to the forecast each morning on the weather radio. Write it down here." Turning, he points to the south. "There's the weather station. Go on down early and record the dewpoint, wind speed, and temperature. And raise the flag. Take it back down each evening."

We turn to the window. Beyond the far end of the parking lot lies a fenced area with a flagpole where an American flag flaps in the breeze. The fenced area to the left of the flag is the weather station. I look over at Jack. He's standing with arms crossed over his chest, forehead beaded with sweat, nodding at everything Arizona says. I imagine he's thinking that as a good hippie, there will be no flag worship on his watch.

"Cool," I say.

Arizona taps a pad of graph paper, pointing out multiple lines connecting a series of dots. "Each line's a ridge, closest to farthest from the tower. Locate all the ridges you can see," he says, "and graph them here. Use the firefinder and draw the ridge contours by calculating multiple coordinates. Knowing the degrees of the ridges helps the firefighters find a smoke after dark." Arizona goes on about nighttime bushwhacking and the men's boiling blood when they can't find the smoke. "Don't let 'em down, kids."

We nod, looking to each other for support. My stomach drops, thinking it will take forever to map all the ridges I see in the distance.

Arizona pulls out the strike log where we're to record lightning bolts during a storm. I raise my eyebrows, looking around the room to distract myself from an imagined thunderstorm hammering the territory. To the left of the entrance is a row of low cupboards. At the end of the counter sits a small propane refrigerator and stove;

a green easy chair with glass insulators cupping each of its four wooden legs is pushed up against the south wall. Another counter spans the space between the southwest corner and the bed. To the north of the firefinder, pushed up against a bank of windows, is a green picnic table and a single bench.

My eyes turn to the stained twin mattress flopped on a wooden box with two drawers built beneath. The first thing I will do is cover the dirty, striped ticking with an orange-flowered sheet. Then I'll spread the quilt I made from sewing scraps over the top. We'll open our sleeping bags over the quilt until summer comes full on, as the nights up here will be freezing cold for a bit longer.

All the cupboards and walls and the picnic table are painted the same color as Arizona's truck: forest-service green. The countertops are unfinished Masonite. Behind the door sits a tall aluminum Igloo watercooler with a spigot that Arizona says to fill with water from the spring at the bottom of the hill. He says, "Take the bladder bag down to the creek and haul five gallons of water back up top. If you can lift it, that is." He laughs heartily. "Maybe just half-full. Or let Nance carry it!"

I raise my eyebrows. Like that's going to happen.

Arizona chuckles. "Corral Hill opens when the snow melts off. We close her back up in the fall when she socks in. The guys bolt the shutters down so the glass don't break out in high winds. I'll let ya know when it's time to come down." He goes on, "There's a trapdoor at the top of the stairs. Gets secured with a padlock over winter. You can shut it at night if you want."

He takes off his hat and runs a big hand over his balding head. "Gal up there on Pilot Knob," he says, pointing to the east, "hauls in supplies on her back. That and a pack train." He snorts. "She's one tough cookie. You can radio her and other towers after dark for company, unless there's a fire, of course. Use a different frequency if you do."

Arizona goes on about food and propane deliveries. The outhouse over the bank to the west needs a sprinkle of lye after each use. And most importantly, he tells us where to sit during a lightning storm. "Stay away from metal objects—never stand between the stove and firefinder, lightning can arc between the two metal objects. That green chair's got glass insulators. Sit there or on the bed," he says. "May be okay to sit on the picnic table." He laughs a big belly laugh as he turns to leave the tower. "Guess you'll find out."

He clicks his tongue and turns back to us. "Oh, and the telephone," he says, pointing at the big black pay phone-like apparatus. "She works every once in a great while. Line's been repaired, but I guess the guys missed a break somewhere between here and the farmer's house. If it works, call your folks collect. They'll be glad to hear from you."

The tower shakes as our boss clomps down the stairs. After a few minutes, we see a plume of dust lift between the trees. I take a seat in the green chair and look over at Jack. He squints with concentration, his lips pinched in a straight line. Bending, he grabs the bladder bag from behind the Igloo cooler and fusses with it until he gets the cap open. "Think I'll wander down the road," he says. "You comin'?"

I nod, but for some reason I'm unable to get up from the green chair where I sit staring out the window. Road dust drifts from Arizona's truck across the forest. Beyond that, the faded prairie bakes in the noonday sun. Everything is silent.

Finally, I push myself up out of the green chair and walk to the door. My legs feel shaky as I step out onto the catwalk. Everything is vast, green, milky, chilly. I hold onto the rail as I descend the tower. Once on the ground, I walk slowly down the road next to Jack.

Kinnikinnick, thimbleberry, and huckleberry bushes line either side of the steep gravel road. The brush reminds me of Priest

Lake. I recall walking back to Luby Bay campground one night, following the lakeshore path from Hill's Resort where we worked. Finding our way in the dark through heat and blackness was like being blind. Jack walked ahead of me that night, his hand reaching back to hold mine. I clung to him, feeling the roughness of his fingers comfort me in the dark. But even with his guidance, I tripped over tree roots and scratched my legs on the low brush. I was terrified, though of what I'm not sure. The darkness didn't last, of course. In no time we were back at the campground. Jack struck a match and lit the lantern. We crawled inside our tent.

I'm still afraid. I reach over and take Jack's hand as we walk down the road away from the tower. I can't shake the feeling that something catastrophic might happen. I've heard of mad men who cut through the sides of tents with knives and hack the inhabitants to bits with chainsaws or axes. Just last summer, our friend's campsite was torn up by a marauding grizzly who ate all the food and, in its fury, destroyed their tent, cooler, and backpacks. Who knows what we'll encounter here on Corral Hill. When I think this way, my fright is like that pitch-black night on the trail. We're completely blind to what comes next.

Hermit and Swainson's thrushes sing sweetly. I recognize their calls—the same birds sing at Priest Lake. This comforts me a bit, but still my stomach tumbles. Finally, I get up enough courage to speak. "Jack," I say, "I'm scared."

He laughs. "Of what?"

"I don't know . . . we're so isolated here. And vulnerable."

He squeezes my hand. "If someone's on the road, we'll see their headlights and hear their engine long before they reach the tower. We can close the trapdoor at the top of the stairs if need be. And, we have a Pulaski, remember. Pick on one end, axe on the other."

"The twenty-two," I say. "We should keep it in the tower." I hang my head, wanting to believe we're safe. Already the shadows are lengthening, turning dead trees and brush into lurching animal shapes. For a moment I think I see a black bear, then I realize it's just a charred stump. At last, we reach the spring and Jack splashes the black rubber bag into the shallow water, pushing it under the surface to fill. I stand close, watching the clear water pour into the opening until the bag fills and settles to the bottom of the icy stream. He caps it and tugs it up onto his back, wrestling the dripping straps over his shoulders. Once Jack is steady on his feet, we begin the long trek back uphill.

"Better boil it," I say. "We don't want to take chances, like Dave, the dishwasher at Hill's Resort. He was poisoned by pesticide. They sprayed the forest to kill the gypsy moth and the pesticide washed into the streams when it rained. People and animals got sick from drinking the water. Not that boiling water will protect us from pesticides and fire retardants, but it will keep us from getting giardia."

Jack grumbles beneath the enormous weight of the bladder bag. He's always grumbling these days. And he's pushy, which is why I moved out of my parents' house as soon as I turned eighteen. He said, "If you don't move out, I'll leave you behind." I knew he didn't mean it; he was just feeling desperate for us to get on with our life together. Still, I wasn't ready to live on my own. I couldn't even balance a checkbook. The only work I'd ever done was for my stepdad and for the Hills. Still, I found a place in Browne's Addition, a studio apartment with silverfish shuffling back into dark corners when I switched on the light in the middle of the night. Jack continued to live at home while I lay awake in my new apartment, terrified of being alone but happy to be away from my stepdad's midnight visits.

I shiver in the growing dusk. "When we get back to the tower, I'm making us a cup of tea." Sipping a cup of hot Lipton always makes me feel better.

Jack climbs steadily, groaning beneath the thirty-five pounds of water sloshing in a rubber pack strapped to his back. I follow him up the stairs with bags of groceries from the truck, stepping up the four flights to the cabin. My load is heavy, but not as heavy as Jack's.

I set the grocery bags on the counter and help him wrestle the bladder bag off his back, spilling most of the water into the Igloo cooler and some onto the wooden floor.

"Bladder bags," Arizona had said, "have multiple purposes. Hang them up in the sun and you've got a solar heated shower. Attach a hose and you can douse coals along the perimeter of a burn. Firefighters call them piss bags."

When we're done with the water, Jack opens two beers, handing me one. We clunk bottles together, toasting a job well done. We step outside and round the catwalk to the west side of the tower. There, we take in the view of Camas Prairie and surrounding mountains: Buffalo Hump, the Gospels, and the Seven Devils. Everything is immense and milky and beginning to glow pink. Wind rustles the treetops, ravens croak, and what I imagine to be static buzzes down forty-five feet of copper wire into the ground far below.

Jack heads back inside. He opens cupboards, checks out the attic crawlspace, opens and closes the drawers beneath the bed, and turns to the Osborne Firefinder. I lean over the south railing and take in our new environment: the weather station, the American flag, the roof of our avocado-green bread truck, the outhouse in the woods to the west, and the giant propane tank to the east.

The vastness of our surroundings stirs my jittering stomach. I know I'll hear my own heart pounding when I crawl under the covers tonight. That and coyotes, owls, wind, and perhaps distant thunder. And of course, Jack's steady breathing as he sleeps next to me, which will make me feel safer, I guess.

Turning, I grab the railing and shuffle back inside. My legs feel shaky. We've been hauling supplies up four flights of stairs ever since we arrived. The bedding is packed in the green plastic garbage can that Jack has positioned behind the green chair. He wants to learn to strike beer, proofing the yeast for each batch of home brew that he'll ferment in the giant garbage can.

"What if Arizona looks inside?"

"He won't," he says.

I reply to Jack's rebellious shrug. "He might!"

"No matter what, it'll be filled with green beer soon. Maybe it won't taste like Coors, but we'll have plenty of beer to drink all summer. I'll mix it up tomorrow."

"Far out!" I say, and let it go.

The rest of the beer supplies remain in the bread truck: bottles, caps, a metal capping device, ale yeast, hops, malt, fine corn sugar made especially for brewing, and a glass meter that looks like a candy thermometer and floats on top of the brown liquid, measuring the alcohol content during fermentation.

The .22 pistol and the hunting knife remain below for now, though I remind Jack that I'd prefer they resided in the tower. Last summer, when we practiced living off the land during the week and working at Hill's Resort on weekends, we learned how to set traps for catching meals. The wilderness survival book I bought explained that both rabbit and fish will kill you if that's all you eat. Meat is too lean to exist on for long. We were able to catch a lot of fish, but we never trapped a rabbit. The book said fat was necessary for survival. "I wish we'd brought chickens along," I say. "Then we could have fried egg sandwiches for breakfast every day."

We won't starve, of course. We can make food runs to town. Jack says he could survive on beer, beef jerky, green olives, nuts and seeds, and a couple of glasses of milk a day. I have no interest in what he calls the Caveman Diet. Ever since I turned twenty, a tiny roll of fat has begun thickening my middle. Though the drinking age in Idaho is twenty, I'm being careful with my beer consumption and try not to scarf down every delicious morsel in sight after a few hits of weed. I'm like Mother, though; I don't want to gain an extra ounce of weight. Jack, however, never gains an ounce no matter how much he eats or drinks.

I look around the cabin at the green walls, cupboards, and picnic table. I don't mind green, but the orange-flowered sheets I remove from a box make me feel happy. Jack continues to make trips up and down the stairs, stacking boxes of clothes and books in the corner. I flap a sheet over the stained mattress just as he walks in with another load of stuff. Groaning, he wipes his forehead with the back of his hand. He squints at the sun, lowered enough in the sky to shine directly through the mullioned windows into our eyes. "It's too hot," he says.

I push the window open. A breeze flutters in. "Are you finished bringing up boxes?"

He grumbles something in reply as I fluff out the handmade quilt, tucking it in at the bottom of the mattress. Pillows fluffed and resting at the head of the bed next to the north window make the cabin look like home. "Where's Jude?"

"Down below," Jack says. He picks up the binoculars and walks out the door, waving a hand for me to follow. "Come on. Let's check it out."

I step outside, holding onto the rail as I walk around the catwalk. Funny, I'm in no danger of falling through; it's just that forty-five feet in the air is pretty far off the ground. All this open air around me feels precarious.

"Look," he says, handing me the high-powered binoculars. He shields his eyes from the sun and points west.

I lift the bins, focusing on vapor trails carving bright orange streaks through the peach-colored horizon. "Far out," I say, amazed at the mountains, patchwork prairie, and view of an uninterrupted sunset. "All I did was fill out the application and mail it in. And now we're here."

Jack nods. "Surprised the shit out of Squeak."

I recall Squeak's—Jack's nickname for his father—disappointed face when he heard we were leaving town again. Seemed he'd just gotten used to having us around after we returned from our honeymoon road trip. Sure, we'd been away at Priest Lake for the winter, but he'd visited us there, staying in Cabin #10—the same cabin he and Jack's mother always stayed in. Now that Jack's mother is gone, it's just Jack's sister, Diane, and their dog, Pokey, to keep Jack Sr. company. Diane's still young, but clearly her dad dotes on her. She doesn't seem to need a female to mother her, though I help when I can. Jack's dad says that Gladys was his only true love. He will never marry again.

While we stayed with him after the funeral, we slept in Jack's old bedroom. I took Diane shopping and bought her a training bra. Back home, I coached her as to what to expect when her period came and helped her with sewing projects too. Diane didn't seem to mind Squeak giving her female advice—like how many days made up a female cycle. I cringe at the memory of my stepdad asking me if I was on my period. I snapped at him once, saying, "It's none of your business." He just laughed, then gave me a stern look.

But Squeak was easygoing with Diane, much more so than with his son, whom he was always ordering around: *cut your hair, don't be late, change your clothes, get a job, don't get married, and keep that thing in your pants*. Finally, Squeak pronounced us *in love*. "I didn't believe you were at first," he said. "What a relief to know that you truly are in love."

We do love each other. In fact, Jack often says he loves me. I asked him once what he meant by that. "But why do you love me," I'd said, feeling particularly unlovable that day.

His eyes closed halfway. He had a goofy look on his face when he said, "I love you, I want you, I need you. And I'm horny." He shrugged his shoulders, grinning. "I just do."

I raise the binoculars and study the prairie that's beginning to burn the same color as the flowered sheets on our bed. The flag down at the weather station flaps in a breeze. The sound is steady and comforting. The clink of the metal clasp on the end of the rope reminds me of boats rocking on the wake at Hill's marina. I know Jack will give it the old college try, though raising and lowering the flag may only last a week or two before he gives up.

We're not anti-American, but kids are dying in Vietnam and we're not happy about it. My thoughts turn to my brother, who returned from the war with shrapnel in his head and arm. He's always wiggling a foot, scratching at his forearm, and chain-smoking Camels. He doesn't have much to say, even when I try to get stuff out of him. He just raises his eyebrows and grins, making a grunting noise as he takes another drag off his cigarette. Jack was lucky, I mean, he didn't even get called up for a physical. It was a miracle that he got such a high number in the draft: 364.

I hand the binoculars back to Jack and grab hold of the railing as I walk back inside. The first time we climbed the steps to a lookout tower to take in the vast landscape beyond was when we lived at Luby Bay campground. We survived on mashed potatoes and occasional hamburgers purchased with refunds on pop bottles gleaned from campground garbage cans. Life just out of high school was exciting, unplanned, and wild with sex and pot parties, which always seemed to be accompanied by Led Zeppelin or Pink Floyd blaring from an eight-track tape player. We finagled rides, because the car situation was always iffy, especially since most of our friends drove junkers. When my brother got back from Nam, my stepdad took away my Chevy and gave it to my brother, Bruce. Did he think I had enough money to buy a car? All I had was what I earned at his office. Then he called me into work and chewed me out for being late the day after he took away my car, saying he'd get someone else, someone he could depend upon. I held back tears as I walked out of his office. I never went back.

I step inside the cabin, my innards tangled from thinking about my stepdad. One day, while I was dressed to sell Avon door to door, he showed up at my apartment. I stood back as I always do with him—careful not to make eye contact. They say that about wolves, you know. You challenge them by meeting their gaze and if you turn and run, you're considered prey. I kept my eyes lowered, but when my ears started to buzz over my racing heart, I could no longer think straight. It was then that I wanted to be anywhere else but near my stepdad, Dick.

Dick said he came by my apartment house to see how I was doing. I was making a call on the hall pay phone to Avon central, who explained to me why my order was late—because I'd called it in late. Which meant the woman who ordered sunscreen, shampoo, and other sundries for her vacation at the lake wouldn't receive her goods on time. She was going to be super pissed at me. Perhaps I *was* undependable, like Dick suggested I was.

"Nance, Nancerella."

I pull myself back to the present moment. "What?" I say, blinking to take in my surroundings again.

"Didn't you hear me? I was calling you."

"Sorry, I was thinking about my stepdad."

"We bought pickles, right? I want a deluxe burger."

I smile. "You love pickles almost as much as you love beef jerky. And beer. We've got an extra treat tonight—potato chips," I say. "Where's the rest of the kitchen stuff?"

Jack points to the corner. I remove the fry pan from a box and take a pound of hamburger out of the fridge. The meat case in Grangeville's only grocery store is like the one in Spokane where Mom used to order pot roasts and ground round from Joe the Butcher—all that bright red beef pressed in neat rows in a long, polished case. And they make their own jerky at the Grangeville store. We bought a whole pound. Pretty expensive, but we saved a bit of money last summer while working at the resort. A better and more consistent job than selling Avon, which I quit doing altogether once we were married. I did, however, keep the tiny lipstick samples—creamy, colorful, and sweet-smelling—applying Perky Pink while looking in the truck's rearview mirror.

I flatten burgers and sprinkle salt and pepper and garlic powder over them, returning the spices to the countertop. The mayonnaise and mustard are in the fridge, along with other perishable items we bought at the store before we hit the ranger station. And we have plates: Melmac, yes, pale green dinnerware, stored in the cupboard beneath the counter. Mismatched tableware and a few cooking utensils are kept in the only kitchen drawer in the cabin just above the dinnerware.

I light the stove with a stick match and soon the tower is full of cooking smells and circling flies. We won't go to the store very often because the truck is too cumbersome to take up and down the logging road on a regular basis. Jack can ride the motorcycle to town and fill his backpack with groceries. He'll be able to carry quite a bit in the backpack and more items strapped to the back fender of the bike. Then, later, perhaps we can buy an International Scout so I can drive to town for supplies, laundry, company, and hot showers.

In the night, wind shakes the tower, rattling the grounding wire and squeaking an open window. I wake, sitting up in time to see flashes of pink lightning flicker across the horizon. "Shit," I say, my stomach lurching. I nudge Jack to wake him.

"Leave me alone," he groans, rolling toward the window, drawing his knees up like a child.

"Lightning," I say, shaking him harder. "There's lightning."

He bolts upright, rubbing his sleep-crusted eyes. "Where?" he groans.

"Over there." I grab his hand and lift it in the darkness toward the storm. "There," I say, "to the southwest." Just then, lightning flashes cloud to cloud.

"Fuck!"

"What should we do?"

"Chill out!" Jack's voice sounds sleepy in the darkness. "Arizona says we're safe on the bed."

"We don't know that for sure. Remember, he was laughing when he said it!"

"He was laughing about the picnic table being lightning-safe. They've never lost a lookout attendant. I asked him," he said, leaning heavily against me, swinging a leg over mine.

"What are you doing?" I say, my voice sounding shrill in a cabin surrounded by windows. "We're not doing . . ."

"What? Heck no! I'm going outside to watch the storm." He rolled over me.

"Don't leave!" I say, wrapping my arms around his bare torso. I break his momentum and hold on, smelling his salty sweat, his skin sticky from our day of moving. "Stay, please."

Laughing, he leans in and kisses me. He kicks a leg out to the side and steps down to the floor. "Out of here," he says, and dashes out onto the catwalk in his birthday suit.

I tug the covers around me, propping up the pillows for a better view. Jude jumps onto the bed, nudging me with her head. I pet her, cooing, "Good kitty." She begins to purr.

Several bolts of lightning flash across the horizon, each burst illuminating the surrounding cumulonimbus clouds, brightening the sky to sunset pink. The pit of my stomach grips. I have a sudden urge to go down to the outhouse. *No way. There could be bears in the woods.* I breathe, trying to relax my bowels so I don't have to use the outhouse in the dark, in a lightning storm, no less.

With each blaze of lightning, booming thunder rolls along distant hills. I think of my childhood bedroom on Audubon Street. Storms rumbled through Spokane frequently, lighting my second-floor room with brilliant flashes, followed by claps of thunder so loud they rattled the thin windowpanes of my little sister's and my room. We counted the seconds between flash and thunderclap to see how many miles off the storm was, estimating how long it would take to reach us and how scared or relieved we should be.

A bright bolt arcs sideways, splitting into two jetting curves that arc toward the horizon. Jack lets out a joyful yelp. A clap of thunder follows. I think of the strike log Arizona asked us to keep. I'd have to get up and light the gas lamp, use the firefinder to mark down the degrees of each bolt, missing the next strike while lining up the one just prior.

"Shit," I breathe. "I won't do it." I feel a pang of guilt but remember the motto: *Never trust the Man*—which includes Arizona.

The storm follows the mountains, circling east. It looks like it might peter out as it passes. I feel relief and disappointment at the same time. An occasional distant bolt flashes to the southeast in the direction of Pilot Knob. Thunder echoes. As I watch, the time between bolts lessens. Eventually, the thundershower is nothing more than a cloudy night sky.

Jack returns to the cabin, revved up and blubbering about the "fucking" lightning. He climbs into bed, his back chilly against my front. I wrap an arm around him and hold on tight.

He reaches around to pat my hip. "Fucking far out, Nancerella!"

Jude readjusts her nest at our feet. Soon both cat and man are asleep. I, however, lie there feeling restless, my body pinging, worried that an errant bolt will find its way through the window at any moment.

The next morning, we get a call on the radio from Arizona. Jack jumps to answer it. "It's early," Arizona says, "sorry." He goes on to coach us on checking the forest closely after an electrical storm. Even a small storm, like the one that rolled through last night, is cause for concern. Arizona's words rattle around in my mind: *It only takes one hot strike to start a wildfire. Cold strikes aren't as dangerous because they aren't continuous current.* I turn down the flame under the camp coffee pot, which boils vigorously into the glass knob.

Eggs sizzle in the frying pan. I'm easing the spatula under the edge of one when Jack runs inside shrieking, "Fire." He points out a thin column of smoke rising south of the tower. He pulls at his mustache as he turns the firefinder, lining up the smoke with the crosshairs. Soon, he's calling in coordinates, wiping sweat from his forehead with the sleeve of his T-shirt as he stammers over the radio.

Signed off now, he takes a seat at the picnic table, continuing to pull nervously at his mustache. I set two plates of eggs and white toast on the table and sit down next to him. "You did good," I say. "I'm terrified of the radio. It's a bummer, I know." I smile weakly, touching his bicep. "Thanks for taking our first smoke."

"You're next," he says, flexing his bicep as my fingertips graze his arm. "Arizona says the fire crew may need our help with locating the correct ridge. He wants to know if we have the ridge map started."

"We just got here yesterday," I say, sipping my coffee. "Later."

We finish our breakfast in silence. While I wash dishes in a plastic tub and stack them on a towel spread across the counter to dry, Jack heads back outside to monitor the fire. He lifts the high-powered binoculars to the territory. We brought along our Kmart pair, the ones we take hiking, which work fine, but they don't have near the power of the large pair. They're light compared to the forest-service issue—huge black things that weigh more than my SLR camera. I dry my hands and follow.

Jack grumbles about the possibility of another smoke and suggests we remain vigilant. He doesn't mention mixing up the home brew. Instead, he studies the territory like a hawk. His lips tighten beneath weighty binocs pressed hard over his eyes. They're leveled on the clear-cuts and treed parcels traversing the ridge that jumped with lightning last night.

Back inside, I lay a sheet of graph paper on the firefinder and line up a ridgetop in the crosshairs. I think I know which ridge the firefighters are searching. I start at one end and work toward the other. It's time-consuming, sighting random points, the definition between ridges blending with cast shadows and mist. I mark the graph paper one dot at a time, moving the firefinder in increments, making tiny pencil marks for each coordinate. Once I begin drawing a line between the dots, the shape of the ridge will begin to appear.

As time passes, a widening column of smoke rises into the pristine morning air. I work until lunchtime, getting down enough information to satisfy the firefighters, should they radio us. Jack handles our other chores, copying down the weather forecast from the radio. Despite his dyslexia, he finishes his notes. He starts for the door, kissing my cheek on his way out, and heads down to the weather station to gather details of the current weather conditions.

I've had enough mapping of ridges for one day. Sighing, I make tea and sandwiches and sit in the green chair. I flip through the photo album while I wait for Jack to return for lunch. I have postcards and journal entries of our adventures, both driving around the United States and other events, all arranged in an album that Jack's dad gave me. One of my favorite pictures is of Jack and me embracing on the catwalk of Hughes Ridge Lookout. In the photo, Priest Lake is a tiny, shining speck in the distance. I remember our friend, Alice, using her Instamatic to take the shot. I touch the photo of us and smile. We were madly in love then.

I hear Jack's footsteps on the stairs, the tower shaking lightly as he climbs. I used to throw my arms around his neck all the time, kissing him with abandon. I don't do that as often now that we're married. I'm not sure why. I look up from the photo album. "Lunch?"

He nods, his serious look securely in place. He grabs his sandwich and walks back out onto the catwalk, lifting the big black binoculars with his right hand, taking a bite of peanut butter and jelly with his left.

I can no longer see his angular chin—his beard has grown shaggy and his fine brown hair has grown long. I remember the day we drove up a mountain to Hughes Ridge, the first lookout we ever climbed in order to see the view. We'd piled into Alice's Dodge Dart and wound our way far into the hills, navigating the dusty, rutted road, parking in the shade at the trailhead miles from the resort. The four of us: our astrologer friend Alice, her sister Christie, and Jack and I hiked the steep trail, huffing our way to the top of the hill. Horseflies and mosquitoes buzzed around us. By the time we reached the tower, we were sweaty, winded, and covered in bites.

We climbed the forty-five-foot tower, crowding inside the small cabin at the top. The wild-eyed fire attendant didn't move from the corner where he sat on a counter looking worried. His tentative expression still comes to mind—not shy, possibly more startled than anything—maybe from living alone for weeks at a time. Soon he was talking our heads off, explaining his job as a lookout and pointing out landmarks. Far in the distance, we could see Priest Lake where we'd left from earlier that morning. Lush forest and grassy clearings dotted with wildflowers surrounded us, much the same as our tower here on Corral Hill.

The Hughes Ridge attendant pointed out the weather station, the watering hole, and the outhouse. Christie said she needed to run down and check it out, since she was on her period. She didn't seem to mind talking about *the curse* in mixed company, nor digging through her daypack for a tampon. I was embarrassed by her candidness. I mean, I once freaked out when I thought I'd lost a tampon on the trail to the outhouse at a friend's lake cabin. As it turned out, it'd slipped through a hole in my pocket and was hidden safely inside the lining of my jacket. Thank goodness!

I run a finger over the photo again. I'm wearing a green sleeveless top. He's wearing his usual white T-shirt and raggedy cutoff jeans. My arms wrap around his neck, his hands wrap around my waist, pressing tightly against my back. We'd just graduated high school: Class of '69. I'd moved into my studio apartment in Browne's Addition and we'd married the following spring at Riverside State Park. It wasn't that long ago, really, but a lot has happened since the wedding: the trip around the United States, Jack's mother's death, my parents' divorce, and my miscarriage. And, of course, there was my stepdad's estrangement from me. I rest my hand on my abdomen. It's a habit of mine, checking, I guess, for the baby that's no longer there.

I remember a heated argument in our family room one night. My stepdad belittling Jack, telling him that he didn't make me happy. And Jack defending himself, saying that the reason I was crying was because of the things Dick had done to me. Jack knew about the abuse, but didn't say, "because of the abuse." So many terrible situations my stepdad has created. I don't remember how we resolved the argument, but it sticks in my mind like tar in a pipe.

I do remember my stepdad calling me one morning after I'd moved into my studio apartment. He said he didn't want me dating Jack. I said, "But I love Jack, just like you love Mother." My words hung in an awkward silence, me imagining him on the other end of the line wanting to tell me something. Finally, I said, "You do love Mother, don't you?" More silence. After I hung up the receiver, I understood that his motivation all along had been to have me, not my mother, as his sexual partner. I felt sick to my stomach knowing the truth of his intent.

Now that I'm out from under his perverse rule, I do what I want. Sometimes I even wander around naked. And I swear like a sailor—my mother's saying. I never wear nylons, which my parents insisted on whenever I wore a dress. And my hair, well, it's no longer cut short like Mother always believed it should be. I see in the Hughes Ridge photo how Mr. French's cut had grown out a bit. And I see how much in love I am. That's something to be happy about, I know that for sure.

I put the book down and proceed to eat my lunch. While chewing a bite of peanut butter sandwich, Jack continues scanning the territory. The fire crew's been active on the radio all morning. We've heard bits of conversation now and then. They are in the area of the strike tree. I imagine them crashing through the woods, bladder bags on their backs, Pulaskis and hard hats and steel-toed boots marking them as firefighters. Though the weather isn't overly warm, they are sweating hard and slapping the backs of their necks. The black flies are fucking thick.

I wonder how many lookout attendants and firefighters are born in the sign of Aries. Alice said a fire lookout job would be a good job for me since I'm a fire sign. And it would be a good one for an Aquarius, which Jack is, since Uranus rules Aquarius. Alice says that the planet Uranus is the ruler of lightning. It's a lot to understand, but I bought a little astrology book and am making my way slowly through it.

The Hughes Ridge Lookout attendant said he'd gone a couple of weeks without a single visitor. He laughed a little too loudly and his mannerisms were awkward, like he hadn't spoken in a very long time. When he invited us to stay over, we wholeheartedly accepted. He said the four of us could sleep in the tiny floor space surrounding the firefinder, sharing the extra sleeping bags and blankets stored in the attic. For dinner, we handed around the snacks we'd brought along. He said he'd shot a bobcat with his .22 rifle and offered us a taste, spearing a chunk of meat with the knife tip from inside a big pot. Everyone groaned at the idea, but I tasted it, because I didn't want him to feel bad. It tasted okay, but now I feel terrible that I ate a bite of a wildcat.

I know what it feels like to be overly eager for company. You can go stir-crazy spending loads of time alone. Already my heart feels like it wants to reach through my chest and grab someone, anyone, just to talk to them. But there's no one here to grab hold of except Jack, of course. It's a bummer, in a way. One thing I know for sure, I wouldn't be able to do this job alone like the girl up the hill manning Pilot Knob.

Though longing for company is one thing, having so much wide-open time is exhilarating. There's plenty of time to read a book or write in my journal, knit, photograph plants, play cards, pick at the guitar, draw, and have sex. It's far out, really. But of course, all of it happens between rounds of searching for fires. No one cares if we hang out, since everything we do here is done to pass the time, as long as we keep watch over the forest, that is. Like now, Jack is back inside picking "Blackbird" on his guitar and I'm taking a turn searching the territory.

The column of smoke is leaning southwest now, perhaps due to the surface air heating up the forest this afternoon. I move the binoculars to revisit the mountains beyond: Buffalo Hump, the Gospels, Mount Baldy, and Seven Devils. And to the north, a huge clear-cut that pisses us off each time we turn the bins in that direction. Some argue that the forest is safer with clear-cuts. Lightning striking a too-thick understory can burn tens of thousands of acres a year. Loggers cut and haul the timber out. Mostly though, I think it's the loggers preaching the benefits of clear-cuts, since it provides them with a livelihood. The rest of us get the leftovers: scabbed land piled high with rusty slash—a tinderbox come mid-July. And it's butt-ugly too.

The firefighters call on the radio. I turn to see Jack through the window setting his guitar aside to grab the mic. I hear some mumbling and Jack hangs up the receiver.

"They found it," he shouts. "We can chill out now."

Tonight, we'll have Hormel chili for dinner. When I was growing up, we ate canned chili topped with onions and cheese most Sunday evenings. Mom served this dish in the fall when football season started and my grandparents came over to watch the game with us. The men drank Hamm's and ate potato chips while the teams moved the football down the field. During halftime, Mom and Grandma served chili with saltines and sometimes a piledhigh platter of hot dogs dripping with catsup and mustard. We scarfed it down!

It's not fall, but an early summer chill that feels like fall is in the air. The chili's heating on the stove. The burner hisses, as does the radio. While I stir the chili, Jack picks up the handset and talks to one of the firefighters. I hear the firefighter complaining that it wouldn't have taken so long to find the fire if we'd completed the ridge map sooner.

"They're pissed at us? We just got here!" I say under my breath. Having people pissed at me is a real downer. Really, we haven't been here long enough for me to complete this graph.

I dish up two steaming bowls of chili and set them on the table. Jack grabs a beer and takes a seat. He crushes saltines between his palms, stirring the crackers into the beans and meat until it's so thick a spoon stands upright in the middle. It's what he does with clam chowder too and his dad's homemade chili. Squeak makes his chili with finely diced sirloin. He brags about his chili, relaying the recipe to me every time he cooks it: steak, beans, onions, tomato sauce, and lots of chili powder. It really is good. And spicy hot!

We drank tall glasses of cold milk with the chili Mom served. The spicy version made my stepdad sweat profusely. Out came his handkerchief to wipe his face and forehead. Jack's that way too, sweating easily. Though, his sweating comes more from nerves than from hot food, which is embarrassing as all get out. Like when Arizona first showed us how to do things around the tower, Jack kept bending forward and wiping his face with the tail of his T-shirt.

He generally extinguishes spicy food with cold milk, which will be hard to come by on the tower. I can see now that it will be difficult to get to town for supplies. Jack rode his motorcycle down to the turnoff yesterday and scored a quart of raw milk from the farmer. The same one who waved at us on our maiden voyage into the Clearwater National Forest. The raw milk was a real treat.

I take a seat at the picnic table and butter a cracker. I don't crush them into my soup like Jack does. In my family, we smear crackers with butter. In fact, my brother and sister and I once made a waitress furious when we asked for extra butter for our crackers, scattering a mess of greasy crumbs all over the table while our parents drank highballs in the bar. They were always stopping off somewhere for a drink during our Sunday drives. We were left to fend for ourselves in the café area—if there was one—or in the car.

Jack takes several swallows of beer and turns to me, smiling. He has hazel eyes with a patch of brown in his left iris. I heard that means his internal organs are not doing well. I always notice eyes, especially blue ones. I have since I was a young girl. Once I told my seventh-grade best friend, Jody, that her eyes looked like snowflakes, white lace patterns against a gray background. Jack's irises aren't lacy like that. Mostly, they're narrow and sharply fo-cused. And hard to read, though I most always bet on "pissed-off" as their meaning. Right now, he looks playful. He pushes aside his chili bowl and raises his arm to wrestle me. I take a swig of his beer and settle into an arm-wrestling match.

I don't understand why men think women are weaker and have less endurance (and brains) than they do. I give him a sly grin. The truth is some of us are bigger and stronger. And many of us are smarter. I like to prove my strength by taking Jack up on his arm-wrestling challenges. I grab hold of his hand, anchoring my elbow next to his. I stick with his resistance until my bicep burns like a hot pepper, finally relaxing my muscles and falling over on the table. We both laugh hysterically. He leans over and kisses me. I kiss him back.

Really, all the women on Mom's side of the family have great arms. Lulu, my grandmother, was not a petite lass, nor were any of the other female McKees seen pictured in the old photo album. But all of them had good-looking arms that I'm sure would cut the mustard.

Even though everyone has always said that I have a good pitching arm, Jack is forever flexing his muscles, proving his strength over mine. I can't touch him without a bicep or a deltoid contracting into a finely honed swell. Clearly, he's the stronger of the two of us, at least physically. I'm emotionally stronger, I'd bet my heart on it any day.

His real name is John Morse Nelson. Morse is after Samuel F. B. Morse, several greats back, his grandfather and the inventor of the Morse code. We don't tap out messages to the district when trees burst into flames from a lightning strike, just pick up the radio and call in the coordinates. And, I don't know the code for SOS, for if I did, I'd have used it when my stepdad was molesting me. Of course, he made me promise not to tell. That's how it goes with abuse.

I did manage to speak up to my best friend, Jody, saying, *Dad loves me too much, way more than my sister. I don't know what to do.*

This was my code for what was really happening; he was forcing me to be still while he fondled and kissed me whenever he got me alone. I guess my code wasn't clear enough to get my friend to warn her parents about what was happening, so I could be saved from the terrible situation. When I presented my problem, she said sweetly, "Why don't you talk to him about it? I always talk to my dad."

I didn't know how to talk to Dick about it—I still don't. Instead, I suffered from bouts of extreme fear, anxiety, and weepy depression, afraid I'd be caught alone at home or at work by my stepfather. I tried to outsmart him, but he was crafty and caught me often.

At sixteen, I learned that he wasn't my birth father. After my mother told me that the man I called Daddy had adopted me when I was three, I decided that I didn't have to do anything he ordered me to do. It was then that I quit calling him Dad. I recall a family visit to the Manor, a senior home where my step-grandparents lived. My stepdad was bossing me around as usual when my grandmother interrupted him. She said, "Richard, do you have to be so hard on her?" "Richard," aka Dick, looked embarrassed and eased up on me.

That evening, I touched my grandmother's hand while walking down the hall heading downstairs to dinner at the Manor. It seemed I might have an ally at last, though I was never candid with her about my plight.

It's hard to talk about someone molesting you, but Jack's willing to listen. And some of his buddies know my secret too. Dr. Gilmore, the minister of our church, knows. My mother knows. And one of these days, I'll tell my sister—and find out if it happened to her as well.

We've finished dinner and clean dishes dry on a dish towel spread over the counter. I take a seat on the bed and open the book *To Kill a Mockingbird*. Jack takes a seat in the green chair, closes his eyes, and leans his head back to listen. Because of his dyslexia, I sometimes read to him from one of my favorite books. Tonight, Scout and her brother are attacked in the dark while walking home from the school play. Boo Radley saves them from the villain.

My voice has begun to crack and it's getting a little too dark to read. I close the book and turn to the sky. There's a band of yellow light illuminating the sky beneath a bank of dark clouds hovering above the horizon. It's like a Maxfield Parrish painting, which we both love. I think about bed, wondering if Jack will want to have sex tonight. Or maybe we'll just get stoned and fall asleep. Or maybe some strange natural phenomena will take place out there in the universe, like a fireball speeding past. Next month, on the Fourth of July, maybe we'll see fireworks bursting like sparkling flowers over the prairie.

When I was young, we watched fireworks on the Fourth at Natatorium Park in Spokane. The sonic booms—or whatever those bright flashes and deep bass rumbles vibrating our chests were called—seemed to wake up an old, pissy anger resting in me like a sleeping dragon. I got so grumpy with all the cheat grass stuck in my socks and the extreme summer heat that Mom said, "Knock off the whining, Missy, or I'll wind up my right arm."

So, when it was time to leave and I climbed in the car, shoving my sister because she was leaning too close to me, I was really in trouble. My stepdad got into the act and threatened that I'd be spending the next day in my room if I didn't *straighten up and fly right*. I wasn't mad at my sister, more like I was mad at what was happening in the bedroom when no one was around. Sometimes the abuse I was experiencing made me act like I was on the edge of crazy about to step into some great pit of despair that would swallow me whole. Really, I didn't know how to act as I moved through childhood carrying a secret as big as a forest.

Jack lights up a pipeful of weed and hands it to me. I take a hit, holding it in like he taught me. When I first met him, I'd never smoked marijuana, just drank some beer, sips of wine, sometimes a taste of a cordial with my parents' friends, and champagne on New Year's Eve. And the occasional phenobarb, of course, that Mom would give me for a headache—but no pot.

I remember when Jack asked, "What do you think about marijuana?"

"I don't know," I said. "I've never really thought about it."

I had, however, thought about LSD. The lady leading our church Sunday school class told us how dangerous acid was. She said we could be slipped a drop without even knowing it, because it was odorless and tasteless. Then we'd go crazy and get hauled away in a straitjacket.

I felt baffled over her plea to never take LSD. It all seemed so strange to me, drugs and altered states of consciousness, as it didn't take much for me to be out there flying through the stars, seeing auras, or dreaming of aliens landing spaceships in the backyard. Not much at all.

Wasted, Jack and I grin at each other for a while. Finally, we decide to go to bed. He kisses me gently around my mouth, then on the mouth, moving slowly down to my throat and then down my neck. Eventually, we get down to what matters. When we're finished making love, I hope beyond hope that we've made a baby tonight—the one thing I want most in life.

The next morning, we are up early, with breakfast finished and the weather stats copied in the logbook by eight. We're out on the catwalk perusing the territory when we hear a vehicle coming up the road. Hanging back from the railing, we look east to where we know we'll first spot the rig. If it's our boss, we'll have to race around the tower, cleaning up paraphernalia from last night. If it's a visitor, it won't matter as much—but still, I'll probably straighten up a bit. When a muddy mint-green rig rounds the curve, I recognize it as a forest service truck. We run back inside and in a flurry, toss empty beer cans into the cupboard and straighten the bed, hiding the pot in the bottom drawer beneath it. We step back out onto the catwalk and act casual as hell.

Three sooty guys climb out of the cab. The men stretch their legs and stomp off their steel-toed boots. One looks up, sees me standing there, and waves. In return, I flip him the peace sign. Jack runs down the stairs to greet them. I duck back inside and put on a pot of coffee.

Their voices are deep and parched. I overhear one guy saying they finally found the fire, then worked all night digging a back-fire, rendering it cold around three in the morning.

My stomach jumps, imagining that the unfinished graph Arizona asked me to draw was the cause of the crew working all night. I hope my hospitality makes up for my inadequacy as a fire lookout attendant. My job is to report fires but now, I'm guessing, it is to help firefighters find the smokes too.

I imagine them walking inside, dropping hunks of dirt in the shape of cleats across the cabin floor. I'm learning to deal with dirt here on the tower. Soot is the worst of all smudges to clean up. Soot takes soap and hot water to wash off. In the old-mare house—the roof was like a swaybacked horse—where we lived when I was pregnant, I washed soot from the trash burner and the burn barrel, both from my hands and from my soul. I can't help feeling guilty for losing Jason Breeze—yes, I'm sure my fetus was a boy.

Yes, I think as I measure coffee grounds into the aluminum pot, *soot from my soul*. I light the flame, recalling lighting the cookstove inside the tent while visiting Vancouver Island. I shouldn't have eaten those mussels at Qualicum Beach. The split-ting headache that came on afterward could have been the cause for losing the baby. Or perhaps the baby would have lived if I had gone to the doctor sooner. Whatever the case, I feel responsible.

The minister at the Greek Orthodox church our high school church group visited said the reason women have painful periods and miscarriages is because we're sinners. I remember the girls eyeing each other nervously: monthly cramps from eating an apple? Bummer! I didn't buy that theory then, and I don't now. I have bad cramps because my uterus is tipped back, that's what the doctor said. Not because Eve ate from the tree of knowledge of good and evil. How ridiculous is that?

The universe will provide, Dr. Gilmore had said, leaning back in an overstuffed chair, his feet propped on his wooden desk in the plush church office. Across from him, dressed in raggedy jeans and T-shirts, Jack and I slouched in comfortable armchairs. Having a mother raised in Virginia meant I wasn't to leave the house unless I was dressed *all proper-like*. This included stockings for most occasions. As soon as I moved into my own apartment, I gave all that up. No one tells me to *act like a lady* these days. I look down at my clothing—what a mess. I do wish I looked a little prettier for these firefighters. I fluff my hair and put on lip gloss. It's the least I can do for our guests.

When we first met Dr. Gilmore, he called us into his office under the guise of getting to know the members of his new congregation. We learned later that Mom had asked him to talk to us, as she was worried sick that we were on drugs.

After we told him that our parents had resisted us moving away from home, he said, "Often, enlightenment requires a journey through the dark night of the soul. The hard things in life are what wake us up."

That's when I told him that my stepdad had been molesting me. He said without hesitation, "Tell your mother."

As coffee percolates on the stove, two sooty guys smelling of smoke and BO enter the cabin. They say hello and drop heavily onto the green picnic bench. They say that their buddy is down below using the latrine. I hate the outhouse more than anything, always fearing a spider lurks beneath the seat ready to crawl onto my butt and bite me. It hasn't happened yet; still, I can never truly relax while sitting on the two-seater. And now, after a stranger has sat on my commode, I will definitely feel weird the next time I use it.

I try not to think about the outhouse and offer the two men coffee.

"Not now," one firefighter says. Then he changes his mind. "On second thought," he says, and stretches out a dirty hand to take the coffee cup I hold out. I get a strong whiff of BO and woodsmoke and hold my breath, taking a step back as soon as the cup is secure in his dirty hand.

"We couldn't find the smoke," he says. "You didn't give us the right coordinates."

"Oh?" I say and am about to add *sorry I didn't have the ridge map finished* when Jack takes his wrestler's stance, arms crossed over his chest.

"The coordinates were correct," he says. "It was dark out there. You missed the road."

The firefighter looks like he might jump up and take Jack on. I step between them, offering RyKrisp crackers, since I haven't gotten around to baking cookies yet. "Thanks," he says, taking a couple and chomping them down.

"You guys must be hungry and tired."

They grumble in agreement. The guy farthest from Jack adjusts a red suspender that has fallen off his sooty shoulder. He says, "We found it anyway. It's out now, that's all that counts. Better finish the ridge map before the next storm rolls through. It helps when we're hunting for a smoke in the dark."

Jack mumbles something and I escape outside to where the vibes are less combative. The sky is the color of deadly nightshade. I stare off into the distance, remembering Dr. Gilmore teaching us how to see auras. We worked with his ideas, staring at each other in a dimly lit room, trying to see the faint outline around each other's bodies. He also taught us how to relax into a trance and gather information from the other side. He saw my real father camping on a river island. It was after Mother took my brother and me away from our home in Portland to our grandparents' house in Pocatello, Idaho. My real father had an angry aura that my mother couldn't tolerate.

With auras in mind, I return to the lookout to check out the firefighters' auras. Just like Dr. Gilmore taught me, I relax my gaze, taking them in. Their auras are red, of course. And so is Jack's. Hotheads, the whole mess of them, including my real father, who beat my brother. That's the reason Mother gave me for taking us away from him all those years ago.

I hear boots on the stairs. I bend to pick up clumps of dirt and soot that have fallen from the men's lug soles. When I look up again, the third firefighter enters the cabin. He looks just like Paul Newman. A blush warms my cheeks. I turn quickly away.

Paul says something about my smile and I spill coffee on the counter as I pour him a cup. I wipe up the drips with a dish rag and, giggling the whole damn time, hand him coffee. Our fingers touch as he takes the cup.

Jack frowns at me and I look away, struggling with the same tight feeling inside that I used to have when I lived at home, only now it's my husband who's setting high standards for my behavior. Perhaps Jack is jealous like my stepdad used to be.

The three firefighters finish their coffee and clean us out of RyKrisp. They've been up all night, fighting fire, but who hasn't? I mean, there's always a fire somewhere to put out. Dr. Gilmore says I shouldn't think that way. He says we create with our thoughts and that I should think as though everyone can hear my thoughts. "Tell your mother about the abuse," he repeated.

The night I finally did, Mother sat there at the dining room table, rolling the glowing tip of her cigarette around a glass ashtray. She said quietly, "I suspected as much."

That's when I started to cry.

For some reason, I couldn't say to my mother, *Why the hell didn't you stop him?* Instead, I just sat there, tears spilling down my face. I cried and cried, unable to speak the rest of the time we sat together. She reached out and patted my hand. I pulled it away and, finally, got up and left the room.

I stop listening to the testosterone-laden firefighters stinking of smoke and BO and gaze out the window. Storm clouds build on the horizon. Maybe we'll have these guys back in a day or so. I feel excited about seeing the one who looks like Paul Newman again. Next time, I'll bake cookies.

I snap out of it. Smiling, I offer to put on another pot of coffee. Miss Suzy Homemaker living in the remote woods of Idaho, wearing jeans and T-shirts, acting like—*I know, I know, I know*—a flirty Bond girl. But they're *out of here*, as Jack likes to say, and I'm left feeling embarrassed and lonely all over again.

The sound of multiple boots descending the stairs is thunderous and tremors the tower. The truck roars to life. Scrapes of gravel, then shovels and Pulaski axes rattle in the bed, clanking as they bounce down the rutted road. Jack sucks his breath through his teeth, crossing his arms over his chest. "What the hell was that all about?"

I turn my back to him. Of course, I know he's pissed. I flirted right in front of him. Not that he doesn't flirt right in front of me: there was his high school locker partner, and the girl in his piss-ant college class he nearly flunked, and the bikini-clad chicks at Priest Lake rumbling up in their daddies' Chris-Crafts, asking Jack to fill their tanks with stinky gasoline. I've seen those sly eyes checking out their tits, his mischievous mouth, his twitching tongue running along his upper lip. Oh, that devilish smile could entice anyone! It did me.

"You should talk," I say, under my breath, spooning coffee into the basket and lighting the burner for another pot, whether he wants any or not.

Sometimes the day is perfectly calm. There are no planes, no wind, and no birds chirping. During the calm, a wildfire could be following roots beneath the ground, burning for weeks before igniting to blaze above ground.

Up here, we watch for smoke, which might not be visible if the lightning strike catches fuel beneath the ground—a bigger fire waiting to happen once ignited by oxygen-rich air. Arizona says the roots can burn for a long, long time. Sometimes, a hole is left beneath the forest floor and the ground collapses into the space where a root once grew.

Above or below the surface, fire calls to me. I have stared into beach fires, campfires, and the blazing logs on the resort lobby grate. I've stared at Pres-to-Logs burning in my family's fireplace, pine sticks burning in the kitchen trash burner, and the converted oil stove in the living room of the green old-mare house.

Starting fires is a gift of mine. Once, I caught my hair on fire when I leaned too close to a candle while looking through a microscope. My sister yelled, "Nancy! Your hair." Smelling my burning hair, I shook my head hard and the fire went out. Then the bottom of a fry pan heated too hot and, *poof*, blue flames leapt around the base of the pan and just as quickly died out. When I was in high school, my stepdad put a plastic platter in the oven and turned the meat on warm, accidentally turning the dial to broil. Shortly that plate was popping and melting and making a horrible stink, filling the kitchen with toxic smoke. He grabbed the platter with a potholder, ran it outside, and flung it into the backyard. We went out for hamburgers that night.

When we were kids, my sister pushed the pink-flowered, up-holstered stool that had belonged to Auntie Van up against the wall heater and shortly it began to smoke. Just as it was about to burst into flames, Dick arrived, smothering the scorch with a towel. Then there was Auntie Neil who flicked the lighter she'd just filled with fluid. The whole thing whooshed, curling a blue flame around her hand, the cigarette, and the lighter. Fortunately, she wasn't injured and continued to smoke like a fiend.

My mother and brother also smoke like fiends. My grandpa too. Dick used to smoke cigarettes, although now he smokes a pipe. The smell of vanilla-flavored tobacco is pleasant, unlike his personality.

When Jack and I were first together I caught my apartment on fire. We'd made several mushroom-shaped candles on the beach at Priest Lake. Though I'd blown out the one I was burning, the string-wick reignited, starting my kitchen table on fire, the curtains, and then the kitchen wall.

We weren't gone long, just down the stairs visiting our friend, Michael. I'd blown out the candle before we closed the door. Time passed, and I began to smell smoke. When I got to the top of the stairs, smoke was pouring out from beneath my apartment door. Jack ran in and my cat ran out. While he tried to douse the blazing kitchen table with water tossed from drinking glasses I'd left sitting in the sink, the firemen passed me on the stairs. I was bawling my eyes out and hugging my cat, Jude, who wasn't harmed, thank goodness. Inside, the firemen hosed down the wall and tossed the burning table out the second-story window in a volley of sparks. All that remained was the charred stink and blackened walls. We painted and sanded, but in the end, I had to move into a different apartment to get away from the smell.

And then there's the stoner's popping match and an ember jumping to the front of a down coat, burning a tiny hole in rip-stop nylon. There's the ash from the end of a joint that falls on the bed quilt. The blazing *zapper* that burns, dripping bits of flaming plastic to the ground below. The zapping noise it makes as it melts into the night is fascinating to ripped partygoers.

Even though fireworks can cause house fires and forest fires, people set them off anyway. The summer after I graduated, I dropped a burning sparkler on the hull of a Chris-Craft that belonged to a friend's father. My friend wasn't supposed to use the expensive boat that night and got in a lot of trouble for damaging it. All of which was my fault!

I've heard of fires set for money. It's hard to believe that someone would set a mountain on fire so they could get hired to fight it—but it happened at Priest Lake across from where Jack and I lived at the resort. After we got married, the caretaker told us the story about how he'd watched the forest being systematically lit, beginning at the top of the mountain, all the way down to the bottom of the mountain.

Taxpayers' money is spent on planes hauling water, fire retardant, pay for pilots and firefighters, and lookout attendants like us who report the fires. Everyone has heard of firefighters getting trapped in a rocky canyon where heat and smoke did them in. There are firewalkers who can step barefoot across glowing coals, but trapped firefighters can't walk through flames, not without injury or death. And then, of course, there are widows and widowers who need money to survive after the firefighter's demise.

We stand on the catwalk watching heat rise off the forest. The eerie, high-pitched cry of a red-tailed hawk sends a shiver down my spine. There's something frightening about high heat. It just keeps going and going, melting pavement, scorching skin, and damaging paint jobs.

When it comes down to it, there isn't much sense in fire; I mean, besides heating our houses, people don't need to smoke and fires for recreation aren't essential. However, if you've ever sat around a campfire in the dark without logs leaping with flames, you know that a burn ban can be a real bummer. No marshmallows blazing away on the ends of charred sticks, no flame to keep away the chill. No smoke to ward off mosquitoes. No flickering flames to mesmerize the mind.

Thoughts about Marriage

Marriage builds community.

You get married for life.

Why marry when the goods are free?

Shotgun weddings are a no-no.

Get engaged before leaving high school.

If your guy's heading off to Nam, marry him first.

A big wedding is a sign of prestige.

It's sinful to divorce.

Marry as many times as you like, like Zsa Zsa Gabor.

Stay married for the kids.

Men can stray, women cannot.

A wife's duty is to her husband.

A husband is in charge of his family.

You don't want to end up as an old maid.

three

Contrary to popular belief, marriage isn't bliss. We've manned Corral Hill Lookout for nearly a month now and already Jack and I have had several blowout fights. I blame our irritability on the close quarters—sixteen by sixteen feet—but even before we got married, he pissed me off to no end, his sexual demands reminiscent of Dick's constant advances. Once I lobbed an unhusked coconut at Jack's head. Another time I threw a glass of water, including the glass, at him. There was the alarm clock, the hardback novel, and one of his steel-toed boots. Fortunately for me (because he's retaliatory) and I guess for him too, I always missed.

I say "fortunately," because once I slapped him across the face as he relentlessly taunted me during a silly game of cards. "You're a loser! Loser! Ha, ha, ha!"

My hand shot out. *Slap!*

Whack! He struck me back.

That was the night we stayed with his grandmother in Hanover, Pennsylvania, on our honeymoon road trip. She wanted me to go with her to her monthly knitting circle so she could show off her "new granddaughter."

Jack said, "No, your place is with me."

I was upset by the disappointment in her face—clearly, it wasn't the answer she'd hoped for. She smiled and walked out the lace-curtained door and down the street to her knitting party in her granny pumps.

Most of the time we're passionately in love, but right now, as I hang my head over the railing so Jack can help me wash my hair, I feel hateful. My hair is soaped and dripping with Dr. Bronner's. My eyes are pinched shut as I wait for him to pour heated stream-water over my head. "Come on, man," I plead. "I'm dizzy, and there's soap in my eyes."

"Quit your pissing and moaning," he growls, splashing the pan of water over my sudsy hair.

Soaked and spitting, I take advantage of the deluge that continues to drown me. Water runs into my mouth and down my neck as it rinses my hair clean. Gasping, I sputter as I jump back.

Jack laughs, pointing at my small chest. "Wet shirt contest."

I look down. My nipples stand alert beneath the soaked T-shirt. "Fuck you," I say, wiping water from my eyes, pushing my hair out of my face.

I smell like mint, the magic of Dr. Bronner's peppermint soap. It's not only the bracing smell, it's the mysterious quotes written on the label that make us ponder life and the fine doctor's meaning. "Love is like a willful bird, do you want It?" Dr. Bronner says. "It flies away! Yet, when you least expect Its bliss, It turns around and It's here to stay!"

I love Jack, but he can be a real asshole. I fly off the handle at him, but not far and not for long. Still, he isn't smiling when he tosses me the towel and that makes me feel even more alone than I already feel. I wrap my head, turban-style. "Now it's your turn to suds up."

"Fuck it!" he says, hurrying inside to grab his stash. He comes up empty-handed and strides past me, heading below to the truck where he often hides a little weed. It's one of the things he can't seem to do without.

"Whatever," I say, and stomp inside. I know he's out of weed. He will tear apart the truck looking for a roach or a few flakes of grass. He gets weird when either his stash of pot or beer runs out, turning sour, flat, and ornery. I try to shake off the bad vibes, combing out my hair before the mirror hanging over the Igloo cooler. No matter how I comb this bad haircut or scrunch it into curls, it still looks terrible. At least I now feel and smell clean.

A mutual friend whom I ran into one night at a downtown Spokane bar told me that my usual beautician and her close friend had moved to California. *Rose is nothing but a goddamned alcoholic,* she'd said. I felt so disappointed. I loved Rose's haircuts. I'd like to find her and tell her not to waste her time or talent. It's selfish of me, I know, but she can cut a shag like nobody's business. I hope she comes back to Spokane someday. And I hope she stops drinking. That goes for Jack, as well. I'm afraid he has a problem.

Every time something super bad happens, like the miscarriage, I get a haircut. I'm not sure why. Maybe it's the only thing I really have any control over. I once read in a dream-symbol book that hair represents power. Well, powerful this cut is not. I'll never go back to the girl in Lincoln Heights. I walk away from the mirror, feeling disgusted with myself and with my marriage.

Mom claimed that we're short-haired people, always deciding when Mr. French would cut my hair, until I started high school and decided for myself, that is. Then I found a beautician who said I had perfect features, like Elizabeth Taylor. I switched to him. What a relief not to sit through another one of Mr. French's torturous haircuts, the skin of my scalp pinching between the teeth of his metal clips. He'd resection my hair and clip it again, pinching my scalp in a different place. I never spoke up, unable to advocate for myself—a silence I learned from Dick's unrelenting intimidation. I just sat there, tears filling my eyes. *Urgh!*

I wore my hair short all through high school—the English in-fluence—Beatles-esque. I rolled it nightly in curlers, ratting it in the morning before school and combing it into a smooth bob, which I sprayed heavily with Aqua Net. I coveted the long, smooth 'dos of the '60s, the slick, ironed hair that all the skinny girls wore. Twiggy girls with their kohl-outlined eyes. I tried hair straighteners and juice-can rollers, but nothing much worked to smooth my curls. Now it's the '70s and my hair has a mind of its own, my bangs curling up across my forehead. But like Rosemary once said, "One thing about hair, it continues to grow."

I open a can of chicken noodle soup and dump the contents in a pan. The strike of a match and a blue propane flame erupts beneath the pot, bringing the soup quickly to a boil. The salty smell of Campbell's fills the cabin. I grab from the cupboard two green Melmac bowls. The tower begins to shake. Jack steps onto the catwalk, his untied logger boots looking far too big on his cutoff-clad legs. His face looks triumphant.

"Find some?" I say as I fill bowls with steaming soup and set them on the picnic table.

Jack nods, pinching the brown-stained relic between the teeth of a roach clip. He lights a wooden match on the back of his cut-offs and raises the clip to his lips, touching flame to paper. There's no time to bogart the joint as the miniscule roach vaporizes prac-tically before he inhales.

Slowly releasing his breath, he drops to the picnic bench and begins crumbling soda crackers into his soup. His eyes are nar-rowed, and his demeanor is fuzzy. Maybe he did get a tiny bit high. He turns the soup into a thick, salty mush and digs in. Relief floods me. He is so much easier to get along with when he's a little bit high.

Dick was the same—saltines in chili and oyster crackers in clam chowder. And, of course, bourbon to settle him down when he arrived home from work. The last meal we ate together . . . well,

I can't really recall the last meal we shared. Perhaps it was the family dinner after my parents separated. Dick finalized things by saying he no longer loved Mother. He put my mother and sister out of our family home and quit speaking to my brother and me, because we were his stepchildren.

Mom said that my stepdad couldn't afford to keep the house in the divorce. The tiny apartment she rented on busy 37th Street got robbed shortly after she and my sister moved in. In the last letter I received from her, she said the thief used Vise Grips to crimp the doorknob and break in. She lost the cameo Bruce brought her from Japan while on R&R from Vietnam. Many other pieces of expensive jewelry Dick had given her throughout the years were pilfered. Fortunately, she was wearing her diamond wedding rings still, even though their divorce was final months earlier.

Jack finishes his soup and sits staring out the window, idly stroking his beard. I'm sure he's ingested little THC, but he has that settled, sleepy look, which is good. I'll take over watching for fires once I finish the dishes. I imagine Smokey Bear leaning on his shovel at the entrance to the Clearwater Ranger Station, the arrow pointing to the blue area, indicating the fire danger remains low. After all, it is only May, and the forest is still damp.

All last night, heat lightning flashed along the horizon. We watched the clouds building, a flickering glow illuminating each negative charge attracting its positive charge—cloud-to-cloud lightning. Nothing came of the storm. It was pretty though, all those jagged bolts forking through banks of pink cumulonimbus clouds, lighting up their insides like Christmas lights buried in angel hair.

Jack says heat lightning is like dry lightning, coming through with no rain. He happily explains direct current and alternating current and how generating current from turbines and other sources works. I just say, "I don't really understand electricity, because I can't see it. Now, lightning, that I understand. That I can see."

"Sometime we should try a Kate and Randy," he says, out of the blue.

"What's that?"

"Unravel the end of an extension cord and plug it in, hold hands and one of us touches the wires just as we come."

"Sex isn't worth killing yourself over," I say, rolling my eyes. "That's insane."

"It'd be fun," he says and smiles his sexy grin, touching the tip of his tongue to his upper lip.

I return his smile. The battle is over, thank goodness. "It's not going to happen," I say, getting up from the picnic table to put on a kettle of water.

I step out onto the catwalk, binoculars in hand, eager to get a closer view of the dusky clouds. In the distance I see a sliver of sunlight lighting the horizon. The building clouds don't look threatening, but they're approaching anyway. Lowering the binoculars, I fluff my bad haircut with my fingers and suddenly turn toward the road. I can't hear a car, nor do I see dust, but I sense company is on its way. I turn to the cabin and call through the open window, "We're going to have company."

"You and your premonitions," he calls back.

"You'll see," I say, seeing in my mind's eye a white truck driving up the mountain.

Even though we live way the hell out in the middle of nowhere, people do stop by. Visitors usually sightsee during the day. The smart ones are home fixing dinner or drinking a cool one by nightfall. The roads are so winding and narrow. Lots of animals run out from the shadows: bears, deer, coyotes, and skunks. And an occasional vehicle—poachers, perhaps—driving from the opposite direction, headlights blinding.

Jack points out a plume of dust lit by orange rays of sunset. "How'd you know?"

"I feel it," I say, touching my stomach, then my forehead. "And see it in my mind's eye." Soon, we'll hear a vehicle groaning as it wends back and forth along mountain switchbacks. For some reason, I'm suddenly imagining chainsaw massacres and other grisly events. After that camping fiasco I heard about on the news a couple of years back, I've never felt completely safe alone in the woods. But here we are alone in the woods. And we aren't entirely safe, I'm sure.

Jack pulls out the last beer chilling in our propane refrigerator. He rocks off the cap with a US Forest Service can opener and takes a seat on the bed. "We need to make a food run," he says.

"Uh-huh," I say, watching him press his thin lips to the rim of the bottle and tip it back. He lowers the bottle and turns to look toward the plume. I can tell by the way he's sitting on the edge of the bed, nursing the bottle of beer instead of guzzling it down, that he feels apprehensive about the possibility of visitors at this hour.

I follow his gaze. We both see the flash of headlights through the trees and know we have about twenty minutes before the truck turns onto the final stretch of road.

I turn off the propane stove, leaving the water I've been heating to cool enough to wash the dishes. Taking a seat on the bed next to Jack, I listen carefully for the truck. It is time for *Green Acres*, which we hate to miss, but neither of us moves to switch on the radio and tune in the local TV station. Instead, we sit perfectly still, listening for the vehicle rolling up the final grade to the parking lot.

More than once I listened for my stepfather's footsteps on the stairs. I never knew what to do with myself during those terrifying moments prior to his arrival. If I hid from him, I knew he would find me and drag me out by the arm. Mostly I just sat stock-still, silencing my breath so as to better hear the predator. Like now, I'm listening hard for coming danger. I am a deer frozen in plain sight.

At last, the sound changes from the whir of a truck traveling along Elk City Wagon Road to a whining engine climbing the last rocky stretch to the tower. Our eyes meet. We look at each other, exchanging an idea without speaking—we can close and latch the trapdoor, remaining hunkered down inside the tower until "they" retreat. Unfortunately, we've left the .22 in the truck. Jack is fast; with his wrestling background he can have someone pinned to the ground in a split second. But there is only one of him. I get up from the bed, switch off the gas light, and return to Jack's side.

There are certain angles from inside the tower that give us views of the road as it curves around the hill, arriving at the parking area below. From one of these vantages, we see a white pickup with a man standing in the bed. He leans over the cab, his rifle pointed toward the woods where a spotlight illuminates a swatch of brush and trees.

"Poachers," Jack says. "Stay down."

I move away from the window, swallowing over the knot in my throat. "What should we do?" I whisper.

Jack shrugs. "Wait it out."

The men stop the truck and get out. Looking around, they take in the tower but don't move toward the stairs. The man in the back swings a long, black braid over his shoulder and climbs down from the vehicle. He walks over to the edge of the trees and pisses. The shorter one climbs into the back of the truck and leans over the cab, turning the mounted rifle back and forth, looking through the sight at the forest. The other one climbs behind the wheel, backs the truck around, and starts down the road again. The bright spotlight illuminates the woods, flicking through the tree trunks, ready to nail a startled deer frozen in the beam.

We wait for their headlights to disappear and the rumble of the truck to fade. I gasp, realizing that I've been holding my breath the entire time. "I need the bathroom," I say. "Will you go down with me? I don't want to go alone."

Jack shrugs, stepping out onto the catwalk to piss.

The poachers spooked me. Weirdly, I think of my real father, a man I can't recall as I was only two years old when Mom piled my brother and me in the car and left Portland for good. He must have lifted my brother or me over his head and made us squeal. He probably tickled our tummies and cooed at us, but he also took a stick to Bruce's backside. A poor little deer caught in the crosshairs. I wander out on the catwalk and pee in the coffee can. I can't hear anything but wind in the trees and a stick snapping in the woods.

"You still need to go down?" Jack says.

"No, I'm okay." I zip up my cutoffs and head back inside.

Jack lights the gas lantern and watches me brush my teeth. I pour a glass of water and swallow it down. He drains his warm beer, continuing to watch me. We remain silent as we undress and climb into bed. We tangle limbs together and begin to kiss.

My friend, Alice, says that the urge comes from low in the spine. She says it's called Kundalini rising, the serpent energy. She knows about metaphysical stuff and says that lots of sex will blend Jack's aura with mine. "Sex is good for you," she said one day while we sat on the dock sunbathing. "And it will make your legs strong."

I laughed but said nothing. It was embarrassing for me to talk about sex. And thinking it's good for a person was a completely different message from the one my mother had given me: *You must do what your husband wants.* And Dick's message: *Don't go getting all bent out of shape.* That's what he said when my first boyfriend was about to move to Alaska. I thought he meant, *Don't go getting yourself pregnant.* How could we? We'd barely done anything more than light petting. After that, he tried to keep me from dating, practically turned me into a nun—until I met Jack, that is. Then Dick's controlling nature rendered me secretive.

Jack wanted me naked almost immediately. Got a little pushy even. It was exciting at first and then I got scared. I barely knew how *it* happened let alone if I wanted *it* to happen. I was only seventeen, he was one year older. He said he could be thrown in jail for statutory rape, if caught. Dick was a catcher; I knew that for sure. Anything I did was suspect. We eventually carried on despite the danger.

Alice said, "Kundalini rises from the base of the spine."

It must be fickle, as the first time Kundalini rose, I was surprised. "Don't stop," I'd begged. Jack looked excited. Afterward, he said, "Haven't you ever had one?" I shook my head.

Even so, I'm no prude; it's stupid to say that about a person when you don't know where she's been. You know what I mean? Has your father kissed you while feeling you up? So, calling someone a prude is dumb. And so is suggesting I would lie about being hurt by my stepdad. "Oh, he wouldn't do that." Or even more insulting: "You're crazy."

I'm afraid I'll upset people by talking about being molested. Besides, I promised not to tell. Yet, one night while sitting around the campfire at Luby Bay campground where I was staying with Jack and his buddies, Jack said, "Go ahead; tell them what happened."

Everyone was quiet as I relayed the story of the abuse. I felt much better afterward. Then I started to shake hard. Real hard. The next day, Jack's best friend asked if I'd been drunk when I said those things. I said no. That's how I remember it, not drunk; oh, I may have had a beer or two, but drunk I wasn't. The shadows of the night woods surrounded us, and the beach sand took on a yellow cast from the licking campfire flames. The smell of lake and campfire smoke was in the air. Everyone was silent as I broke the secret: "Dick touches me any chance he gets."

I've heard that some folks who've been molested don't like sex. To my best friend's face when asked what the big deal was about sex, I said, "I wouldn't know." Hopefully, nothing bad had happened to her, but I was embarrassed to talk about the pleasures of sex with anyone except Alice. And I didn't want to give away the fact that I'd been doing it with Jack since I was seventeen. Yes, statutory rape if caught, but who would know? Well, my stepfather, of course, but fortunately he didn't figure it out until after I turned eighteen. We were seniors in high school when he forbade me from seeing Jack. "I haven't seen him," I lied when asked. But, of course, we saw each other every day.

Now I'm twenty-one and living on a lookout tower with hubby. The baby we made when I was twenty died after three months. I still cry over losing our child. To be a mother is what I want most in life. To love and nurture a child will mean everything to me. "Things happen for the best," the doctor said. "The egg probably didn't attach correctly to the uterus wall." I don't know—should I give back the booties and crocheted baby blankets friends and relatives made for me, or keep them for the next baby? In any case, they are safe in the chest with the towels from our wedding, stowed in Mom's basement—the basement where Jack and I slept before heading to Grangeville to keep fire watch at six thousand feet. That night in the basement we made love on the foldout bed that Mom got in the divorce, the same one we stained with love the night it snowed a skiff.

The night I lost my virginity, I swept the snow off the front porch afterward. I didn't want my stepdad to see Jack's footprints. Such a sleuth, right away asking, "Was someone here?"

"No, no one," I said.

He stared at me, his eyes saying he didn't believe a word of it. And somewhere deep inside, I felt a terrible transparency. Like he knew exactly what I was up to.

Tonight, forty-five feet in the air, we entwine beneath a brilliant starlit sky. Heat pulses our spines as the shivering serpent readies to uncoil. The curse may or may not come this month, but I don't think about that right now. Ordinary life is as far from my thoughts as Kundalini rising is from my understanding. I close my eyes and let go.

Clouds

Cirrus: Thin, white, wispy clouds made of ice crystals.

Cirrocumulus: Cloudlets arranged in rows, seen in winter or when it is cold and fair.

Cirrostratus: High, sheer clouds made of ice crystals, causing a sun halo or a ring around the moon.

Altocumulus: Most common, smaller than stratocumulus, and can signal thunderstorms.

Altostratus: Sheer clouds at medium altitude. The sun can be seen through them.

Cumulonimbus: Thunderheads with anvil tops. Clouds span low, medium, and high altitudes.

Cumulus: Fair-weather clouds.

Nimbostratus: Thick, dark layer of precipitating clouds.

Stratocumulus: Low cloud covering with blue sky seen between.

Stratus: Clouds that resemble fog.

four

A giant anvil cloud looms over Grangeville. The towering top is brilliant white and shaped like popped corn. The bottom is flat and stained black as a smithy's iron. Dick taught me to recognize thunderheads. "See the shape," he said. "See how the top flattens with the updraft? It's shaped like a blacksmith's anvil."

I feel the coming storm in my bones: air crackling with static, my body weak with humidity. My skin smells sharp of sweat. I taste salt on my upper lip. Trapped heat hunkers inside me and blackens my mood. Sighing, I stretch out on the bed and face the prairie, watching the building storm.

Even though my body has finally gained its strength back from the miscarriage, my emotions remain unpredictable as lightning strikes. I try not to think about the baby washing away, tumbling down the pipes into the septic tank, but I can't help it. Especially here in the middle of nowhere. In all this silence, my mind reviews all the mistakes I made. I should have looked at my child, seen whether it was a boy or a girl. All that blood, all those horrible contractions, all the excruciating pain. And the bath, afterward—the water staining pink. Now I will never know for sure the sex of my baby, though I believe it was a boy.

Earlier today, I begged Jack for us to try again. He just hissed, "No baby."

"My clock is ticking," I argued. "Let's try. I'll see the doctor in Grangeville. If he says it's okay, then we can."

Jack stood there staring out the window at the growing pileup of thunderheads. He pulled at his beard, sticking stray hairs in his mouth. He's extra nervous today. I know to stop pushing when he gets like this. I turned away and flopped on the bed. Now we're both as silent as our surroundings.

My underwear remains stained—three months' worth pouring from me like a gully washer. My pregnancy hormones disappeared along with the baby. Gone is my mothering instinct, the gagging at the scent of bay leaf, the repulsion over a small bit of shell stuck to my hard-boiled egg; gone is my nesting urge. Now I feel nothing. No flutters. No cravings. No backache. *Nada!*

I punch my pillow, raising my head higher so I have an eye-level view of the spreading anvil. "Winds," Dick said, "are turbulent around thunderheads. Dangerous to fly into."

The day he flew me from Spokane to Priest Lake to visit my girlfriend for a week, he brought along an airline pilot to co-pilot the small Cessna. He feared the black clouds towering large at the end of the airstrip, and so did I. My friend's family waited, parked on the side of the highway. I could see them watching as he set the Cessna down. I jumped out, suitcase in hand, and ran across the field. The Cessna roared to life, turned around, and immediately took off again, hurrying to stay ahead of the storm.

During that week at the lake, I Frenched a boy for the first time. And I drank too much beer and threw up in the small bathroom at the back of his cabin. Last summer, while perusing the Avon catalogue with a customer, I learned that the French-kissing cabin was the same cabin the resort hairdresser lived in with his ex-wife and their baby and his new wife too. *Weird*, I think, studying the flat bottom of the cloud, *all of them living together like that.*

Jack comes in from outside and announces that he's hungry. I pull myself up from the bed, shuffling through the electrified air to the counter. From the cupboard I take out a loaf of bread, a jar of peanut butter, and one of jelly. In slow motion, I make a sandwich. As I slide it on the green Melmac plate, I turn to him. Jack's drying his hands on a not-so-clean dishtowel. He catches my eye. His are dull and bitter. The baby standoff continues.

"Here," I say, shrugging. "Fuel for the big storm."

He takes the plate and mumbles, "Thanks."

I turn back to the counter and make another peanut butter sandwich, only I add pickles instead of jelly to mine. I've never been a fan of the jelly-and-peanut-butter marriage.

We wander outside to eat, pulling up seats just in time to see the first strike arc across the prairie. Both of us exclaim, "Far out," at the same time. We turn to each other, connecting this time with quick smiles and raised eyebrows.

The anvil cloud joins others, growing into a giant comforter of cumulonimbi—black bottoms with giant white tops blanketing the sky between the tower and Lewiston far to the west. We've seen a few distant flashes, but since lightning doesn't strike until the rain falls—at least that's what I've heard—we're in no hurry to go inside. The storm's far enough off to give us time to finish our sandwiches. As we chew, we begin to smell rain—that distant wet grass and asphalt scent everyone recognizes. The sun disappears behind the clouds. Goosebumps run up and down my arms. It won't be long before the first fat drops sting our faces, bare arms and legs.

Camas Prairie blurs with virga—rain evaporating before it hits the ground—hazing fields of blue camas, farms, and foothills in a wash of gray. I imagine cattle huddled along barbwire, rumps turned to sideways rain, farmers curtailing fence-mending to stable skittish horses and back their loaded hay trucks inside barns to stay dry.

The wind gusts. A bright bolt curves across the sky. Jack whoops. I shriek and jump up. "Come on," I shout over my shoulder as I hurry around the catwalk to the cabin door.

Through the window I see Jack's rebellious face loosen and his fixed expression turn to wonder. Shaking my head, I want to make him come inside, but I know he'll challenge the elements no matter what I say. I close the windows and kneel on the bed next to my cat, watching the storm's progress through the safety of glass panes.

Not every storm follows through, but this one appears to mean business. I can tell by the snapping flag down at the weather station that the wind is blowing toward the storm, the anvil drawing air upward, shooting it skyward on a powerful updraft. The whole prairie will soon be ablaze with flaring transformers and arcing lines. A forked bolt lights the sky several miles off. I open the window and shout to Jack to come inside. A thunderclap drowns me out. I give up, latching the window again.

Three bright flashes to the south and Jack turns in circles on the catwalk, his head thrown back, arms raised. He's in his John Muir-mode. This is not the first time he's dared the elements. Once, he stood in the middle of a dust devil; another time he jumped from galloping dock to galloping dock at Priest Lake during a treacherous gale that sank several expensive Chris-Crafts.

He has climbed trees in high winds and scaled Chimney Rock without a rope. Once, he swam dangerously close to the edge of a waterfall. Now he's leaning over the catwalk, arms stretched toward the darkening sky, playing chicken with Zeus.

Lightning will travel underground and come up beneath a fence post or tree, electrocuting unsuspecting ranchers or cattle. I've always heard that in the open, you're much less likely to get hit—though the highest object acts as a grounding rod. How does this make sense? You'd be the highest object, right? In that case, where is the safest place to ride out a storm? Perhaps the tower, since it has a lightning rod attached to a copper grounding wire thick as my little finger. It runs from the peak of the cabin forty-five feet down to the ground, attaching to a grounding rod buried deep in bedrock.

Jack sticks out his tongue, turning his face upward to catch the rain. His hair is plastered to his head, his shirt soaked. Lightning flashes overhead, forking off to the north. He's one with the electrical storm, practically glowing with static electricity. I pound on the window, but he can't hear me over the booming thunder.

Another blinding flash and he sprints around the slippery catwalk, banging open the door and leaping inside. He slams the door behind him and bounds onto the bed next to me. Wet and shivering, he cries, "Fucking-A," over a rolling peal.

"You could have been killed," I shout over another thunderclap and several flashes in quick succession.

With the rumbling thunder, pounding rain, and excited whoops, Jack doesn't hear me. He grins like a hyena, exclaiming, "Fuck, fuck, fuck!"

The rain falls harder, bouncing off the catwalk and back up to the top of the railing. Bolt after bolt lights the sky, brightening the blur of rain with each arc. Jack shouts, "Yes!" swinging his fist through the air like a spectator at a Frazier fight, then laughs as he sits back on his heels.

The truth is, I'm terrified. The lightning flashes and flashes and random rumbling has turned into nonstop booming. When we signed up for this job, I never imagined the blinding light in the darkness, screaming wind, and cracking thunder. I close my eyes to it all, but even then, flashes of light sear clean through my lids. The rain beats harder. Torrents thrum against the roof and shutters and bounce off the catwalk, spraying the windows. I cower on the bed, hands covering my ears, for what seems like an eternity.

Jack touches my shoulder. I jump, uncovering my ears momentarily. "Is it over?"

"It's over," he says.

I sit up, leaning close to his soggy outdoor scent. A few distant zigzag bolts light the sky behind him, but that's about it. Rain continues to drench the forest. Jack sits quietly next to me, his hand resting on my back. The heat of his palm calms me. Jude is an unmoving lump beneath the covers. I forgot all about her. She knows where to go to feel safe. Always on our honeymoon road trip, she traveled beneath the covers, hiding whenever spooked.

Beyond the tower in the dark forest, I imagine giant trees split down the middle, burning from the inside out. Far beneath the ground, roots could be smoldering in forked branches, stretching out from the trunk toward other trees. Fire in tree roots takes a pickaxe and a lot of digging around the base of the trunk to render cold. Once it's out, firefighters crawl on their hands and knees, feeling the ground, drawing fingers through the soil to make sure there is no remaining heat. A fire must be completely out to be considered a cold fire.

I imagine the forest on fire to the south. A blaze could roar up the hill toward us. What would we do then? Run, I expect. For me, fearing fire is right up there with being afraid of men, a lack of money, or a physical malady. It's hard to breathe when I get so frightened that I can't think straight.

Jack says he needs to piss. I look at him, then turn to the rain streaming off the shutters, deciding it looks iridescent. "Hah!" I say, realizing that my voice is hoarse. "Don't piss into the wind."

"Right on," he says, and steps out the door into the stormy night.

A waft of ozone-saturated air drifts inside. Once he returns, we brush our teeth and strip naked, climbing into the twin-size bed. Spent, we both fall fast asleep. I dream a mumbling dream about lightning. A strong gust shakes the tower, waking me. Arizona's words and imagined laughter linger in my head: *Your first storm will scare the bejesus out of you.*

He's right. I touch the back of my neck where the static electricity tickled me earlier. Lying awake, I realize I didn't write down the lightning coordinates in the strike log. I imagine lining up the strikes with the firefinder. There were far too many to record. Besides, I would have had to leave the lightning-safe bed to follow through with Arizona's request.

I turn on my side and wrap an arm around Jack's sleeping form, kissing his still back. Steady rain falls, pattering the shutters and roof, reminiscent of the sound of fingers drumming bongos. Wind buffets the tower, whistling through the guy wires. I try not to think about what's going on outside, but it's hard to shut it out. A twinge of pain has me curling more tightly around Jack. I shift my hips, readjusting my arm around his waist, trying to relax. Eventually, I fall back to sleep, dreaming of lightning bolts and cattle huddled beneath trees.

I wake up late, shaking off the dream of Jack daring lightning. Rolling onto my side, I see him outside leaning against the catwalk railing, high-powered binoculars raised to his eyes. He's studying the clear-cut to the north where the storm hit the hardest. We may have a fire to report.

Jumping out of bed, I scamper barefoot across the cool floor to the stove. I put on a pot of coffee and while it perks, pull on jeans and a T-shirt and comb my hair. I grab a Melmac cup and study the steam spirting from the spout of the coffee pot. I think of the vaporous mudflats in Yellowstone Park where we camped on our honeymoon road trip. Jack decided to go walking across the restricted sulfur flat where eggy fog rose in gagging clouds. I begged him not to go, imagining him falling through a thin crust into a boiling mud pit. He scoffed at me, "If the buffalo can do it, so can I."

His adventuresome nature didn't kill him when he jumped into the middle of a swirling whirlwind, nor while running toward a furious volley of lightning. High winds, bear encounters, and mogul-racing in the pitch dark haven't slowed him down. He seeks the pinnacle, the fast lane, the coldest and the hottest water, all to prove what? That he's invincible?

His friend, Slow Bull, is also a daredevil. Once he jumped off a bridge from high above the Columbia River. His buddies encouraged him by offering him the reward of all the hamburgers and fries he could eat once they reached the next town. Slow Bull promised us he'd come for a visit this summer. We can't wait to sit out on the catwalk with him and hear all about the water's hardness, the bruises and sore muscles, the difficulty he must have had walking for weeks afterward.

"For burgers and fries? Are you crazy?" I'll say. Then we'll all laugh, swigging brewskies and staring out at the fading prairie light, high on the bomber Jack will roll for us to smoke.

Squinting, I strike a match, lighting another burner. My eyes feel sensitive to light from hundreds of bolts cracking open the darkness the night before. I melt butter in a skillet and break an egg into sizzling fat to make a fried egg sandwich.

Jack walks in, binoculars hanging around his neck. "Mind-blowing," he says, pouring wheat germ, honey, and milk into a Melmac bowl. "No smokes that I can see."

"Better keep careful watch today," I say. "You want a fried egg sandwich?"

Jack grumbles. "I've got wheat germ!"

"Coffee?" I say, taking the coffee pot off the burner.

"Sure," he says.

Thank goodness my daredevil hubby isn't as physically radical as our friend, Slow Bull. Though Jack takes other risks that our friend does not, like eating dried bits of the Amanita Muscaria we found while hiking up on Mount Rainier. Despite my pleas to throw it out, he prepared the deadly mushroom just like he'd read about in a book on ingesting hallucinogenic mushrooms and other plants.

Why he wants to partake in thrills like these is beyond me. I'm so happy he didn't take our friend up on the peyote buttons he brought back from Arizona. Maybe it's his nervousness that drives him to experience heightened states of consciousness. Unlike me, he craves stimulation in multiple ways: mind-bending drug experiences, deafening rock 'n' roll, screaming fast motorcycles, and tons of sex.

The poisonous mushroom he swallowed left him feeling lethargic and forgetful. And then there were the morning glory seeds he experimented with. They made him feel queasy, even though he'd soaked them, attempting to wash off the pesticide and antifungal agents applied by the seed company.

There are chemicals in our drinking water and traces of DDT in mother's milk. DDT is sprayed on forests to kill the gypsy moth, and then people drink from the streams it pollutes and they become violently ill. That's what happened to the dishwasher at Hill's Resort. From what I understand, you don't have to be a daredevil to get sick from chemicals found in the woods.

When my brother, Bruce, came back from Vietnam, he had Agent Orange poisoning. We know pesticides and herbicides are bad for the population, but how can we stop their use? Perhaps we can boycott the products the chemical companies make. Like I've been doing, boycotting Nestle ever since I heard that they push formula on breastfeeding women in third-world countries, claiming it is so much better for infant health. When what is true is that babies on formula die far more often from a lack of natural immunity.

I *punch the yolk in the nose*. That's what my sister calls breaking the yolk. While it cooks, I pour two cups of coffee, which isn't a poison, though I'm sure some people think of it as one. I set the cups on the table and return to the stove to flip the egg. I spread mayonnaise on two slices of Wonder bread and slide the cooked egg between.

Taking a seat at the picnic table next to Jack, I say, "A friend of mine got struck by lightning while hiking. She blew it off, saying she just got licked. Licked! Can you believe it?"

I take a bite of fried egg sandwich, imagining Jack getting nailed last night during the peak of the storm. I wipe my mouth with a napkin. "You could have gotten struck last night, you know."

Jack narrows his eyes. His jaw tightens as he glares at me. "Better get used to it."

"I can't get used to you doing dangerous shit like that," I say, meeting his defiant gaze. "I need you to be the father of our child. Fucking stick around!"

Growling, he jumps up from the table and storms out the door.

I follow him. "We need to talk about getting me a car to drive to town. I don't want to be stuck here all summer with an asshole like you."

In the lengthy silence of the day, I imagine Jack flying down one dirt mountain road after another on his Bridgestone motorcycle. Who knows how long he will be gone. I press my hand over my heart, amazed by how much pain one can withstand without dropping dead on the spot. As I lift the binoculars to the forest, my stepdad's words come back to me. Despite the calming feel of soft, hazy skies and the smell of warm pitch and damp greenery, I can't make his words stop rattling around inside my head: *You don't know how to love. You never have.*

As much as I pleaded my love for my parents, he kept repeating: *No, you don't. You don't love us. You never have.*

I lower the binoculars and close my eyes. I look into my mind's eye like Dr. Gilmore said I should. "Pretend your mind is a blackboard and erase whatever appears on it." I imagine the blackboard I cleaned in my fourth-grade classroom, wiping away my stepdad's words with a felt eraser. I wipe it again and again, and still his steely gaze glares back at me, his words magically re-appearing in my mind. I shake my head, trying to dislodge him, but he refuses to go.

"Shit!" I say, opening my eyes again. I lift the high-powered binoculars and train them on the territory. Taking in the clear sky and the milky horizon, inch by inch, I realize that this is a totally different day than yesterday. Though it's beautiful, I don't feel amazed by the thriving forest, the vast prairie, and the lush damp woods all around. I feel flat and vulnerable and wrung out from last night's storm. And now, Jack has left for who-knows-where.

It's silly, I know, as Jack'll probably only be gone for an hour or so. When he yanked on his leather jacket, he said he'd be back when he was *good and ready*. He bolted down the stairs and raced off, spinning gravel as he fishtailed out of the parking lot.

The isolation on the mountain is getting to us. A little over a month in, and already cabin fever has us antsy as cats. Hopefully, Jack's shooting the breeze with the farmer we saw waving from his garden as we passed his place on our way to the lookout. I know company will make him feel better.

I move around the north side of the tower and study the hazy territory looming large through the binoculars. My brain rattles on, replaying other fights my stepdad and I had. We fought over the messiness of my room and his assertions that as an artist I'll surely become a drug addict, that secretarial school will give me a proper career, and that the people I call friends are merely step-ping stones to getting ahead in the world. "Who have you been talking to?" he often said. "Those kids you hang around with are a bad influence. Stay away from them."

I know those fights were smoke screens for the molesting that took place when no one was around. He wanted it to appear as though I'd ventured down the wrong path, when in fact, he was the one who dwelled in darkness. He could go to jail for molesting me if I reported him. I turn to the prairie and study the landscape.

After one such fight, I threatened to run away from home. He left me sobbing in the kitchen to join Mom, who waited by the front door to leave for the evening. She was dressed in her beige designer suit, sheer stockings, and suede heels, with a matching handbag looped over her arm. Once she and my stepdad were gone, I ranted to my little sister about running away. She became hysterical and crawled under the kitchen desk and hid. I begged her to come out, promising that I hadn't thought it through. I said, "If I run away, he'll find me. And he'll give me hell for worrying Mom to death."

Through the high-powered binoculars, I study a pileup of distant rain clouds lingering just short of Lewiston. Virga fuzzes the atmosphere into a bruised band stretching across the prairie. The clouds don't look like they'll amount to much, though we won't know for sure until later in the day. The weather report did call for a possibility of thundershowers this afternoon. The woods are only moderately dry at this point, which is good. I don't think I can take another night of zigzagging lightning and booming thunder. I walk around the catwalk and view the territory to the southwest, checking the clouds: stratocumulus, altocumulus, cumulonimbus.

I've learned a lot about nature through observation and because Jack's always explaining things to me, though I'm not certain if I'm getting the facts straight when I quote him. When he's around, he corrects me if I'm wrong. And I'm wrong a lot!

Just like Dick, I guess, always correcting me. I lower the binoculars and say to my imaginary stepfather, "Of course I love you. You're my parent, aren't you?"

The day of the bad fight, my parents sat at the breakfast table not looking at or speaking to each other. Cigarette smoke hazed the air. I waited outside the kitchen door while they discussed me riding on the back of a motorcycle with my sweetheart—such a small request.

At last, Dick turned to me and said that once I was eighteen, I could do whatever I wanted. At eighteen, he'd no longer be financially responsible for me. That April, he was mostly true to his word, giving me the go-ahead to do whatever I wanted.

I've written to him, telling him about the lost baby and our exciting summer job manning a fire lookout tower. I haven't heard back. It's like I'm dead to him now. Sure, I'm adopted, but being adopted when you're three—or at any age—requires the same parenting commitment as raising a natural child. No matter what he's done, I need a father.

Or do I? Now that I'm twenty-one and married, I'm free to tell the world anything I choose. I sigh aloud. It's hard to talk about being molested. For one thing, it's embarrassing. And another: Who'd believe me? I've heard that people often reply to such claims with disclaimers: *Oh, he'd never do that. He's such a nice person. You've misunderstood his intentions. Don't be disrespectful; he's your father, for Christ's sake. Maybe you brought it on yourself.*

And even though I told Jack's buddies that dark night while sitting around the campfire at Priest Lake, who else would I tell? My sister? I tried telling her that Dick was treating me badly, but she got furious and snapped at me, "He's *my* dad. Don't say bad things about him." So, I shut up.

I walk to the north side of the tower, raising the binoculars to the territory to study undulating shadows cast by the morning sun. The trees are thicker in the valleys and thinner over rocky ridges. Heat rises off the forest as the sun heats rain-sodden bark. The mistiness is beautiful and should bring me joy, but it doesn't. I listen hard for the rumble of Jack's motorcycle but hear nothing. I head back inside to make myself some lunch.

Feelings

Lonely
Sad
Fearful
Angry
Grieving
Frustrated
Lustful
Needy
Suffering
Betrayed
Longing
Jealous
Mistrustful
Suspicious
Affectionate
Fondness
Warmth
Tenderness
Satisfied

five

It's early afternoon when I hear Jack's motorcycle coming up the road. My heart leaps with relief. While he was gone, the eerie quiet had me jumping with every creak or groan of the tower, and with each snap of branches down below. I can't imagine manning a tower alone. The chick up on Pilot Knob must be freaked out half the time. But now, my hubby is back. And there's a bonus in it for me—he's in a good mood.

He grabs the binoculars and rounds the catwalk. After checking the territory, he pops back inside and sets the bins on the green picnic table. He grabs the bladder bag and shrugs it on. "Heading down to the stream for water. I'm going to mix up the home brew. Want to come?"

"Nope, I'm making spoon bread for dinner."

"Spoon bread?"

"Corn bread, only more like custard. I found the recipe in my *Fannie Farmer* cookbook."

Jack shrugs, turning to leave. The tower shakes as he runs forty-five feet down to the ground. There's the scuff of his boots on the gravel road below, then nothing.

Back to baking. I turn the oven to 350 degrees and light a match. A whoosh of gas and the circle of blue flame flickers at the base of the oven. I close the door. As the oven heats, I change my mind and mix up a batch of honey bread, substituting half the whole wheat flour with a combination of cornmeal and sunflower seed flour. While the loaf is baking, I take out the plastic dishpan and wash up the dishes, stacking them to dry on a well-used towel. I need to either get to town soon and visit the laundromat or carry items down to the stream and scrub them on the tiny washboard I brought along. I imagined I might have to wash clothes in the stream like the women who traveled to Elk City in covered wagons during the Gold Rush did.

When I moved into my own apartment at eighteen, Mom bought me the household items I needed: sheets, bath towels, iron, ironing board (now stored in her basement), and dish towels, which I brought along. The toaster, stoneware, and silverware were wedding gifts that I left in her basement. The tower came with a set of green Melmac dishes and mismatched flatware. I'm glad we didn't bring our wedding dishes up the winding, potholed logging road. The tower cupboard is outfitted with a few pots and pans—a similar banged-up version can be found in the kitchens of Hill's Resort cabins where I worked on the cleaning crew last summer.

Once I was on my own and paying my own rent, Dick laid me off at his office. I had been working for him for years, doing mostly secretarial work. Of course, why not punish me further for not being the submissive daughter he wanted? He said he would get someone else, someone more responsible. Granted, I didn't come to work the day after he took my car away, but I gave it the old college try. I took the bus—which I wasn't used to doing—and ended up on the North Division line instead of the one heading out to East Sprague. By the time I retraced my steps, it was late in the afternoon, so I gave up and went back to my apartment in Browne's Addition. He called me into the office the following day to talk to me.

Jack gave me a ride in his mother's car across town to East Sprague. He dropped me off and waited at the feedstore nearby, petting cute puppies and poking chameleons while I made my way across the busy street to Dick's office.

When I walked in, he was sitting behind a huge desk with this pissed-off look on his face. Even now it makes my stomach hurt to think about facing him across the huge wooden desk piled high with letters and invoices, a calculator the size of a small TV flashing numbers across the screen behind him, the nut-and-bolt man playing golf next to his name marker, and a huge raised relief map of Washington state covering the entire west wall.

By the time I got back to the feedstore, Jack was furious. "What took you so long?" he said.

I burst into tears as I explained the situation—being lectured for my inadequacies, my stepdad's decision to hire someone more responsible, and finally, the brutal firing.

"Fuck him," he said, hugging me tightly. "Everything will be all right, Nancerella. He's jealous. He doesn't like me being in the picture," he said. "It's okay to hate him!"

But I don't hate him, I think as I wipe up the counter. *I just don't understand how he could abuse me and then act like I am to blame? I know I can get over these bad feelings on my own.*

The scent of baking bread fills the tower. I expected Jack back from the stream by now. I step outside and call out to him. Listening hard, I hear nothing. I decide to wander down to the weather station and try taking the dewpoint. It's complicated, all that spinning and calculating and the resulting numbers that make little sense to me. I still don't understand why the dewpoint is necessary to our job.

Jack says it's all about humidity and the dryness of the forest. I didn't listen to his explanation very closely so I cannot repeat it, but like Jack says, it's important in determining fire danger.

When I reach the weather station, the smell of wildflowers is sweet as violets. The sun is warm, a slight breeze flaps the flag, and puffy clouds scud past overhead. There's even a sun dog refracting a sparkling rainbow over the prairie. A camp robber flies so close to me that I think it's going to land on my arm. One did once, while I was camping with Jack's sister. I stood statue-still watching it cock its head, thrilled by its boldness.

The bird squawks and lands in a nearby tree. A flutter of excitement vibrates my chest. My mood picks up. I spin the hydrometer and write down the reading.

Finished recording the weather stats, I make my way to the outhouse to pee. Since the miscarriage, my body has continued to grow stronger. Now I can easily run up the forty-five feet to the cabin, which I proceed to do. At the top, I'm hardly winded. I consider what we'll eat for our dinner besides honey bread. Canned soup again?

After Dick fired me, I bought a sleeping bag and headed north to Priest Lake where Jack camped at Luby Bay campground with his buddies. He lived in space #19 most of the summer, occasionally getting the boot from Forester Stump. Jack would move his gear from one campsite to another and carry on.

I called the resort and left a message that I'd be at the train station in Priest River at 1:00 p.m. Red suitcase in one hand and my Avon makeup bag in the other—complete with a new product catalogue—I climbed aboard the eastbound train to Priest River at the Spokane train station. Maybe Dick did me a favor. I would learn to support myself without him.

Jack and I were both poorer than poor at the time, but we were so much in love it didn't matter if we half-starved that summer. We were together and that's all that counted. When Jack got off work, he raced back to the campground on his Bridgestone motorcycle, leapt off the bike, and grabbed me up in his arms, twirling me around like in the movies. The two of us wandered along the lakeshore, wading in the chilly water, stopping to kiss any chance we got. When we got back to camp, we made love in the army pup tent that he'd borrowed from his dad, Squeak.

We frequently ate mashed potatoes and wild mushrooms cooked on a Coleman stove. We savored ripe huckleberries and caught silvers in the lake. We'd share the occasional hamburger at the local marina—purchased with change collected by turning in empty pop bottles for a refund. Or we chowed down at Hill's Resort summer barbecue when his mom and dad came for a visit. They never questioned seeing me at the lake with their son; they must have thought I was staying with a girlfriend or by myself at the resort. They trusted me completely, something I had never experienced at home.

One weekend, while back in Spokane to pick up my Avon order, I stopped at the family home to see my mother. She sat at the kitchen table smoking a cigarette, her face pinched and pale. My stepdad just happened to be home and was strutting around the kitchen, pissed as a wildcat. He said he knew I was living with Jack at Priest Lake. He'd hired one of our friends from the resort to snoop on us. My stomach dropped. *He had us spied upon? Fucker!*

He paced the kitchen floor while Mom sat there at the table wringing her hands. "What you've been doing," he said, shaking his head, "is disgusting. You might as well turn around and shit on your mother."

His words shocked me. Even now, when I think of what he said to me, I feel horrified by his crudeness. I mean, he'd been molesting me ever since I was a little girl. How had I become the bad person here? Sure, I was living with my boyfriend, but Dick had been climbing in my bed weekend mornings ever since I entered first grade. What he did was far worse than sleeping with my boyfriend at eighteen.

Frequently, after Mom was out with her friends, Dick sneaked into my bedroom. And when she went away to Arizona to visit her sick mother, things totally went south. I remember once pleading with her not to go. She didn't know what was bothering me, because I couldn't say what my stepdad did when she wasn't there. He'd warned me not to break the secret and I obeyed. That day as I watched her pack, I started to cry. "I'll be lonely without you," I sobbed. She just laughed and kept packing.

If I could have told her about Dick's visits, and if she had believed me, perhaps he would have gone to prison for sexually assaulting a child. Later, if I had been emotionally stronger, I'd have hauled him off to the police station myself. But I did nothing, because I had been silenced.

Unlike him, I'm not a cheater. I am not the other woman, although sometimes I feel like I am. And I'm not a nympho like Sally from high school, a waif of a girl with slick, ironed hair. I didn't hang with the high school sluts, wearing short skirts, sleazing down the halls, swinging hips and long, shiny hair. In fact, Mom often coached me in how to walk without a wiggle. "You don't want to draw unwanted attention from men, do you?" she'd said.

I know I don't look like a whore as Jack's friend once said I did. But after I dyed my hair red beneath the campground spigot, we stopped to visit him in town. His friend said, "Nancy, you look like a hooker."

I just laughed. What could I say?

Back at the tower, I find Jack absent still. Perhaps he stopped at the outhouse after he returned from the stream. I turn my attention to the little mirror hanging above the Igloo cooler, scrunching my hair with my fingers, trying to make myself look prettier. I haven't had a shower in weeks. I lick my finger and rub a dirty smudge off my cheek. My bangs are still too short, curling high above my eyebrows. At least they show off my Ram's horns—arched eyebrows being the physical characteristic my astrologer friend attributes to Aries. She once told me that every sign rules a physical characteristic. Even my hair was Mars red for a while. Now I'm just a dirty brunette, literally, with a bad haircut.

Disappointed, I turn away from the mirror. I put on an afternoon pot of coffee. Soon it will be perking over the gas flame, popping and sighing, popping and sighing. Along with the spicy scent of baking bread, my mouth begins to water. It's then that I hear Jack's boots on the stairs and my fear falls away like dishwater tossed over the railing. I'm so glad he's back.

When he arrives at the top, I grab hold of him and kiss him with enthusiasm. Surprisingly, he returns the affection, kissing me quickly as he tugs at the straps of the bladder bag.

"Where have you been?"

"I hiked a bit before filling the bladder bag. There's a bunch of bear grass growing north on Elk City Wagon Road." He whips a stem from behind his back and hands it to me.

"Thank you," I say, taking in its citrusy scent.

"I was hoping to find us some berries, but there weren't any." He steps inside and walks over to the green plastic garbage can. He hikes the water bag up, balancing it on his shoulder, the spout pointed over the can. He's already proficient at pouring stream water from the bladder bag into the five-gallon Igloo container. The green garbage can with the wide opening is no challenge at all.

I stand back watching while he grouses about the two guys and the girl living on the farmer's land in an abandoned shack, supposedly working for room and board. I don't know why it bothers him so much. Perhaps because he'd rather be doing something like that himself.

I pour two cups of coffee, and he takes the quart of milk the farmer sent home with him from the fridge and splashes a bit in each cup. Raw milk and brown eggs make us happy. "Thank heavens for fresh food," I say.

We take a seat at the picnic table and drink our coffee, waiting for the bread to finish baking. "I tried something new this time: sunflower seed flour mixed with the whole wheat flour. It smells good."

Jack nods, his eyes watery and narrow. "Those New York hippies are using the farmer. Tom's the nicest of the squatters. The other guy, the blond one, showed the farmer his art portfolio. Like art will get you anywhere in this neck of the woods. Tom seems okay. Even gave me some pot! Says he'll come for a visit soon. I hope he does." Jack shakes his head. "The artist and his girlfriend are fuckers, but Tom's a good head."

He finishes his coffee and goes to the cupboard to retrieve the can of ale hops. He opens it and pours it into the garbage can of water, stirring the contents with a wooden spoon. Next, he pours in the entire bag of fine corn sugar, adds brewing yeast, and stirs the concoction again. He gives me a mischievous smile as he sets the alcohol meter in the center of the brew where it bobs just above the surface. "It will settle as the alcohol increases. It won't take long to ferment, then we'll bottle." He clamps down the lid and tosses the can and sugar bag in the trash.

It's then that I hear the whine of a truck engine and wander outside. Jack follows, standing beside me on the catwalk. "I missed this one."

"Losing your edge?"

"Maybe!" I say, watching the USFS vehicle groan up the last stretch of road, pulling into the parking area next to our bread truck. A cloud of dust wafts over the camper and nearby brush. Jim climbs out. Jack gives a loud hoot. Then Nan climbs out of the passenger side and I squeal with joy. Company at last!

At the top of the stairs, Nan grabs me in a warm bear hug. Jim grins, explaining that he regularly checks the team's slash-piling progress and Nan decided to ride along. The two men wander around the catwalk, viewing the territory, passing the binoculars back and forth, while Nan and I duck inside, babbling on about Nan's quickly growing baby.

"Oh, I love the view from here," Nan says. "I miss tower life. Jim and I manned this tower for two years before you guys. Never again . . ." She pats her stomach.

"But then you'll have a baby," I say cheerfully, despite the nagging sadness over my loss. "I can't wait," I say, "to be pregnant again."

Nan says, "Maybe we'll be pregnant together."

The men stride inside, their energy a little too big and too loud for the small space. But everyone finds a seat and watches me as I take the bread out of the oven. We're all happy to chow down on the treat, sip coffee, and feel the balm of a new friendship easing our cabin fever.

"I'm not sure about the sunflower meal," I say. "It has a strong flavor; maybe I'll use half as much next time."

Jack frowns, setting his bread aside. Jim says, "It's delicious," humming as he chews. Nan likes it too. She smiles a wide smile. Her dark hair frames her happy eyes. Maybe pregnancy makes some women love food and everything else more than usual.

"I like to experiment with unusual ingredients. We have a hundred-pound sack of soy protein stored at Squeak's house in Spokane. I brought a small bag of it along to experiment with. Maybe I'll try making pizza, substituting soy protein for sausage. It's for the end of the world when people live underground. Jack's neighbor told us, 'Our church is advising people to amass food now, so that when everything goes to hell in a handbasket and people pack guns, we'll have enough stores to survive.'"

Nan and Jim look at each other with raised eyebrows. Nan laughs. "The apocalypse is nonsense."

"You never know," I say. "Her church is selling soy protein—eighteen dollars for a hundred-pound bag. Better safe than sorry, don't you think?"

Jack squirms. "Nancerella!"

"What?" I say, knowing he hates it when I rattle on about weird shit.

He frowns at me, then turns to Jim and engages him in a conversation about buying a beater for us to drive back and forth to town. Jim says that one of his crew members has a beat-up Scout for sale. Jim makes rounds daily, checking on the men's progress. He'll tell the guy to get in touch with us. "Wait, I have his address," he says. "You can stop by next time you come to town."

I hand him a piece of paper. He scribbles down the phone number and address and hands it to Jack. "Why not continue working for the forest service after you come down from the tower," Jim says. "We need men after fire season is over. There's always slash-burning and other jobs to do."

"And you," Nan says to me, "can work at the diner. You know, fry doughnuts and dust 'em with powdered sugar. The locals will love your honey bread. Great tips too!"

"Good idea," I say, thinking about powdered-sugar doughnuts and the way they puff sugar down your shirt when you bite into one. "I've worked in the resort kitchen. I'm experienced at making flavorful stews and soups to feed sixteen."

I offer our guests more coffee, but they decline.

"It's a long way down to the outhouse. I used a coffee can when I was up here. Who wants to go up and down those stairs all day long when no one's around? Or in the middle of the night?" Nan says. "But the good thing about drinking coffee is you don't get constipated. Being a fire tower attendant is pretty sedentary."

"Yeah," I say, cringing at the thought of sitting in the dark outhouse with spiders crawling around my bum. "I'm arachnophobic.

Last summer, the outdoor resort bathrooms were crawling with spiders. I was constantly looking around while I showered or sat on the pot. And when we opened the cabins in the spring for cleaning, I freaked out each time I walked into a web or when a spider dropped down in front of me. So now I prop the outhouse door open and check for spiders before taking a seat."

Everyone laughs. I've had too much coffee and am blabbing on and on. "Fortunately, I don't have astraphobia—fear of thunder and lightning. Or acrophobia—fear of heights. We'd really be screwed then."

Nan and Jim chuckle as they get up to leave. We follow them down the stairs to their rig. When they climb in and say goodbye, a wide emptiness drops my stomach. A cloud of dust wafts from the tires as they drive off. I stand waving until they disappear around the bend, then wander down the path to the two-seater, feeling like I might cry.

After I pee, I find Jack waiting for me next to the bread truck. He waves me over, wrapping an arm around me, kissing my cheek.

"Let's buy it. We have the address. We can ride the bike down after work today."

"Out of sight," I say, grabbing him tightly. "A Scout and groceries too."

On the drive back, I recall someone telling me that wildfires roar like jet engines. "If you've ever heard one," the person said, "you'll never forget the sound of a raging inferno." I remember the small fire Jack and I lit in the mountains above Priest Lake. We'd stopped to warm up after a long, chilly motorcycle ride. Unexpectedly, the wind came up, fanning the flames so high, they nearly licked the cedar boughs above our heads. Jack kicked dirt on the blaze, smothering it immediately. I shake my head at the memory, marveling over our stupidity and our good fortune. We could have caught the entire forest on fire.

I can't imagine being the cause of a fire that burns hundreds of acres, thousands even. Generally, fires start by accident. A flicked cigarette butt from a car window, a spark off a car engine, a lightning strike, and *whoosh!* You see it all the time. Or, like us, building a small fire to warm our hands and the wind comes up. Things can happen, and they can happen fast. Who would admit to destroying an entire forest? And who could live with themselves if they didn't confess they were the cause of such devastating loss?

After we snuffed out the fire, we wound our way back down the mountain to Luby Bay campground where we'd set up camp for the summer, stopping to see a friend at his cabin on the way. Still chilled from the motorcycle ride, we plunked ourselves down in front of the stone fireplace, holding our palms out to the hot flames. Steve jabbered on about the properties of fire and how staring into the flames was mesmerizing. "If you stare long enough, fire will change you."

As I speed across the Camas Prairie in the used International Scout, I wonder what Steve meant by "fire will change you."

I recall that he went on to insist that Jack and I have two children. "I've been a mortician long enough to know that things can happen. Two children will replace Mary and me. You should do the same."

Jack teased his friend about selling underground real estate and scoffed at the idea of having children. "It's a terrible world to bring children into."

"Okay, two," I said, imagining the impossible—my own child dying before I did. But I guess that has already happened. The miscarriage—though my baby only made it to the end of its first trimester—broke my heart. I feel older now; though I just turned twenty-one this spring, I am emotionally worn out. I'm sure the doctor in Grangeville will give me the okay to try for another pregnancy.

A loaded logging truck careens past in the opposite direction. In the rearview mirror I watch it disappear into waves of heat rising off the landscape, silhouettes of flying tree debris swirling through the orange light. In the distance I hear a long, low rumble of thunder. *Bummer*, I think.

I've heard thunder called many things: brontide, peal, crack, and clap. My mother described it as God bowling in heaven. Any way you say it, thunder spells lightning. Nervously, I note that the sky above the glow of sunset is thickening with storm clouds. I shift down, slowing at the turnoff onto Lightning Creek Road.

Dick taught me to drive. I can still hear him now, saying that it's safer to stay in first gear while driving up a steep hill. And easier on the transmission too. I argue with him in my mind: *Yes, but it takes too long to get up the mountain in first gear. Anyway, a slower speed won't keep me from a head-on, as the hairpin corners are blind no matter what.* As far as I'm concerned, the only problem with speeding up a narrow logging road in second gear is sliding around a dusty curve into a ditch.

Gunning it, I shift into second. And then, without thinking, I pull off the road and roll up my window. Seconds later, a loaded logging truck barrels around the corner, tearing past me. Jake Brakes pop and a cloud of dust engulfs me. I hold my breath, noticing the surprised look on the driver's face. Perhaps mine looks equally surprised. I press my hand against my beating heart and wait until the cloud settles before I pull out and continue up the mountain in first gear.

An hour later, I'm back on the tower with Jack. He took off on his motorcycle as soon as we secured the Scout. Jack excitedly snatches the white butcher-paper-wrapped package from inside the bag I set on the counter. He tears it open, extracting a chunky piece of beef jerky, pinching it in his mouth like a cigar. He grabs his guitar and walks out on the catwalk, glancing over the rail at the Scout before taking a seat facing the prairie. He rests a foot on the railing as he chews and plucks the strings.

As I put the food away, my ears adjust to the elevation, popping and clearing. The heat and the long drive home wore me out. I lie down on the bed with a copy of *Living on the Earth*, perusing the page describing clouds as strains of "Here Comes the Sun" lilt through the open window. The drawings are childlike and make me chuckle. But they are also accurate—the anvil clouds described as "dark nimbus clouds piling up into thunderheads."

The guitar Jack strums has supposedly been to Woodstock and back. He reminds me of this often. I remind him back it's just a story—perhaps our friend's relayed history of the guitar is a fantasy. "All he really wanted was to trade for a lid of grass. He's always bargaining for something. Beer, food, weed."

To me, the guitar does vibe like it's been to a giant rock concert. However, whatever its origin, I'm glad it's ours now. Since I read music, I've been teaching myself to pick out classical tunes on the easy-to-press nylon strings, tunes like I used to play on the Hammond when I lived at home.

Instead of Woodstock, we took in the Seattle Pop Festival at Gold Creek Park. Most folks couldn't get remotely close to Woodstock because of its massive size, about four hundred thousand people, and many never got close enough to hear the music. We, on the other hand, brag about seeing The Guess Who, Led Zeppelin, Santana, Ike and Tina Turner, The Youngbloods, Moody Blues, and a slew of other bands we were too stoned to remember. We laugh when we tell people our story of showing up at a concert, naïve kids from Spokane, Washington, sleeping in an army pup tent while Hell's Angels pushed speed at the entrance to the park.

I recall planes flying over, dropping sugar cubes rumored to be laced with LSD, and people jumping to grab them through the surging crowd. Again, I recall my youth group teacher explaining the nature of the drug as colorless and odorless, warning us to be cautious. "You don't want to go mad, do you?" We never did, not the first time or any other time we split a tab and let it melt on our tongues. We hallucinated as we rode the motorcycle, walked across railroad trestles beneath the starry night sky, or went wild dancing to loud rock 'n' roll music at the armory.

Jack wanders in from the catwalk and asks about dinner. I guess he doesn't have a clue how the meal thing works, and we've been married for over a year now. "Why don't you cook tonight? Pork chops are in the fridge," I say. "And there's applesauce to go with them."

He grumbles something about it being my job and wanders over to sit on the bed next to me. He runs a hand up my leg. "Come on, Nancerella, fix us something nice to eat, please. We can fool around later."

I laugh. "I'm not cooking or anything else tonight. So, fuck off!"

He slides his hand higher. "Please . . . you'll like it."

I push away what he calls his *old man hand*, wrinkled and no larger than mine. Though his hands are small, they're strong. He resists my pressure. "Stop it!" I say, finally managing to remove his hand and place it in his own lap. "Let's just snack tonight," I say, looking past him out the window. "Hey, wait a minute." I sit up, crawling over him to grab the binoculars off the firefinder. "We've got a smoke." I raise the bins to my eyes and focus on the forest southwest of us. "Surprised we didn't notice the plume on our way home."

Jack agrees to set out ingredients for what he calls a Caveman Meal if I call in the fire. I agree and line up the firefinder on the curl of smoke. I jot down the coordinates and reluctantly pick up the handset. Though I'm getting a bit bolder as time goes on, I still feel shy about using the radio. I switch to a different channel and call headquarters: "Clearwater Ranger District . . . this is Corral Hill . . . come in."

"Go ahead, Corral Hill."

Nervously, I relay the azimuth and sign off. I'm back to studying the smoke through the high-powered bins when we hear back from the dispatcher: a crew is being sent out.

"It's getting late, they probably won't arrive until after dark."

"Ten-four," I say and sign off. I feel jittery but happy that I managed the radio without freaking out. I look around. Jack is working away, setting out a variety of food on the picnic table. Turns out, dinner will be RyKrisp, peanut butter, olives, sliced apple, raisins, beef jerky, and Buck beer. "My home brew is ready to bottle," he says. "Will you help me bottle it tonight, before it gets too dark."

"It's already getting dark," I say, finishing putting away groceries, stopping occasionally to look over at the column of dark gray smoke. "Probably a strike from the last storm that blew through."

Jack climbs on the picnic table to check out the attic space. "It's a good place to store home brew," he says. "Dark and hidden." He climbs back down and opens two Buck beers, handing one to me. I take a long drink as I peruse the smoke streaming upward.

"After we finish off the two six-packs you just bought," Jack says, sitting at the table for dinner, "we'll do a taste test."

I shrug. The smoke rises into the sky with increasing vigor. "It needs to age awhile, doesn't it?" I imagine the home brew served like expensive Southern Comfort: shot glasses filled with amber liquid. I take my store-bought beer and load up a plate of snacks. Instead of sitting at the table, I move to the bed so I can keep an eye on the fire. A gust of wind rattles the shutters.

We won't hear from the fire crew until late, so Jack prepares to siphon the home brew through a clear plastic hose from the garbage can into the sanitized bottles. I'll be glad when the beer is stored away, since it worries me that Arizona might open the lid and discover fermenting liquid with the alcohol hydrometer bobbing in the middle. The lid fits tightly so there is no scent of beer when you enter the tower cabin. The last time Arizona visited, he did point to the garbage can and ask, "What's in there?"

Jack said, "Clothes and stuff."

Arizona nodded approvingly.

After we finish eating, we form an assembly line of sorts, Jack siphoning beer into clean brown bottles, me cranking the capper atop each bottle.

"Careful," Jack says.

"I am," I say. The whole situation reminds me of the time my family made root beer in the basement on Hoffman Street, our first house before we moved across the street from Audubon Park. I was five and my brother was eight. Our new "dad" laughed a lot. And he snapped at us equally as often. He ordered me to stand back while they did the bottling. He said I was too little to help, which made me whine. I didn't feel little. But I did what he said.

I can't remember the beatings Bruce suffered from our real dad, but Mother said they were terrible. I do remember hiding in the closet like she hid my brother when our dad came home from his long-haul trucking job. Once, while visiting Old Faithful, I got frightened by a bumblebee and ran shrieking through the cabin to the bedroom closet. I darted between the clothes and slammed the closet door behind me. I was jumpy for weeks after that, thinking even the distant sound of a waterfall was a huge bumblebee coming after me.

My hand slips on the capper and I spill half a bottle of beer on the floor. Jack pinches his lips in a line and hisses at me, insisting that I quit helping because I'm wasting his *fucking beer*. I shrug and get up off the floor, light the gas lamp, and mop up the spilt liquid.

I pick up my knitting, deciding to work until it gets too dark to see. By then, Jack should have all the bottles stored away in the attic and the mess cleaned up.

There's not much to do in a dimly lit tower but rest and sometimes read or play cards by candlelight. Before the season ends, I want to finish reading *To Kill a Mockingbird* aloud to Jack. Some nights I read a few pages, but my eyes and voice can only hold out for so long. I knit a few rows then take a tour outside to check on the smoke.

In the warm twilight, the smoke appears to have thickened into a bluish column. We can tell by the color that there's plenty of fuel being consumed. Even though it's after-hours, we stay off the radio in case the fire crew calls and needs help locating the strike.

In theory, a fire should be easy to locate by using the azimuth and the graphed ridges I've mostly completed. That's strictly theory, however, as it's hard to know for sure which draw they'll bushwhack into, especially if we can't see the crew's headlights from here.

I return to the cabin. Twilight is gone, though it's nearly a full moon, which will be rising soon. Jack has finished bottling and decides to wait until tomorrow to mix up the new batch of home brew. He cleans up his mess and gets out the deck of cards. "Wanna play?"

"Sure," I say, petting the cat, who's asleep on my knitting. I give her a scratch and climb onto the bed. She purrs loudly.

Jack deals a hand of gin rummy. We tally our scores in one long line of numbers. So far, Jack is winning with the lowest score. He gets up from the bed occasionally to search for FS truck headlights visible in the distance. With multiple ridges stacked one upon another and convoluted drainages bordered by thick forest, bushwhacking becomes torturous and usually leads to nowhere but lost. The guys are used to reading maps and locating coordinates, plus, this fire is smoky. Their noses will lead the way. And perhaps moonlight, if the clouds don't block its pale glow.

It's getting too dark to see now, though the moon comes and goes behind the clouds. We give up on the cards and Jack heads out onto the catwalk. He stands alert, looking in the general direction of the smoke. The air is fraught with tension. Not electrical storm tension—though the clouds are thickening—but Jack's nervous energy, which has him pulling at his beard between draughts of beer. When the call comes over the radio, we both startle. He runs back inside, grabbing the handset. "Corral Hill, come in. Over."

"Corral Hill, we can't locate the smoke. Check ridge graphs, go ahead."

I pull out the folded graph paper. The ridges I outlined by connecting multiple azimuths should help the fire crew locate the blaze. A dot every quarter-inch follows along each ridge, just like Arizona requested. I look for the ridge. "Shit! It's not here."

"What?"

"I can't find the ridge the firefighters are looking for." I shake my head, stomach sinking. "I didn't complete that area."

"Sorry, that ridge isn't on our map, over," Jack says.

"Can you see our headlights? Are we in the right vicinity? Over."

"Yes! I'm guessing the smoke is to the east, one ridge over," Jack says.

"Thanks. We'll handle it. Over and out."

Jack replaces the receiver. A gust comes through the window, snuffing out the candle. The night folds in on us.

Firefighters are young and strong and not afraid of wild animals. They are fueled by adrenaline, as well as aggressive testosterone. They have K-rations and water and other necessary firefighting equipment. They have their sleeping bags, mats, and lamps. And they get paid a ton of money in overtime. "They'll be fine!" I say and imagine them visiting us tomorrow. My stomach jumps at the thought. I wonder if the handsome guy that looks like Paul Newman will drink coffee with us tomorrow. I better make cookies.

Jack's worrying his beard. "What's wrong?"

"Nothing," I say. "Just tired, I guess." Jude stretches her neck to the left as I stroke her head, directing my fingers to scratch behind her ear. She purrs so loudly that I laugh, saying, "Who's a good kitty? Who's my girl?"

"You are," Jack says, and from behind, slips an arm around my waist. He gently kisses the back of my neck. I turn in his arms and kiss him back. Soon we're under the covers, wrapped in each other's arms.

The territory steams this morning, mist rising in clouds as the sun bakes moist stumps and dew-damp deadwood. It rained in the night, which hopefully helped douse the fire. Binoculars in hand, I circle the catwalk several times, observing haze to the southwest, but no column of smoke to speak of.

I take a deep breath. I'm feeling more agitated than usual this morning. My nerves are on edge and Jack's too—the full moon is playing havoc with our wits. It'll rise large tonight. I imagine Jack standing on the catwalk and howling like the coyotes we hear in the night. He'd do that, I'm sure.

Mr. Walker, my sixth-grade teacher, loved astronomy. I always say my favorite schoolteacher was Mrs. Ogle, but I'm wondering why that would be when she scolded me so often in front of the class for humming. For God's sake, what's wrong with humming? Most likely, I was supposed to be adding and subtracting like we practiced the following year in Mr. Walker's sixth-grade class. He praised me for reading *The Story of Dr. Dolittle* from cover to cover, a very thick book. Plus, he took us out after dark to study constellations—my favorite subject in school, besides art.

I probably think of Mrs. Ogle first because she did show concern over my upsets. It was hard to concentrate the year my periods started and the secret touching increased. The whole bloody mess rendered me feral. Maybe the smell of puberty drew him to me, like a hungry coyote to roadkill. Whatever it was, I was an emotional wreck, often ending up in the nurse's office sleeping off a sick headache or bad cramps.

My self-consciousness increased tenfold when I started wearing an elastic belt with hooks to hold the sanitary napkin in place. It was cumbersome and embarrassing, though probably not a soul other than my parents knew. In high school, while sunbathing on beach towels in the backyard, my girlfriends and I read a tampon ad in *Teen* magazine. We were thrilled and vowed to try them out.

Later that summer, while visiting a family friend's cabin at Spirit Lake, Mom gave me a small box of tampons. Actually, my parents presented them together, explaining how to insert one properly. They sent me into the bathroom and after a few minutes, I reappeared, embarrassed by their expectant faces. I just nodded, but in my mind, I flew away.

What I wonder now is why Mom allowed Dick to be involved in my personal hygiene. He always acted overly familiar when it came to my body. It would have been so much less embarrassing if he'd left the gritty details of feminine hygiene to my mother. I wish she had told him to butt out of her territory. I wish I'd told him *to leave me the fuck alone.*

I clear my throat as I raise the binoculars to the forest. A raven lands on a treetop, puffing pollen into the blue sky. The large black bird makes a croaking noise, cocking its head to look at me. Though who can say that the bird is actually looking at me.

Dick looked at me pointedly once and said, "We're not close, are we?" I just shook my head and turned away. I should have said: *Maybe it's because you're always reaching under my clothes to touch me.* But if I'd said that, he would have denied it or claimed I was crazy for making up something as gross as that. "What is wrong with you? Do you have a hole in your head or something?"

In Mrs. Ogle's class I drew leaves, one after another, coloring them with orange, red, and yellow crayons—so many beautiful colors and the sweet smell of wax. They say that smells bring back an object or an event. Like the smell of Dick's spicy aftershave that he tried to pat on my face after he shaved. It was a game, of sorts. Everything with him was a goddamned pushy game, trying to make me give him something he shouldn't want and was inappropriate for me to give. Next time he writes to me, I will write back to him and say, *Fuck off, asshole.* Actually, I probably won't say that, because then he'd stop speaking to me altogether—which seems worse in some ways—but perhaps he has stopped already.

The raven lifts off the branch. It has an amazingly large wingspan. Croaking in its strange bird language, it flaps off. I imagine I can feel the air stir with the whisk of its feathers. Then I see a thin trail of smoke curling through the rising mist. I go inside and tell Jack that the fire we reported yesterday isn't cold yet, but no worries, the rain and the firefighters will take care of it.

Just before sunrise, a brilliant yellow light outlines the shadowy, gray silhouette of Pilot Knob, east and slightly south of our tower. As the sun lifts higher, the sky turns pale peach, then orange, and then the edges of the rocky peak flame brightly. Birds sing like crazy, calling out to each other that it is time to get the morning started. All at once, everything whitens and the sun lifts above the mountain, warming the dewy territory, beginning our day.

Mountains have weight, a vibration of sorts, almost a humming that I feel in my chest. When the sun comes up, everything gladdens. Even Jack's face, which has become increasingly flat of late, brightens a bit. He's bummed because he wants more action, actually more interaction. Interaction during high school brought him happiness, as he was loved by his fellow wrestling buddies, and all the rich girls adored him, especially the blond cheerleaders. He was so entertaining, making everyone laugh in assembly with his naughty jokes, his mischievous eyes, his tongue touching his upper lip, suggesting sex. I guess his manipulative ways worked on me.

Now, we're the assembly of two standing in the bright morning sun, drinking coffee before our audience—trees and birds and wildlife—oh, and the occasional visitor who respectfully addresses us as rangers. Once I said, "Rangers get paid a heck of a lot more than we do." We all laughed.

Do we have any stature at all? I mean, are we important in the eyes of the public? Well, I don't think many people know we exist. Except, now, I sense a car's coming. "Company," I say, and we hurry to the east side of the catwalk to watch for dust. When it rises from a certain area, we know how much time we have before company arrives.

A half hour later, Slow Bull steps out of a clunker car parked between our bread truck and the tower. He shades his eyes with his hand and grins up at us. Jack whoops and runs down to the ground to greet him. I wrap my arms around myself, protectively.

Slow Bull is a flirt. More than once he's made suggestive remarks to me, so I'm glad Jack isn't away on his motorcycle this morning. A mutual friend once told me he'd whispered in her ear that he wanted to screw her. I said, "He said the same to me." After comparing notes, we vowed never to be caught alone with him, ever!

He'd also interrupted her extravagant wedding thrown by her proper judge-father when he ran out from behind the stage, past the priest, and jumped over the podium in the middle of her wedding ceremony. The guests gasped and then laughed at the grinning man dressed in a colorful kaftan, complete with Nehru collar.

Now, Jack watches him closely from where he stands nearby on the catwalk. He knows what Slow Bull whispered to me and my friend. I stand near Jack, remaining vigilant. After a bit, I return to the cabin to grab the binoculars. *Fuck these men who think they can say and do weird shit to women.* I return to the catwalk to study the territory.

The sun is warm and there is no chance of an electrical storm predicted in the weather forecast. Ravens croak in distant trees. The guys swig coffee, seemingly studying the heat rising off the forest. I overhear Jack asking Slow Bull if he's still thieving. He shrugs, saying, "Not since my father got the charges dropped the last time I got caught." Slow Bull goes on to say that he keeps his loot in a locked closet that he won't open for his girlfriend no matter what. I imagine Jack hiding stuff from me in a locked closet. I would find a wrecking bar and pry the dang thing open.

But who can judge a thief? I mean, I once stole a package of valentines. And an eraser from Bob's Grocery while Mother went through the checkout line with a heaping cart of food. And Jack and I stole Dee's stash of beer that she kept out on Indian Island at Priest Lake. It was hidden in a moss-covered wooden box on the back porch of her parents' cabin. I'd stayed with her more than once on that island. And when I did, we stashed our six-packs in that moss-covered box, taking a few bottles with us to the boathouse where we talked and drank into the wee hours.

Dee never missed the beer and when I confessed that I'd taken it, we both laughed. I had brought along another six-pack to leave with her when we pulled up at the dock. I consider myself lucky that she has remained my best friend.

Jack says, "You can't go back home, nor can you rekindle old friendships."

"Home is wherever you are at the time," I say. "And friends should be loyal, don't you think?"

"Fuck," he said, "you're naïve."

"Peace, man," I smile, flipping him the sign.

Before we lived on the lookout tower, we lived in our truck at Priest Lake. I wouldn't trade all those mornings waking up in the woods for anything. The most divine feeling would wash over me—the cool air, the sound of chirping birds, the smell of evergreens, and all those colorful sunrises over the lake.

Right now, Slow Bull is giving us his undivided attention as we explain what it's been like living up here on the tower. The storms, wind, low ceilings, the isolation, wildlife, and visitors late at night. He gets up and walks to the other side of the tower and pisses in Jack's usual spot. I turn away. But then I hear him in the cabin, rummaging around in the fridge. He brought beer, hamburger, buns, and potato chips. He returns with three beers and offers me one.

"No, thanks," I say. "I'm working."

He laughs. "Some job you two have."

"Yeah, pretty cushy."

Slow Bull arriving with gifts is unusual, as he generally asks for a handout. Once, when we were living in the green old-mare house, he raided the refrigerator, eating all the special pecans Jack's grandmother had mailed from Pennsylvania for Christmas. Another time, he helped himself to the last of the beer we were saving for a picnic in the woods. The last time, he put a couple of bread rolls in his pocket after lunch—something to eat later. He offers me the bag of potato chips.

"Thanks, Slow Bull," I say. "It's nice of you to bring dinner. I'll make burgers later, but right now, I need to keep an eye on the forest."

I leave the "boys" to their mischief, smoking grass and drinking beer while I study the territory fifteen minutes out of every hour—just like instructed.

I hear snippets of their conversation as I make the rounds. Slow Bull tells Jack the story of how he jumped off the bridge for the burgers and fries our friends offered. I want to join their storytelling, but I'm not done studying the territory through two magnified circles. "Fire watch is almost done," I say. "Then I'll sit with you."

Shortly, I leave the binoculars on the counter and return with my Minolta SLR to record our friend's visit to Corral Hill Lookout. I lift the camera and photograph the boys, one sitting, the other standing, on the catwalk. They are both smiling, the prairie and the clear blue sky a picturesque backdrop. Jack takes the camera from me, capturing Slow Bull and me standing in the corner near the pole with the anemometer on top, whirring as it records wind speed.

After a few more photos and farfetched stories, our friend says he's heading out after dinner to the Rainbow Gathering, a yearly assembly of like-minded, naked hippies smoking dope, singing, and drumming, and making love—not war. He'll try to make it to Colorado by the end of the week.

Smiling, we nod, though I know we're both feeling our stomachs sink even before "alone again" happens. Oh well, what matters most is that we're protecting the forest. Visitors or not, when the morning sun rises over Pilot Knob, we'll drink it in, watching evergreens come alive with morning light, their tops bowing toward the beginning of a new day.

After a day of chatting, laughs, trips to the outhouse, and views of the territory through the high-powered bins, we sit down at the picnic table to eat an early dinner of juicy hamburger patties resting on buns slathered with mustard, mayonnaise, and ketchup. The flavor of the meal blows our minds. Even Jack raves, and really, he has a very particular palate. We keep thanking Slow Bull for the food as we wave yellow jackets away from our dinner plates. We joke that the only thing missing from our fare is the fries.

Slow Bull grins, eating slowly as he is still telling stories at the table. He rattles on about his travels here and there and all the wild fun he's had at other Rainbow Gatherings . . . free love, pot, and cool traded, homemade items. He shakes his head and rolls his eyes, feigning exhaustion. We laugh until our full bellies hurt. And then, just like that, he gets up to leave. He's always been like that—here, and then gone! Like a dust devil.

Jack and I stand looking out over the prairie for a long while, taking in the quiet, leaning over the catwalk at one point to watch dust float up from Slow Bull's car and settle again over the forest. Early and late shadows show us the shape of the land, the ridges running from north to south, the same ridges a plane flew over one day, a vintage craft heading straight for the tower. The sound of its engine was thunderous, growing louder as it closed in on us. Jack and I whooped and waved our arms. The plane soared upward at the last moment, flying over us in a rush of roaring exhaust, wind, and engine noise. It was exhilarating, frightening, and then, a letdown. That's how I feel right now, first excited and now empty.

We go inside and wash the dishes. There is no longer the smell of smoke in the air, just fresh evergreen pitch and damp earth. And some faint sweetness: blooming Syringa, perhaps? Maybe it's good that we have unfinished ridge graphs. Now, as we study everything from distant mountaintop to nearby ridge, we know the territory all that much better. Now, finishing the graph will be a piece of cake.

As Jack dries the dishes, he smiles, though his lips remain pressed together. Who knows what he's wrestling with inside that stoned head of his, but Slow Bull's visit seems to have enlivened him—though he's not completely back to *my* normal Jack. He doesn't like me prying, but I ask anyway, "How are you doing?"

"I'm missing Love."

At first, I think he means sex, then I laugh, recalling his reel-to-reel stereo in the truck and his hunger for loud rock 'n' roll, his favorite musical group being Love. He likes picking at his guitar and inventing catchy riffs, but playing super loud music seems to break apart his anxiety, turning it into an exhilarating vibration.

"I'm gonna try jury-rigging the reel-to-reel in the truck, see if I can hook it up to the battery."

I imagine the reel-to-reel tape player sitting in the cupboard above the driver's seat. When we plugged in the bread truck at KOA campgrounds while on our honeymoon road trip, we could listen to music in the evenings. I don't think it will happen, but I can imagine playing Love's "Alone Again" to the Clearwater National Forest. Only problem I see is, if Jack does get the stereo hooked up, it'll run down the truck battery. Then how will we start the rig when the season is over and it comes time to go down from the mountain?

Anyway, Slow Bull got to see the territory clearer than usual today; all that rain falling in the night washed the surroundings clean of particulate. It's like the limbs, cones, and needles that were coated in dust, pollen, and smoke are now washed clean, rich browns and brightened greens. Even the farthest mountains over in Montana are visible. Maybe, if we look hard enough, we'll see Colorado where our friend is heading to hang out with a bunch of naked hippies drumming and dancing and freely loving each other until replete.

We awaken the next morning to the smell of smoke. To the southwest, a cottony haze blocks what we could see so clearly yesterday; an out-of-district fire is burning and its smoke drifts in our direction.

I rub my eyes, feeling overly tired. I didn't sleep well, probably because Jude didn't come home by the time we went to bed last night. I climb out of bed and slip on shorts and a T-shirt and my Dr. Scholl's sandals. I step out onto the catwalk and call her name. Jack's down at the weather station recording stats. He turns and looks up at me standing forty-five feet above him on the catwalk. I wave, yelling, "Have you seen Jude?"

"Nope," he yells back.

I head down to the ground to search for her. As I clomp down the stairs, the smell of piss wafts up from below. I admit to myself that I also dump my coffee cans of pee over the side of the tower each morning. But I toss mine in a wide arc, whereas Jack whizzes over the rail, day and night, in basically the same spot. He's the main stinker around here, that's for sure. You can even see the dried yellow spatter on the big white propane tank east of the tower.

I hold my breath until I get down the road a way, then gulp fresh air that tastes of sweet wild roses and warm cedar pitch. The wild plum tree to the north with its yellow fruit ripening elicits a sigh of relief from deep inside. Salal blooms along the shoulder, edging the road in clumps of purple-white berries that are said to be edible, though I've heard they're bland, dry, and mealy. You can eat Oregon grape berries too, also bland. Then there are rose hips with their pithy, sour taste. The riper the better, sometimes tasting a little like a sour tomato. Not too bad if you're hungry enough. And I've read that they're filled with huge amounts of Vitamin C—an important food to eat if you're ever lost in the woods.

"Jude," I holler, then stop to listen. Nothing. I call again and wait to hear a *meow*. I get a whiff of the paper mill, a sulphury smell riding an air current all the way from Lewiston, Idaho, a hundred miles to the west. I imagine the road to Grangeville passing patches of blue where the prairie blooms lush with native camas. I imagine flour made from dried and pounded roots by the Nez Perce. I wonder what it tastes like. Bland, I suppose, but nutritional and an important addition to the diet, balancing wild meat and berries with a decent starch.

I wander farther down the road toward the spring, continuing to call the cat as I walk. My stomach growls. My mouth begins to water. A slather of peanut butter on a RyKrisp sounds yummy. I relish the summer tomatoes and cukes and radishes the farmer sends via folks heading our way or when Jack makes a trip down to the turnoff and the farmer loads him up. But right now, I'd kill for a plate of Mom's roast beef and gravy. French fries, pizza, and a pitcher of beer. Bacon and eggs and jam on toast. It must have been the burgers enticing my taste buds to desire scarfing down anything and everything.

I swallow, kicking at the dry ground where it has cracked from the heat. The range cattle's ribs will be showing soon. The potential for drought is imminent. Fire danger is moderately high. The forest could erupt in flames from a single lightning strike at any time. I'm sure Smokey will frown when the arrow points to red on the sign at the district building. *We're on the eve of destruction.*

I pick a thimbleberry, so tiny, no longer bleeding red but dry and tart on my tongue. When I was a child, my grandmother made them into sour jam. Then there are the huckleberries that turn our tongues and fingers purple. The wild blueberries should be coming on in August, if it's not too dry for them, that is.

"Jude," I call again, stopping to listen. Again, I hear nothing.

My heart hurts. I miss the calm spirit T. Lobsang Rampa speaks about. In my dream last night, I struck Dick in the face again and again, my anger pummeling him until I gasped awake, drenched in sweat and tears. I'm so furious at him for the molestations, for threatening me to keep the secret of abuse, for ignoring me now that I'm married. "The asshole!"

He who has no sin, cast the first stone, Dick's office manager said to me one day, raising his eyebrows when I complained about the teens hired not working hard enough. Upon seeing my perplexed expression, he explained how Jesus protected the prostitute against the people's angry stoning.

"Oh," I said, nodding. "I get it. I think." And I did, but he didn't know that Dick had asked me to speed up the workers; we had a deadline to make for Kaiser Aluminum. Two twenty-foot rows of three-by-four-by-one-foot gray metal boxes rested side by side on conference tables and makeshift tables of plywood and construction horses. The room was located next to the loading dock at the back of the building. The low-ceilinged space hadn't been used before the panelboard job. It was long and narrow and smelled like dirt: basically a cellar that opened to the back entrance of the property. Emergency lights hung every few feet down the length of the end-to-end tables. Eight of us teenagers strung wires, each with a personal color to wire around the inside perimeter of the box. The electricians wired in the switches and gauges. Then they organized and strapped together each bundle of colored wires we'd added, cinching plastic ties every three to four inches, checking and tidying the insides. It was an efficient process and a blast working together, gabbing beneath safety lights for eight hours a day over several weeks that particular summer.

We took our coffee and lunch breaks outside on the loading dock jutting into the overgrown strip of land edged in black locust along the back of the lot. From the dock we could see the grain elevators and the railroad tracks to the north. Bums sometimes wandered the few blocks from a boxcar to the back of the building, at times sleeping in Dick's Model A Ford parked beneath the trees. Talk about the smell of piss. The back seat of that old Ford was pulled apart, foam stuffing exploding like a mole's mound, saturated with a gagging stench of a filthy bathroom.

As the boss's daughter, I had to set a good example. So, I ate my lunch fast and encouraged everyone to hurry up and get back to work. I'd march back inside before lunch was over and take my place at the table.

As I contemplate my bossy attitude, I arrive at the bottom of the road near the spring. I was in my head practically the whole walk down to the turnoff, hardly noticing the beautiful sunshine, the smell of summer heat, wild fruit ripening, and the babble of running water. I bend, picking sprigs of mint and watercress, burying my nose in their fragrant leaves.

Dr. Gilmore once said we should take responsibility for everything that happens in our lives. This thought makes my head hurt. If my cat is gone, does that mean I am responsible for her running off? Did I do something that caused my parents to break up? Am I responsible for the abuse? Dick was always trying to get me alone so he could fondle me. Wasn't he the bad one?

The sun blazes. I draw a hand over my forehead, wiping away a bloom of sweat. The stream murmurs, birds sing, crickets chirp. Tears stream down my face.

"Jude," I call louder, beginning to feel a bit frantic. It's not the first time she's run off. The last time was when we lived in the truck at Priest Lake. Someone said, "She's probably up and gotten herself eaten. Yep, a goner. Sorry, kid."

Not true, I think. *She's alive. I know it.*

I call for her until my throat turns hoarse. Nothing. I drop onto a large rock and hang my head, weeping. After a while, I look up, thinking I see something moving on the other side of the road. I wipe away tears with the back of my hand and search the forest beyond the meadow. The sun is bright, light blanching color from the forest. I squint. "It's just a robin," I sputter, hugging myself.

While pining for home or family, I sometimes imagine what it would be like to be a yogi sitting cross-legged in a cave for an entire lifetime. A servant passes a parcel of rice and cup of tea through the L-shaped opening, but the yogi never sees the person delivering the food. Contemplation for a lifetime—so not my cup of tea. I guess I'm just plain homesick, distracting myself the best I can with novels, spiritual books, cooking, radio programs, and sex. I need to get out of here for a while. Then I hear a faint mew coming from off in the distance.

When I arrive back to the tower, Jude's fast asleep on the bed. I figure she's been gone twenty-four hours, maybe longer. At Priest Lake, she was gone a couple of days. I lost it then too, but this time I'm totally freaked out, because I know what danger lurks in these woods: coyotes, mountain lions, bobcats, raccoons, and bears.

Jack's been giving me a bad time ever since I got back. He says I shouldn't hug her and coo at her like that. "She worried you. You should scold her."

"Bad cat," I say, and kiss her head.

"I can't imagine you parenting like this."

"Right!" I say. My instincts tell me to scold her, but I'm just so relieved she's back that I can't do anything but fawn over her. Jack's right. It must be hard for parents to discipline their children. They want their kid to be good, yet they don't want to hurt their child. What a dilemma.

I was scolded frequently. Dick never appeared to want to help me become a better person. He seemed to enjoy power-tripping me, confusing me, or backing me into a corner. I pet Jude, talking to her in a baby voice: "Don't ever run off again, you hear me?"

Jude purrs like crazy, kneading the quilt, her claws catching the fiber of the purple square that used to be a kitchen curtain in the green old-mare house.

Jack's becoming more irritated by the minute. He wears his narrowed-eye look, focusing it fast on me. His arms cross his chest. He's jealous because I'm paying more attention to the cat than to him. He's often jealous when I turn my attention to someone or something other than him. I shake my head.

"I think I'll heat up some soup for lunch." I climb off the bed, hurrying past him to the kitchen cupboard. Crouching, I pull out a can of cream of mushroom, my favorite. "We're running low on supplies. I'll put soup on the list."

Jack grumbles something I don't hear. I say, "What?" but he doesn't answer. I'm happy that Jude is back, but Jack's bad vibes are making me feel tense and angry. Even when we first met, he hissed and growled at me, even barked: *Nancerella!* More than once he grabbed my arm and jerked me around. Twice, I've made the mistake of slapping him in the face for being mean to me. He slapped me back, both times. Once, he put me in a wrestling hold, which hurt like hell. Another time, he pinned me. He's fast and strong and I can't win against him.

I take a couple of slices of Wonder bread out of the wrapper and cut them in halves.

Jack says, "My mother used to cut the crusts off."

"That's nice," I say. "But I'm not your mother."

"My mother made cream of celery soup from scratch."

"I don't know how or I would." I serve up two bowls of steaming soup with buttered white bread on the side. "I'm relieved Jude's back," I say as I take a seat at the table. "I'd die if I ever lost her."

"We all lose things we love," he says, dipping his bread in the soup and gobbling it down. "I dig this soup, man."

"Yep, not bad."

"I'm going stir-crazy."

"Me too."

The Color of Smoke

Brush: red- or brown-tinted
Twigs: white
Dead grass: dark gray
Green grass: white
Trees: bluish or white
Chemicals, tires, etc.: black
Wildfire: dark gray

six

The wind howls all day, guy wires pinging and snapping, shutters rattling. Mid-season is blustery at six thousand feet: some days are warm, some days, cold. It is my turn to collect weather data, which I do, albeit reluctantly. Now I'm lying on the bed, my feet aching from clomping up and down the open stairs in my wooden Dr. Scholl's. I was all the way down to the weather station when I realized I'd forgotten the logbook. I hiked back up the hill and climbed forty-five feet to the cabin to retrieve it. Then I headed back down again without a pencil. Maybe Dick was right—I'm irresponsible. More like forgetful. More like it's my Pisces moon.

"It's worth a million bucks," Dick would say. He was speaking about my experience working as a secretary for his company. "A secretarial job is the only way you'll make any money, Nance."

"Bread, the root of all evil," I say aloud, sitting up, looking around. "What about my famous art career? Did he think of that?"

Jack is out on the catwalk whizzing with the wind. We've been drinking hot tea all afternoon. He's grumpy as hell today, and it isn't over a lack of money. More like a lack of access to a chilled six-pack. He went through the beer I brought back from town in no time at all. Of course, I helped him out a bit. The batch of home brew is fermenting in bottles in the attic. It will remain green for a while longer—but green beer won't stop him from imbibing. We'll see how long he can hold out before he breaks open a bottle.

He bangs around outside, checking shutters, guy wires, and the grounding rod. The wind is supposed to pick up tonight, a real blower. I shiver with each increasing gust, hating windstorms more than lightning storms.

Jack steps back inside. "You could work on the ridge graphs," he says, grabbing the binoculars off the picnic table.

"So could you," I say. "I'm going to make bread." I squat down and pull out my biggest mixing bowl from the cupboard next to the stove.

Grumbling, Jack heads back outside, the door flying open with a bang. He grabs the knob and slams it shut.

"Whatever." I measure yeast, sugar, and warm water from the tea kettle. My childhood best friend and I kneaded dough into balls until they were *as smooth as a baby's bottom*. That's what her mother always said. We oiled the dough and let it rise in ceramic bowls covered with damp dish towels. We baked often in Mrs. Adam's kitchen, serving tall glasses of milk with warm sticky buns, crusty bread, or sweet cookies.

The drawers and cupboards in her kitchen were painted 1950s green—not unlike the lookout's FS-green cupboards. Green is supposed to be mellow, that's why they paint the walls green in hospitals. Though here on the tower calmness is rare. Right now, the wind rumbles and clatters and pings. I chew a torn cuticle.

Mother painted her cupboards, rather she had them painted—orange. She loves anything orange. I'm thinking of making her an afghan for her birthday: orange, brown, yellow, and green.

Money's green, and a driving factor in my family home. Well, it's no longer *my family home*. Mom has her own place, which she bought after she and Dick split the proceeds from our "family home." Not sure how the family business got split up. Mom says she was cheated. *Uncool!*

I realize the family business required me to work at the office Saturdays, holidays, and daily over summer break, while my sister and brother rarely helped. I guess my sister was too young and my brother, too accident-prone. I think being Dick's favorite—for perverse reasons of course—left me feeling hopelessly alone. And afraid.

A burst of wind buffets the west windows. I stop what I am doing and watch the treetops whipping side to side. My main jobs were answering the phone, filing invoices, mailing statements, and typing up letters that Dick read and signed with his big, messy signature. My high school offered me a small scholarship to attend secretarial school when I graduated. It was my exceptional typing skill that drew their attention. Another girl was in the running for the scholarship as well. The school decided to give the grant to her, because her parents made less money than mine. I wasn't disappointed, but Dick was.

I did other jobs at the office too, like working in the back room tinning the ends of wires so they could be bent into loops and screwed to a switch inside a gray metal box or panelboard. Other times, Dick set me up to do direct mail. I was to stamp addresses, embossing metal labels on the big green machine set up in an out-of-the-way room in the basement. As always, working alone in the basement or back room meant he could attempt to kiss and fondle me.

Additionally, he'd embarrass me with his lewd humor. Once he showed me a mannequin sitting on a toilet in a small, unused bathroom in the back of the office. Her skirt was hiked up to the top of her thighs and her red satin bodice hung low. Another time, he took me into the men's room and showed me the plumbed, rabbit-faucet pissing in the sink. His gutter humor, along with the touching, taught me to whip around and hurry the other way whenever I came across the opposite sex in an isolated situation. I would walk blocks out of my way to avoid a man or group of boys heading my direction while walking home from school.

Jack bangs inside and I nearly jump out of my skin. His hair is a hurricane. The tower shakes with a dramatic gust. "Fucking crazy out there."

"Bummer," I say. "Blasted wind. It makes me so nervous."

Once I moved away from home, I carried an Avon bag door-to-door to make money. I walked around a south hill neighborhood, offering lipstick samples, perfume, and lotions to housewives. One hot summer day as the wind gusted wildfire smoke over the bluff into town, I sat with a woman in her air-conditioned house, offering her the catalogue specials of the month. She said, "I don't know how your parents can let you live on your own." All I could do was shrug. I didn't say, "I moved out because my father molests me." It was impossible to talk about my dark secret.

Now, I live with a man who doesn't like anyone telling him what to do. "Do you know," he said the other day, "that there can only be one person—*one person*—in charge in a relationship. And that person's me." He crossed his arms over his chest and looked at me as if to say, "Don't fuck with me."

"We're both in charge," I managed to say softly. "You are in charge of you, and I am in charge of me."

Speaking up is tough. I look over at Jack as I cover the oiled dough with a damp towel and set it in the oven. The pilot light keeps the oven at the perfect temperature for rising dough. I refill the tea kettle from the Igloo cooler and set it on the flame. Maybe it's the wind stirring me up today, or maybe it's Jack's pisspot attitude. Either way, I am beginning to feel like I won't be putting up with Jack's shit much longer.

Alice, my astrologer friend, said, "Never mess with an angry Aries."

Maybe she's right. With the day growing long and shadows darkening the territory, I begin to think that I've made a mistake setting up camp on a mountaintop with a moody husband.

The wind gusts higher. The tower shudders. It won't be long before I punch the dough down. I bite my fingernails as I watch the tea kettle come to a boil. I recall what Dr. Gilmore said about Edgar Cayce and the angelic beings that came to him in his dreams. They helped make his home life easier when he was having difficulty with his violent father. While the bread bakes, I ponder my prescient ability. I've known since I was a kid that there is more to this world than what meets the eye. I have "seen" things in my dreamlike states, events that come true.

Once my mother and I were sitting around the dining room table in the tiny apartment she rented after the divorce. I was talking to her about the ghost I saw in the haunted apartment house in Browne's Addition.

"Do not mess with things like that," she said, blowing cigarette smoke toward me.

I waved my hand under my nose. "But what about your boyfriend? You saw his ghost when he died."

"That's different. It just happened," she said. "I didn't conjure him." She rolled the tip of her smoking cigarette around the glass ashtray, appearing irritated as she brought the Winston to her reddened lips and drew hard. Smoke curled around her face and hair, veiling her expression.

"What?" I said.

"Nothing," she said.

It was after her family moved west from Virginia to the remote Idaho plant where her father inspected the large guns used on navy ships that she saw her boyfriend's face materialize on the glass pane of the kitchen door. It turned out to be the exact moment of his death.

She was only sixteen when she left her first love behind. *I could never leave Jack behind.* I look over at him again, his lips pinched together as he studies the territory through the high-powered binoculars. *Or could I?*

Like Mom, I feel and see spirits and have ever since childhood. Once, after an evening talk that Dr. Gilmore gave at Plymouth Congregational Church about the dead communicating with the living, a car careened around the corner down by the old railroad trestle, nearly running me down as I crossed the street. I knew it wasn't a ghost driver, but with the headlights blinding me and my heart pounding wildly, instead of jumping to safety, I froze in place. Later, I believed I'd been temporarily possessed by a poltergeist, the same one who'd haunted me after visiting Westminster Apartments in Browne's Addition.

Then there was the night Jack and I dropped acid and I fell asleep on my Murphy bed. As I dreamed of Egyptian pyramids and King Tut's gold, Jack stayed up rushing on LSD. Later, when I woke, he was still sitting on the davenport, reading a *National Geographic* magazine. He said, "Look," holding up the page detailing King Tut's gold artifacts sitting alongside a golden Anubis. When I explained my dream, we both said, "Heavy, man!"

I like studying psychic phenomena. Once, after reading a book on psychometry, I wrote to the author at the Paranormal Institute. I told him about Mom seeing the materialization of her boyfriend's face the exact moment of his death. The author wrote back, encouraging me to continue studying the paranormal. I was in the ninth grade at the time. The letter is stored, along with our wedding gifts, in Mom's basement.

With Dick arranging his schedule so he would have opportunities to catch me alone at home or work, I was forced to learn avoidance tactics. If he went one way to grab me, I'd go the other. Eventually, however, he would catch me.

The possibility of being caught frightened me, but it also made my stomach tighten when he said he always knew where I was and what I was doing. Though I wasn't doing anything wrong, I stayed alert for the sound of his footsteps, his car, and the sound of him blowing his nose as he approached the front door after work. I learned to watch for him in my mind's eye, moving silently about the house, learning which stairs creaked and which didn't, and which doors needed oiling. Because of his inappropriate touching, I withdrew, barely opening my mouth at school. My attention drifted. I grew ill easily and was sent to the nurse's office. I cried often.

The wind continues to scour the land, trees swinging limbs, a constant howl shivering the tower. I punch the bread down and cut the dough into two pieces. I twist each piece into a log and gently press it into a loaf pan. While waiting for it to rise again, I pull out the ridge map and add a few coordinates, connecting the dots to complete each draw. In the distance, I see a flash of lightning. Somehow, it brings me relief. The arc of light draws my mind away from thoughts of Dick's abusive nature.

I awaken this morning with a headache and cramps. The pain started in the night, gripping my insides while wind creaked the tower, rain pummeled the shutters, and lightning ravaged the district. I roll over in bed and squint against the day. Outside, plumes of white smoke rise from the territory. Jack is on the catwalk, binoculars glued to the forest. He yells, "Nance, come out here. We're fucking surrounded!"

I lean up on my elbow and squint hard, studying the white plumes dotting the clear-cut. The white plumes can't be smoke. The lightning never came this close. And the plumes are the wrong color. They are too white.

Jack runs inside and grabs the radio. "Clearwater Ranger District, this is Corral Hill, come in." He takes his wrestling stance—feet planted wide, pelvis thrust forward—practically yelling into the handset, "Smokes all around us, sir. Smokes all around."

Arizona laughs. "It's just ground fog, son. Happens all the time 'round here, plumes rising from clearings after a storm."

I smile a little, settling back onto my side. Jude jumps up on the bed, curling up at my feet. Since there is no emergency, I'm staying put under the warm quilt, waiting for Jack to hang up the radio and leave the tower in a huff. The tower shakes as he runs down the four flights of stairs to the ground below.

A while later, the mist thins and the sun breaks through. Jack returns to the cabin looking somewhat sheepish. He makes tea and brings me a cup. I turn on my side and face him, pulling the quilt around my shoulders for warmth. It's still cool in the cabin, even though the gas stove hisses. I try to read but can't concentrate with the throbbing in my head. I close the book and my eyes and think about Dick.

After Dick asked Mom for the divorce, the family gathered one last time for dinner. I was so sassy at the dinner table that night, insinuating things that were hurtful, I'm sure. But I was angry at him for leaving all of us. And for the secret he forced me to keep. Even though I hated him, a part of me still loved him. I felt confused by these conflicting feelings.

After the family dinner, Mom told us that they'd been seeing a counselor. She thought Dick might be homosexual and asked, "Besides red ties, what are the other signs of homosexuality?"

Jack grunted. My brother rolled his eyes.

"But, Mom," I said. "He's living with a woman in a trailer park in Airway Heights."

"His goddamned secretary," she snapped, drawing hard on her cigarette. Smoke billowed around her as she exhaled forcefully.

"So, then he's not homosexual, right?"

"Well," Mother said, and tapped the ash into a glass ashtray. "Maybe he likes both."

"What?" I said, knitting my eyebrows.

Her drunken eyes closed halfway. She brought the cigarette to her reddened lips once again and drew hard. "You know," she said, winking, smoke leaking from her nostrils, "bi-sexual."

"Whatever," I said and downed the rest of my wine. I knew Mom was suffering and wanted to figure out why her husband had left her. I didn't have the heart to tell her he moved out because I married Jack.

I massage my tender belly with my fingertips, rubbing the sore spots with light pressure. My periods often put me in bed for a couple of days. *The Scourge*, my sister called it. *The Curse*, Jack's sister called it. *Hell*, I call it.

It really hasn't been that long since my parents' divorce, about a year after Jack and I married, I guess. And since then, my step-dad has only been to see me twice, once on my birthday, bringing me a giant, all-day sucker, and another time stopping by out of the blue for an awkward visit at the green old-mare house.

The following birthday, I called to remind him that it was about to be my birthday. When he asked what I wanted, I told him exactly what he could buy me—a Minolta SLR. I figured it was the least he could do after what he'd put me through. He bought it for me, though joked that such an expensive present would put him in the poorhouse. I picked it out myself at Huppin's on Main Street in Spokane. I never looked back.

I've been taking lots of photos of plants, hoping to write an herb book someday. Lois, my former boss, who is a bit psychic like me, said she could see the book in her mind's eye. I can see it too. Although the herb book has nothing to do with being psychic. Maybe I'll write a book about that too.

Even if others don't believe me, I know my psychic ability is real. It demonstrates itself often, like when I know someone's coming to visit us on the tower. It's not because I hear an engine humming or see dust rising off the road far below, because there is no vehicle sound until they are just down the road. And there is only one place nearby where the road is visible from the tower.

I just know, like I know what a person is going to say before they say it, or when there's a package left behind the door. I know when something bad is about to happen or when someone's going to call or write. I just know!

"How do you do it, Nancerella?" Jack asked me recently.

"I don't try," I say. "The thought just floats into my mind. If I try, it doesn't work. It must happen naturally. It's cool!"

Dr. Gilmore says communicating with spirits is real. He talks with them just like Edgar Cayce did. Once when Jack and I visited him at the church, Dr. Gilmore stretched out on the floor of his office. He had us stretch out next to him and asked that we relax and clear our minds. Shortly, he went into a trance state and began speaking with my real father. Well, he didn't actually speak to him, but in a trance, Dr. Gilmore watched a movie of my real father sitting on a river island, sick with grief. My father blamed his temper on losing us. He went to the river to console himself. Dr. Gilmore saw Virgil sitting on a log, sadder than sad and burnt to a crisp by the hot sun. The channeling Dr. Gilmore did filled in the story for me.

I turn on my side, hoping the cramps will lessen if I pull my knees up to my chest, like Mom suggested I do when I was a child. Outside, everything is milky from sky to ground, with patches of sunny blue peeking through from far above. Jack's fiddling with his marijuana pipe. He cleans it regularly, running a pipe cleaner through the stem and a tiny brush over the screen. He's wearing sunglasses, as it's glaringly bright in the cabin. His thin lips purse together in concentration. He's said little all morning, embarrassed by the *smokes everywhere* incident. It could have happened to anyone. But for some reason, I want to laugh.

With windows all around and shutters bolted open, light surrounds us. I shield my eyes with my hand and study the colorful quilt warming me. There's a charming square cut from the yardage Mom brought back from Mexico: black-and-white-and-brown-striped with cute children riding *bicicletas* across a yellow background. There's the pink square alive with butterflies and dragonflies that Mom and I ordered through the mail from a book of material swatches. The design is woven. Mom says woven material is the best. I made a pretty shift out of the yardage and wore it all through high school. There are orange squares left over from the bedroom curtains I sewed for the old-mare rental where I lost the baby. All the squares are tied at each corner with a strand of yarn. The polyester fiberfill is warm enough for cool nights at six thousand feet. As I run a finger over an orange square, I turn my gaze to the territory. Ravens play above the trees, twirling and diving and pecking at each other.

If a person has never witnessed a raven flying upside down, it's hard to believe they could do such a thing. But just now, a raven flips over and flies south upside down. He flies swiftly, rolling upright again in a wink. Another bird catches up with him, tips a wing, and croaks a greeting. I laugh aloud. "Look," I say.

Jack turns to the playing ravens, curiosity written on his face. At last, he smiles his beautiful smile.

As the days creep by, Jack becomes more and more antsy. Maybe it's all the solitude or maybe it's just his nature; he is so tightly wound. *High-strung* is what my parents call his type. *Uptight* is what I say. Whatever the reason for his tension, he decides to blow it off by riding his Bridgestone to the turnoff to visit his new friend, Tom.

"Shoot the bull, smoke a bowl, hang loose."

Shrugging, I get up and take a seat at the picnic table. I feel better, though the ache in my abdomen hasn't completely let up.

I begin making out a grocery list. We go through food quickly around here, especially nuts and seeds, olives, and beer. "If you get down to Grangeville, would you pick up these items?" I offer him the note.

He nods, snatching the list out of my hand. Backpack strapped on, he doesn't even say goodbye—just runs out the door onto the catwalk and down the stairs. The tower shakes and the motorcycle rumbles to life, spattering gravel into the silence of morning. As the sound recedes, I stretch out on the bed with a paperback, glad to have a little recovery time without Jack's pissy energy dragging me down.

I crack open *Robinson Crusoe* and immediately get sucked into the story. Time passes slowly. I get up now and then to make tea, pee in the can, and walk around the catwalk, checking the territory through the high-powered binoculars. It's a clear, cool day, not much chance of a fire popping up since we haven't had a storm in a while. I head back inside, leave the binoculars on the counter, and pick up my book again. By afternoon, I've made the rounds several times, been down to the outhouse and back four times, and have read half the book.

The drone of a plane interrupts my concentration. I drop the book face down on the bed and head outside. I stand there like a fool, waving eagerly at the yellow fire plane heading toward the tower. The fire plane dips a wing and levels out as it closes in on Corral Hill. I duck, covering my ears as the plane roars past, its wing a little too near the railing for comfort. And then, like all good fire-plane pilots, he spots a fire not far from the tower, a fire I missed. Missed because I was reading my book or because it was over the rise just out of sight? Or because, because, because—I don't know why I missed it. But I did. "Shit!"

The pilot calls in the coordinates as I stand helplessly by, listening to their conversation over the radio, watching the yellow fire plane grow smaller and smaller as it heads back to

Grangeville. I turn to the north and gasp, for even with the naked eye I see the thin curl of smoke rising above the clear-cut. My stomach sinks. "We're in deep shit!"

I return to the cabin and line up the firefinder crosshairs on the smoke. I hear the pilot laughing on the radio, saying to Clear-water Ranger District: "Your lookout missed a smoke."

My stomach lurches as I jot down the coordinates and grab the radio handset. I'm wishing hard that Jack was back. I had my nose buried in a book; I wasn't paying close enough attention. I repeat Jack's mantra *fuck, fuck, fuck* as I pick up the receiver, back-pedaling thoughts coming to mind. *I made my rounds regularly, checking the territory, and still I missed the smoke. Bad timing is all. Bad timing!*

I begin formulating what I'd say to my boss, who no doubt would be heading up the mountain to reprimand us in no time: *It was a quiet day. A storm hadn't passed through lately. I wasn't feeling well. Jack went for supplies. He's better at this than I am. I'm sorry, sorry, sorry. Sorrier than you can imagine. Please forgive me!*

But I missed what the guys in the plane spotted easily. And now they're laughing at me. Laughing!

I've been calling headquarters on a different radio channel, as I'm still nervous to use the dang thing. Jack teases me about it, but honestly, it's nearly a phobia. I figure if I call on a different channel, not as many people will hear my halting voice seeping across the airwaves. Maybe it's not true, but a different channel helps me feel more courageous.

A cramp doubles me over. I lean against the firefinder po-dium, sweating, apologizing in my head to God, Arizona, his boss Arnie, Jack, and myself for being such a fuck-up—just like Dick said.

"Clearwater Ranger District, this is Corral Hill . . ." I'm tenta-tive as I speak, relaying the coordinates. Then I hear Jack's motorcycle coming up the road. I sign off, practically dropping the handset as I hang it up.

I run outside, binoculars in hand, waving as Jack rounds the corner. He rides up the last stretch of road, a trail of dust ready to tag him from behind. I practically jump up and down as he boots the kickstand and pulls off his helmet. He unstraps the bungee cords from the bags he's fastened onto the back and, with a full backpack, begins a slow ascent.

"There's a smoke," I yell down to him. "Hurry!"

I hear his boots on the stairs running, stumbling, and running again. He's frantic by the time he emerges on the catwalk. "Where, where?"

"There," I say, pointing toward a thin curl of smoke. "A fire plane flew over. The pilot called it in."

Jack grabs the binoculars out of my hands and studies the area, grumbling low in his throat.

I chew a fingernail. "A smoke, Jack. I missed it. I called it in after the pilot did. They laughed at me. Laughed over the radio!"

Jack drops his backpack on the counter and rechecks the co-ordinates. He grabs the radio and calls the district. "It's small," he says. "Over the hill. We didn't see it. Probably the same storm where the firefighters fought the blaze to the southwest. Remember, the cloud put down several strikes."

He hangs up the radio. "They're sending a crew. We could walk to it in less time than it will take for them to get here."

"Man-oh-man," I say, clutching my stomach. "We're in deep shit."

Jack pulls at his beard. "What were you doing?"

"Reading, going down to the bathroom, you know. I made the rounds several times, but I didn't see it. Then the plane flew over, spying it easily. They laughed at me, Jack. Laughed."

Fires are burning all around, smoke smudging the sky in Montana and just over the mountains to the east. And now the fire just over the hill from the tower has taken off; the clear-cut's beginning to lose definition as brownish-white smoke blankets the area. If they hadn't flown over, I would have spotted it shortly. "What a fucking bummer!"

The plume curls like my mother's cigarette smoke clouding the car's interior. My brother's smoke filled the kitchen while on leave from Vietnam, holding his hand-rolled fag inside a cupped palm, a gesture he said soldiers adopt to hide the glow of their smoke from the enemy. Both Mom and Bruce blow smoke rings. I wish I could make a ring that floats away, disappearing into the ethers. It looked sexy when a high school cheerleader did it. But cigarette smoke makes me ill—definitely not sexy.

Jack and I hung out together after school, wandering the neighborhood where we lived just two blocks apart. He knew all the private places where we could make out. Which we did any chance we got. One day he said he wanted to teach me how to get high. We leaned together in an unfinished basement, me watching intently as he stuffed the tiniest roach imaginable into the end of a bummed cigarette. The roach was so small, it burned up immediately when he lit up. He handed me the cig and I took a puff, inhaling the tobacco smoke, which dropped me dizzily to the ground. He helped me home and I went to bed for the rest of the day.

It was because Mother overheard me talking to Jack when I woke up that Dick did what he did. I was just being silly when I said, "Wow, what a trip." But those words seemed to prove to my parents that I was on drugs, thus the visit to Dick's friend, Corky. Prior to the event, I recalled Dick asking me silly questions, hoping, I suppose, to catch me in a stoned state. I wasn't stoned, but I guess my answers, plus what I said after the cigarette-smoking-event, were enough proof to warrant a trip to the police station.

In a tiny upstairs office at the police station, we sat across the desk from Corky, a mean-looking narcotics officer. The narcotics chief interrogated me until I was bawling, blurting out the names of friends who'd sold or had given Jack drugs: one diet pill stolen from Dennis's mother's medicine cabinet, a quarter-inch-long roach—compliments of Gary from the art department—and a birth control pill (oops!) from somewhere. Wonder who swallowed that one? I don't think I ratted out any other naïve drug thieves, but I really don't recall. After I'd been "interrogated," my stepdad drove me home and sent me to my room. He forbade me from ever seeing Jack again. *That didn't work out so well, did it?*

No matter what I said, I couldn't convince Dick that cigarette smoke had made me dizzy. Not surprising, I guess, since I'd been riding around in the back seat of the Caddy, breathing Mom's secondhand smoke since I was in grade school. I don't want to subject myself to that stink ever again. Now, firefighters put out a smoke that has milked the air an opaque, bluish-white. My eyes and nose burn from the particulate. The firefighters are breathing carcinogens and so are we!

I head inside the tower and close the door. I put on a pot of water for tea, thinking about Arizona's words after he said he was coming up to speak to us: *Nearly two million acres of timber burnt in Washington and Idaho last year. Firefighters died. Towns burnt. Forest income was obliterated.*

The tea kettle whistles. I begin to cough.

Jack and I collected wild roses early this morning, dipping each pink petal in egg white, then in granulated sugar. We let the petals dry on paper napkins and, when completely dry, *viola*, we had ourselves a candy dish (aka, FS Melmac coffee cup) filled to the top with delicately perfumed confections. Delicious! We set the collections on the countertop next to coffee cups. Coffee perks on the stove as the tower shakes. Our timing's perfect.

Arizona strides into the cabin wearing his summer cowboy hat and black cowboy boots and plunks himself down in the green

chair with a loud exhale. When I hand him the little bowl of sug-
ared rose petals he snorts. I say in my sweetest voice, "We made
them ourselves."

With big fingers he pinches a tiny petal from the dish and
places the candy on the tip of his tongue. "Huh!" he says, chewing
slowly. "Not bad. You tryin' to butter me up or something?" He
cocks one eyebrow.

I shake my head. "Coffee, sir?"

"No thanks."

Jittery still, I continue to smile. Turning, I look at Jack, who
stands back, pulling at his beard.

"I'm not here for roses," he says. "Why the hell'd you miss a
fire right out your goddamned backdoor?"

"We *were* looking for fires," I say. "Like your boss, Arnie, said
we should—about twenty minutes out of every hour." (I didn't
say that Jack was gone on a motorcycle ride. After all, he was on
the clock too.) The sound of another truck pulling up below
makes my stomach drop again. "Sure you don't want a cup of
coffee?" I squeak.

Arizona grumbles.

Jack steps out the door and calls to us. "Arnie's here."

Arnie clomps up the stairs, shaking the tower more violently
than Arizona. He's a big man too, though not as rotund as Arizona. When he steps inside the tower, the room turns
claustrophobic. We offer him rose petals and coffee. He shakes
his head and takes a seat at the picnic table, his face worried.

Both men study us, eyebrows pinched as we sputter explana-
tions as to how the event played out. We swear we would have
discovered the fire too, and probably about the same time as the
plane flying over had. It was bad timing, that was all. They suggest
we watch more carefully, as the fire danger is growing higher
every day. And more often than every twenty minutes. When they

finally leave the tower, Jack's face is dripping with sweat. My head is pounding.

The plane beat us to it. I try to get these words out of my mind, but I can't. I keep seeing the pilot's jeering face. I didn't do anything wrong. Nothing bad happened because we failed to get a jump on the smoke. But I was reading my book. I could have spent more time on the catwalk, making the rounds. I feel sick about it all and vow to work harder, searching the territory through high-powered binoculars until I go cross-eyed.

The rest of the day, we watch the territory closely, hardly speaking. The following morning, I study the territory inch by inch, slowly moving the high-powered binoculars across the forest. Arizona laughs when I call in the azimuth on the regular channel. It turns out it's Lewiston's paper mill. "Way the hell out of the district, Nance," Arizona says. "But good job, anyhow."

After a few days of being extra vigilant, we relax a little. Jack's back to taking occasional rides on his motorcycle and I pick up *Robinson Crusoe* again and sip tea while relaxing on the bed with the exciting book. We haven't had a storm rumble through in over a week, so a day of rain and wind somehow makes us feel quiet and settled, like damp tinder. Jack pulls out the Woodstock guitar and plays "Quicksilver Girl." As he plays, a suggestive look brightens his face. I smile, thinking he is so good-looking.

Types of Kisses

French kiss
Butterfly kiss
Single-lip kiss
Upside-down kiss
Earlobe kiss
Sloppy kiss
Eskimo kiss
Hickey
Secret message kiss
Hollywood kiss
Vampire kiss
Thrown kiss
Biting kiss
Breath kiss
Forehead kiss
Unwanted kiss

seven

When I first learned to French, I clamped my teeth together, causing my jaw to ache for two days. I decided it was gross having a
boy's tongue darting about inside my mouth. I was hell-bent on
keeping that fleshy thing out of there. I admit that I'd drunk too
much that night and threw up in the tiny bathroom at the back of
the woodsy cabin at Priest Lake. My best friend at the time, Dee,
held my hair back. It was touching in a way, how she mothered
me. I don't remember if I brushed my teeth afterward, but really,
I don't remember much about that night except returning to the
bedroom where the boy's adept fingers proceeded to unfasten my
brazier as he continued to attempt to French me.

I wonder why a man wants to probe a woman's mouth, to
breathe in and out along with her breath, to bite her lips or press
her head hard into the pillow, leaving her lips swollen and bruised
from kissing afterward. Perhaps it's because "man" comes from
the body of a woman. Perhaps the male's inner animal growls and
grabs hold of the female with sharp teeth, attempting to conquer
and penetrate, and to procreate. And, perhaps, to take back control.

We kissed for a long time last night, and now, Jack wants to
kiss again. He hovers behind the green chair where I'm sitting, his

hands on my shoulders. I'm not into kissing this morning. Not only did his mustache rub my upper lip raw, but his nipping teeth left my lower lip tender. "Not now," I say, realizing that sometimes I feel held down, and that reminds me of Dick's visits to my bedroom. Perhaps I'll never get to a place where I don't recall my stepdad sloppy-kissing me like he did the night Mom was away visiting my sick grandmother in her Arizona nursing home. He woke me from a dead sleep with his whiskey-flavored lips pressed over mine. I pushed him away and still he pleaded drunkenly to get in bed with me.

Jack leans over me, pestering me for a kiss. I say *no* forcibly and proceed to knit. He walks away, shoulders slumped. Last night when we slipped beneath the covers and kissed, it felt good; I felt loved. But then he got too excited and started kissing me too hard. I couldn't keep my mind from wandering to Dick, so I told him to stop. He did, though reluctantly. Finally, we ended up spooning to the sound of heavy rain peppering the tower as we drifted off.

Sighing, I recount the stitches I cast on earlier for the left sleeve of the gray sweater. As I cast stitches, I feel bad about being so sharp with Jack. He sometimes presses his lips into a line when I'm bummed, like he's mad at me for feeling reluctant. Or he lights up a joint when I talk about wanting another baby. Sometimes the pain I feel around all this makes me want to run out the door and down the stairs, down the road to where the cows sometimes drink from the spring. But then what? There's no place for me to go where my emotional pain doesn't follow close behind.

I imagine the wind pulling me out the window, wending me along the dirt road, my feet touching down occasionally, scuffing up dust as I sail above the powdery dirt. How far would I get on foot, I wonder? Not far. Yet the impulse is strong; I move to standing, remembering the "new" Scout and the key I left on the counter by the tower door. *No*, I tell myself. *Face the pain.* Finally,

I give up and rest back again, knitting along the first row of cast-on stitches. Now that I have wheels, I can bolt whenever I want. I'll go down to town tomorrow and see the doctor at the free clinic. I want the doctor's okay to go ahead and try for another baby. I so want a baby to love.

T. Lobsang Rampa suggests meditation as a solution for anger, sadness, or for the wandering mind—for everything, really. But the idea of sitting in a cave and seeing nobody for a lifetime scares the bejesus out of me. I feel lonely enough without wishing for more solitude than we already have living in the Clearwater National Forest. There's enough isolation at six thousand feet to last us a lifetime.

Jack's out on the catwalk peering through the bins, studying the territory north of the prairie. No storm is predicted tonight. Not even a shower, though the horizon is growing hazy. *Knit, purl, knit, purl.* I study hubby through the window. He's wearing a serious face, mouth flattened into a line so thin that his lips nearly disappear. If he keeps his mustache clipped, the narrowness of his lips remains visible. Though they quickly diminish when pressed together with concentration. Suddenly, I want to know his lips better, maybe even draw my tongue across them, feeling their slimness, tasting their saltiness. But the feeling doesn't last. I mean, I just need a moment to myself sometimes. Such close quarters here on the tower. Such terrible, suffocating nearness.

Arizona said anytime I need a shower, I can stop by their place. His wife will be home today, so no need to bother her, just enter through the side door. "The bathroom's just down the hall on the right," he said. "Just let me know ahead of time and I'll warn the missus."

We haven't done laundry in a long time, so I rinse out my underwear in the sink, checking my figure in the bathroom mirror. I'm tanned and angular, having lost weight since we've been on

Corral Hill. My hair is greasy. I have a new smattering of freckles dotting my nose. I remember my friend Dee's neighbor at Priest Lake saying that after three months of roughing it in Alaska her hair was in better shape than it had ever been in her life. It was from the grease that didn't get sudsed away daily. I'm hoping for the same results.

I press out my underwear in a dry towel and hang them over the towel rod. They'll still be wet when I'm done showering, so I decide not to wear them under my cutoffs until after I see the doctor. I don't want an embarrassing wet spot soaking through the seat of my pants.

I turn on the shower and step in. Streams of hot water cascade over my skin, the feeling luxurious and soothing. I am truly amazed by this simple pleasure. As I drink in the comfort of running hot water, I consider how people take electricity and running water for granted and decide to stop wasting water when I get back to Spokane. But right now, all I want to do is stand beneath the showerhead *forever*.

By the time I arrive at the health clinic on Main Street, it is a hundred degrees in the shade. I hang my bikini underwear on a hook in the dressing room, hoping they'll be completely dry by the time the exam is over. White gown pressed tightly around me, I pad barefoot to the exam table and take a seat at the end next to the metal stirrups covered with white socks. My palms are sweaty and my feet are cold. My stomach hurts.

The doctor arrives shortly. He's friendly and down-home-looking. He checks everything: pulse, blood pressure, heart, eyes, ears, throat, even the crooked place in my spine. Then he has me lie back for the pelvic exam. I do as he says, tightening with anxiety as he pulls out the stirrups and lifts my feet into them.

"Just relax," the doctor says.

I do my best, feeling the pinch, then the swab. Then I feel his large-gloved fingers probing my insides, his top hand pressing down over my lower abdomen. He says, "There's a mass in your pelvis the size of an apple."

I experience a split-second leap of hope. "I'm pregnant?"

He shakes his head. "It's near your left ovary. More the size of a lemon or small orange."

"Is it because of the miscarriage?"

"Probably not," he says, continuing to palpate.

I flinch. "That hurts."

"Sorry," he says, and removes his hand. Gloves snap and he tosses them in a wastebasket. "You can sit up now." He picks up his clipboard and writes on my chart. "I'm referring you to a specialist in Lewiston. He'll determine whether it is cancer or not. You may need surgery."

I feel faint, like I did when I skipped class and Jack and I drove to his friend's house to drink beer. I should have known my stepdad would track my odometer. Busted beneath his disappointed glare, I fell through the stars, sliding into a faint on the floor below. Now, the room begins to darken the same way. "Cancer?" I say, my voice catching.

"Can't rule it out. The nurse will make the appointment for you. Stop at the desk on your way out." He smiles. "Nice to meet you," and he closes the door.

I can't move for several moments. "Cancer," I breathe into the sterile room, regaining my equilibrium. Then I sit up, sliding off the table onto unsteady feet.

The lingering dampness in my underwear feels cool against my skin. I wander numbly down one grocery aisle after another. The mass in my belly isn't a baby. I recall Grandma's dumplings, round and doughy. Perhaps it's the size of a dumpling or a hard-boiled egg.

I'm hungry but I don't feel much like eating. I think of Mother's mashed potatoes and gravy. I recall her proclaiming chicken gravy as worthless. "It's not real gravy unless it's dark brown." She made gravy from what she called brownies, the drippings left in the pan after roasting beef. Mother taught me to sear meat until it is almost burnt. I recall pouring the flour and water mixture into the sizzling meat brownies, adding salt, Kitchen Bouquet, and boiling water, stirring the mixture into thick gravy that we would spoon lavishly over mounds of mashed potatoes.

"Delicious," I mumble as I drop an assortment of Campbell's soup in the cart. Jack likes chicken noodle. I like cream of mushroom. And, unlike Mother, I've always loved chicken gravy. I head toward the meat case to buy a hen. On the way, I fill the cart with apples, potatoes, peanut butter, RyKrisp, Coors, eggs, Wonder bread, chocolate chips, brown sugar, and an icy Coke for the trip home. At the meat counter, the butcher wraps up a hen, jerky, pork chops, and a pound of hamburger, which I can't help noticing is the color of blood. I turn away, thinking enough is enough. The lookout tower's gas refrigerator has a tiny freezer. I buy only what we can use in a few days, plus a few items to cram into the icy eight-by-eight-by-ten-inch compartment.

We're lucky. Not all towers have refrigeration. Everything's hauled in on horseback: dried fruit, canned milk, grains, and tins of meat. And of course, K-rations—but nothing perishable needing to be kept cold. Things that need to stay cool, like flour, are stored in a cold cupboard, screened and open to the breezy mountain air beneath the floor.

Near the store's back wall, I look through multiple colors of Red Heart yarn and choose several skeins of orange, yellow, brown, and green to crochet an afghan for Mom. Once checked out, I step outside into the blazing sun and push the cart across sizzling asphalt to the Scout. By the time I've loaded the groceries into the passenger seat, I'm sweating like a pig. Before I head home, I make one more stop: the bookstore to purchase a book I want to read titled *Psychic Discoveries Behind the Iron Curtain*. I'm excited about telekinesis. When I learn the secret, I'll try bending a spoon with my mind. I imagine lifting it and floating it through the air, scooping up a spoonful of chocolate ice cream on its way to my mouth. I buy the book and hurry back to the Scout before everything spoils.

Lightning

Intra-cloud
Cloud-to-cloud
Cloud-to-ground
Ground-to-cloud
Heat lightning
Ball lightning
Sheet lightning
Dry lightning
Bead lightning
St. Elmo's fire

eight

Jack's New York friends live halfway down the mountain in a rustic shack located across the road from the farmer's place. Tom, along with James—the long-haired, blond artist—and his girlfriend, Kate, trade living space for odd jobs. James told Jack that when he showed the farmer his art portfolio, he convinced him to let the three of them stay the summer. I imagine the farmer removing his hat and scratching his head as he gazed at James's abstract art. For some reason, he agreed to let the three hippies occupy the rustic shack at the back corner of his acreage.

A little after lunch, New York Tom clomps up the stairs. He announces that he's tired of the others' constant bickering and needed to get out of there. "They act like jerks. They got a new kitten," he said. "It jumped on the woodstove and back off, licking its burnt paws for hours. They just laughed at the stupid thing."

Tom shook his head, unloading the bag of crooked cukes and knobby tomatoes, setting them on the counter along with a pint of raw milk. "The farmer must like you guys. The only food we get is what we work for by weeding vegetables, feeding chickens, and milking the cow."

"Jack visits him sometimes," I say, biting into a salted pickling cuke. "They've become friends."

Jack's mouth slides into a sly grin as he licks cream off his upper lip. Moving to the refrigerator, he exchanges the pint of milk for a couple of chilled Coors. He pulls the tabs and hands a cold one to Tom and swigs the foam off the other. While Tom tips back his beer, Jack strikes a match with a *pop*. He lifts the flame to a fat joint and takes a puff, holding the smoke in until he can no longer. He hands the burning doobie to our friend, releasing the smoke in a burst.

Grinning, Tom takes the joint. He is happy to be here, having caught a ride up the mountain with a hunter. He takes a deep drag off the doobie, leans back against the stove in the south corner of the tower and closes his eyes. Beyond his tall frame, a small black cloud stains the perfect blue of midday.

Ignoring their stoned banter, I step around Tom and raise high-powered binoculars to the sky. Magnified, there's no mistaking the roiling brute speeding toward us as anything but a thunderhead. As I think this, a searing bolt arcs toward the ground. I shout over the thunderclap, "We're gonna get hit!"

Jack and I make a dash for the bed. Pointing to the green chair as we leap on the mattress, he shouts, "Sit there, Tom."

Tom jumps into the Naugahyde chair, and just like that, the thunderhead is upon us. There's a searing bolt and simultaneous sonic-like boom, *CRACK!* And we're struck!

"Fuck, fuck, fuck," Jack swears.

"Shit," I say, falling back on the bed, heart pounding, eyes watering. I turn my head and look over at Tom. A sheet of white and his mouth agape, he begins to laugh hysterically. I turn my head in the other direction, watching the little cloud barreling on, already past the adjacent clear-cut to the north. It's not large, but it's supercharged with static electricity. The perfect natural phenomenon for Jack's growing list of John Muir-type experiences.

Now he has a new story to impress our friends with: *You should have been there when lightning hit our tower.* Our story won't quite match John Muir's exciting tale of a night spent lashed to a one-hundred-foot Douglas fir, riding out a Sierra Nevada windstorm. However, Jack's list keeps growing; he's doing his best to one-up the naturalist with his own natural wonders.

I leave Tom and Jack sputtering expletives and step outside. Inching around the catwalk to the west side of the tower, I peek at the ground wire. The lightning-shined copper buzzes like a swarm of yellow jackets. I whirl around and sprint back inside. "Lightning's in the grounding rod," I shout. "It could have arced, killing me."

"Not likely," Jack says. "It's discharging harmless static. That's all!"

"Static? You sure?"

"Positive," he says and relights the joint, takes a hit, and hands it to Tom.

Tom continues to laugh. His tall frame remains folded into the green chair, knees to chin. He reaches a shaking hand toward Jack. He takes a long drag off the joint and noticeably relaxes.

Jack seems to know everything about electricity, so I decide static it is. Still, I'm shaky, my heart pounding fast. I move weak-legged to the stove to put on a kettle of water. *When in doubt,* I think, *make a cup of tea!* I strike a match and light the propane burner, noticing beyond the blue propane flame a thin curl of smoke rising between the evergreens down by the road. Pointing, I shout, "Fire!"

When Jack and Tom return from checking out the fire, they act like they are on speed. Jack jots down coordinates and calls in the smoke, speaking loud and fast into the handset, "The tree's sliced open, burning in its roots," he says. "My friend, Tom, and I can handle it. We have a shovel and Pulaski."

"Get it done," Arizona says. "Consider him on the payroll. And tell Nance to watch for more smokes."

Jack hangs up the handset. "We're lucky motherfuckers. The lightning rod saved our asses," he says, turning to Tom. "Come on, man. We got a fire to fight."

The tower trembles wildly with the two men running down the stairs. I watch over the railing as they gather the Pulaski and shovels from the shed, hard hats obscuring their faces. Jack wears his steel-toed boots. Tom wears torn high-tops. There's excitement in the air.

Once they're beyond my view, I walk around the catwalk and touch the penny-bright grounding wire. It shines from the lightning rod up top all the way down to the ground. I still feel shaky from the direct hit, the crashing thunder, the blinding flash of light. And we weren't killed, which I consider lucky. I wander back inside, take a beer from the fridge, and open it. Tipping it back, I appreciate the cold brew and the feeling of warmth flowing through my veins. Well, it was more than luck, I guess. Lightning protection must be a science. Thank goodness they have it figured out.

I decide to refrigerate the second six-pack. When the men return, the first thing they'll want is another cold one, and something to eat, of course. They'll be sweaty, soot-covered, smelling of smoke, and exhausted from digging out the base of the tree, making sure all the roots are cold. We'll eat dinner and call it a night.

I could have gone with them. The forest service hires women firefighters now. I imagine firefighting chicks stumbling into camp, dead-tired, smudged black, tugging off their boots in the parking lot to bandage blisters. Women have demanded equal rights and now they carry Pulaskis, shovels, and canteens, and wear safety glasses and hard hats, the same as men. I can see them dropping their equipment outside the shower barracks and tripping inside. They remove hard hats and let their hair fall to their shoulders. They throw blackened, stinking clothing in heaps and step under sprays of hot water, sighing gratefully.

I've also heard stories of firefighters getting hemmed in when a backfire flares up or killed when a tree explodes. It's risky work, but I'm not worried about Jack and Tom. From the sound of it, this fire is straightforward. I lift the binoculars and look in the general direction of the smoke I saw rising between the trees earlier; it has widened and now catches the pink light of late afternoon. Amazingly, a dangerous thing has turned into a thing of beauty. I swing around to the north, studying the path of the thunderhead. I see nothing but the usual, thickly treed mountains, clear-cuts, and the late afternoon sky beyond.

Before me, there's a pile of garden veggies strewn across the counter that Tom brought from the farmer's house. In some ways the brilliant tomatoes and radishes seem unreal. And Tom showing up on our doorstep seems to have happened far in the past. I pick up a small tomato and bite into it. Its sweet juiciness surprises me. I feel giddy. It must be the shock of lightning hitting our tower. All my senses are on hyperalert.

Jack doesn't like taking things from people, not even vegetables. Neither does my stepdad. Both men think that if you accept a gift, you owe the person something in return. Dr. Gilmore says generosity is a coin, one side giving, the other side receiving. I enjoy giving. Perhaps it's more of a female thing. However, it is much harder for me to receive. Perhaps something I learned from Dick.

I love that the women's liberation movement encourages us to leave behind subservient roles and learn to assert ourselves. Jack is old-fashioned like his dad, or maybe he's just lazy, thinking I should do all the cooking and cleaning and washing. After our wedding in the state park a little over a year ago, he asked me to iron his jeans and T-shirts like his mother used to do. Of course,

I said, *No way!* I do a lot for him, anyway, and still he grumbles if I ask him to put on a pot of tea water or scramble me an egg when I'm feeling under the weather. Mostly I agree with the division of labor around here. I mean, he can have jurisdiction over the vehicles. Though I do know how to rebuild a carburetor, he still argues that I could have kept the Bridgestone upright the day he tried to teach me to ride. He climbed on behind me—that was his mistake. I've told him a million times that we fell because his body pressed against mine from behind, pushing my hand against the accelerator, revving the engine as we rode Lakeshore Road.

The more he leaned against me from behind, the less control I had. As I careened toward the drop-off and the lake far below, he kept yelling, *Let off the gas!*—but his weight kept my hand jammed against the throttle. The engine roared as we closed in on the bluff, skidding on nettle-covered ground and dumping us just short of the bank. Jack jumped up and stomped around, shouting, "Shit! Fuck! Piss! What's wrong with you?"

Sitting up, I brushed off my scraped knees and elbows and started to cry. "Don't ever ask me to drive again."

"Don't fucking worry. I won't!"

Of course, I'm not the only one who's wiped out on the bike. Once, he laid it over as we rounded the corner onto Luby Bay Road. We went down, the two of us sliding along the dirt, the bike spinning like a skipped rock, turning and turning until we finally came to rest. Jack most always wears his brown leather jacket and helmet. I wear my helmet and sunglasses, more for my hair and contacts, since the dust blinds me and the wind tangles my curls. I don't have a leather jacket like Jack does. That day I was wearing the same thing I'm wearing now: summer top, cutoffs, and tennis shoes. We were scraped up royally.

I guess I'm a bit of a tomboy, even though I was raised to be a lady. My parents enrolled me in charm school the summer prior to junior high. I recall my stepdad picking my girlfriends and me up after class one Saturday. Next to me in the back seat sat my best friend, Jody. Next to her, on the opposite side of the car, sat my other best friend, Mary Ellen. We each had our new makeup kits open on our laps.

"Now that you know how to behave like ladies," Dick said, "I expect you to do just that."

"We are," I said, smiling at my reflection in the rearview mirror, my newly rouged lips parting to show off my white teeth, my face tilted slightly upward, as if for a kiss. I remember wanting to believe I *was* beautiful like my stepdad said I was. But it's harder to be charming than it looks. It takes strength to squat gracefully in a skirt and stand again so it doesn't ride up. Strength like it takes to climb four flights of stairs or grip the driver from behind while riding on the back of a motorcycle. And, of course, quad strength is needed during sexual intercourse.

I guess I've turned into a women's libber now: braless and brazen. I say *fuck* whenever I want. I remember the closest I ever came to swearing while growing up was when I said, *Jesus*.

Mother said, "Shame on you, Nancy. You swore."

"No, I didn't," I said. "Jesus is plural of geez." Now that I think about it, I'm not really brazen. I mean, in some ways I'm as timid as a mouse . . . take the mic on the tower radio, for instance.

Dusk is falling. It won't be long before I will need to strike a match and light the gas lantern. I think of the guys working away in the darkening woods. They don't have headlamps to fight the fire with, which would help if they end up working after dark.

I slip the binocular strap over my head and walk outside. Leaning against the railing, I lift the heavy binoculars toward the territory. A thin curl of smoke continues twining upward between the trees. I drop the field glasses to my chest and stroll around the catwalk to the north side of the tower. I lift them again to the path of the little cloud. Nothing!

Sighing, I wait, imagining wrapping my legs around Jack's nakedness tonight. A flutter bubbles up from low in my abdomen.
Jack and Tom should have a cold fire by late evening. Jack can
give Tom a ride back to the farmer's house so we can be alone
together later.

Mother taught me that sex wasn't to be engaged in out of wed-
lock. In high school, when Jack started coming over to the house,
she said to me one day, *I know what you're doing down there*—meaning
downstairs in the family room where we were making out on the
couch. But she didn't really know what we were doing. That
couch was where I had my first orgasm. And later where I lost my
virginity. I promised her that we weren't doing anything. She
frowned at me, blowing cigarette smoke out her nostrils.

Mother said that getting married was sacred. And that her family believed that couples married for life. But Dick's my
stepfather—which means she was married before to my real father. This essential bit of information didn't come to my attention
until I turned sixteen. That's when my stepbrother moved in with
us. Prior to that, he'd been our skinny cousin who came to visit
on weekends. Dick had adopted my brother and me when he married my mother. I was three. Bruce was six. You'd think someone
would have told us the truth before our stepbrother—alias
cousin—moved in when he was in high school.

I hear muffled voices and my heart leaps. The guys are back
from the fire. They stomp up the stairs, stumbling past the bank
of tower windows to the door. Filthy and soot-smeared, I say,
"Wait outside. I'll heat water so you can wash up on the catwalk."

The fire's cold and Tom's back home after spending last night on
the floor of the cabin, which was disappointing, though I understand it was too late for Jack to give him a ride back to the farmer's
house. The guys were exhausted from all that digging, so after
washing up, we opened beers and slurped down tomato soup,

dipping leftover stale bread in the creamy red liquid. They took turns stopping to take a breath, describing the sliced trunk, the intense heat, the roots burning, and how hard and dirty the work was. Smoke burned their eyes and made it hard to breathe. After each outburst, the men went back to eating and drinking in silence.

This morning, we keep an eye on the path the thunderhead took, searching often for new smokes. But everything is dull. No new smokes and very little radio activity. We fiddle around, reading a little, knitting (my gray sweater is nearly complete), playing the guitar, and sighing. We throw each other occasional wistful glances. All that excitement and now, zilch. I think we've made up for the "missed fire incident."

Jack decides to haul water. I walk to the stream with him. There are flies galore right now, some of them biting. I swing my arms, smacking them away, certain they can smell my stink. We need baths like the dry forest needs rain.

Back at the tower, we fill the Igloo cooler with cold water. I heat a pan of it on the stove for sponge baths. I smell sweaty and Jack smells of smoke and BO. The bath ritual feels good: hanging our heads over the railing, taking turns shampooing each other's hair, toweling off, feeling refreshed by the smell of Dr. Bronner's peppermint soap. Jack moves in close, touching my back lightly. I turn to him, smiling.

We decide it would be fun to have a little party tonight. We arrange peanut butter and slightly wilted celery, slices of cheddar cheese, and a few rectangles of RyKrisp on a plate. We nibble small pieces of beef jerky purchased at the Grangeville grocery and the farmer's tomatoes and crooked cukes. We savor the last of the organic dried apricots we bought at the health food store in Spokane. Then there's Jack's chilled home brew served in green forest service cups—their size more suited for gathering thimbleberries than for drinking dark beer. And, of course, we have each other's sweet lips to savor in between sips.

We sit on the bed, eating and making sexy faces, licking peanut butter off each other's fingers. Sliced pickles make us pucker. The green beer goes down fast, hoppy at first, and then the high alcohol content warms our veins and makes me feel tipsy.

Jack reaches over to touch my breasts. "I love your perky breasts!"

Giggling, I think of the colostrum leaking from my nipples when I was pregnant. How they widened and darkened, the areolas rising around each nipple. For a short time, I was slightly more buxom than I am now. For a short time, I was with child, replete with womanhood, happier than I've ever been.

With no smokes in sight and a horizon beginning to color peach in the west, the two of us seem to be on the same wavelength. We kiss greedily, stripping off our tops, then our bottoms. Now we're naked, sitting with our dinner spread across the bed between us. The brightness of the setting sun bathes the cabin in orange light, the color flooding the prairie and igniting the forest with its glow. Ravens *groak* from nearby trees. The cat stretches, turns, and sleeps again.

"I love you, Nancerella."

"I love you, Jack."

That night I dream that I've hurt Jack's feelings. I didn't get up and pour more beer, nor close the door after he opened it, or was it that I left it open after he'd closed it? I didn't let the cat out or in. I didn't look at him right or kiss him just so or stroke him like he likes. In my dream I sail off the tower, crash-landing in the gravel parking area. Heart pounding, I jerk awake. A motor idles below.

"Jack," I whisper. "Jack!"

He turns over in his sleep, mumbling, "What?"

"Listen," I say, shaking him. "Someone's down there."

Groggy, he leans up on his elbow and cocks his head. Out of bed in a flash, pulling cutoffs on over his nakedness, he steps out onto the catwalk. "Who's there?" he calls. No answer. Quietly, he closes the trapdoor and locks it. Standing back, he calls out again, "Who's there?"

The sound of grinding gears and spinning gravel breaks the silence. Headlights flick off the trees. A shadowy truck spins off, bouncing down the road, away from the tower. Poachers again? Someone thinking they could camp out on the lookout? Someone meaning us ill will? I cover my heart with a trembling hand. It races like the sound of the engine fading into the night.

Jack pisses over the railing. He returns to the cabin, drops his cutoffs to the floor, and climbs under the sheet next to me. As he runs a hand down my thigh, I turn to him, circling his waist with my arm. "I wonder how long they were down below. They could have climbed the tower while we were sleeping."

"Everything's okay now," he says. "They're gone."

He continues his exploration, palming my pubic bone as he heads lower. I'm still wound up. I move his hand to my hip bone—safe territory. An artist friend of ours once claimed the hip bone was the sexiest of all the body's bones. Our friend smiled devilishly while staring at my waistline. Shrinking away, I turned from his gaze to grip Jack's arm.

"Please," Jack says in the dark.

"Can't. I'm freaked out still."

He touches me again. "It'll take your mind off of it."

"I'm not so sure of that," I say, and roll away.

Several days have passed without lightning activity. Today started out sunny, but this afternoon, the smell of rain wafts through the open windows. To the west, clouds gather and sheets of virga cross the prairie. Jack points out the virga and says there's another natural phenomenon visible to the naked eye. He takes his stance of authority and says, "It's called prana: sparkling particles of life force."

Still acting a bit standoffish from last night when I turned down his sexual advances, he takes my hand and leads me out onto the catwalk. I go willingly, happy that he wants to mend fences—though I don't know what there is to mend, since I have the right to say no.

In the distance, the storm gathers energy. Anvil clouds spread wide on updrafts. Maybe we'll get some action, after all.

Jack leads me around to the west side of the tower. Facing the prairie, he says, "Now look, without trying, at the air directly in front of you."

I do what he says, relaxing my eyes. As I do so, tiny dots of light begin to dart around like sperm beneath a microscope. "Are you sure it's not just tired eyes causing this? I mean, the sun was intense earlier."

"It's life force, you know. God," he says. "Remember when we climbed Gunsight Peak?"

"Sure, that was way cool!" I recall sitting on the pinnacle, my legs hanging over the rocky edge of the seven-thousand-foot peak. Sparkles swirled all around us. The curve of earth at the horizon was obvious and blew our minds. The sound of universal *om* was nearly deafening.

"Everything's saturated with life force," Jack says, narrowing his eyes. "And if you watch closely, you can see it."

I linger at the rail while Jack returns to the cabin. He usually doesn't act so "out there." I shrug, watching the distant storm clouds build beyond the darting life force. Soon, I hear the familiar jingle of *Green Acres* and give up on the prana. Back inside, I gather my crocheting and take a seat in the green chair. As I spread several granny squares across my knees, admiring the beginning of Mom's afghan, the last bits of sunlight break through the clouds and warm the cabin. In my last letter to Mom, I described how I was crocheting an afghan made of granny squares in her favorite colors: orange, brown, green, and yellow. If I keep adding to it for the rest of the summer, it could end up as big as a bedspread by her birthday.

Jack sits on the bed, angled so he can watch the building storm as he listens to *Green Acres*. Occasionally, he points and blurts out, "Cloud-to-cloud lightning."

"Record it in the strike log," I say.

"Fuck the strike log," he says, taking out his pipe and his stash of weed.

"Right," I say, and we both laugh. "It's impossible to get them all down. I hate the strike log."

Soon Zsa Zsa Gabor's character, Lisa Douglas, is chasing escaped pigs around the barnyard. One has gotten inside the farmhouse. Jack doubles over laughing. I shift in the chair, unbuttoning the top button of my cutoffs. I'm not sure why I'm feeling so uncomfortable. It's not my time of the month. The idea that I could be pregnant makes my heart quicken.

Although I've wanted a baby since I was sixteen, my cat may be the only child I raise this lifetime. She's curled up next to Jack right now, sound asleep. I recall the glowering looks she gave him when we first started sleeping together. A stray who showed up on the apartment house steps just after I moved away from home at age eighteen. From the beginning, Jude slept curled against my belly beneath the bedcovers. When Jack moved in, she left my side and sat at the end of the bed, glaring at the intruder. It's clear that he loves her. Perhaps it's a good indication of the kind of dad he'll be if we ever get pregnant.

Lisa chases squealing pigs around the kitchen. Jude startles awake. She jumps from bed to counter, looking around the room for the source of the noise.

"It's just the radio," I say, catching a flash of light beyond her. "There's one!"

Jack nods and continues to listen to the television show on the radio. *Green Acres*, as usual, is a fiasco. The Douglases have finally corralled the porkers and Oliver heads off to town to do some banking. It becomes hard for me to listen, since I suddenly feel a headache coming on. I recall having a murderous migraine before the miscarriage. People say miscarriages happen for a reason. Everyone seems to have a story about the one, two, or five miscarriages they had before delivering a full-term baby. The stories are usually relayed with cheer, as if God's plan to wash away a child in a flood of red is no big deal.

I should have gone to the doctor sooner, but I'd read in Adelle Davis's book, *Eat Right to Keep Fit*, that it isn't necessary during the first trimester. The nurse was surprised I hadn't been seen by the doctor yet, but thankfully she didn't scold me. Over the phone she said, "Stay in bed until you see the doctor on Monday. And try not to worry."

Right! I was terrified. I turn back to the building storm. The sun's hidden in a bank of clouds. I put away my crocheting and light the propane lamp. I put water on for tea. Maybe I lost the baby at three months because Jack was so angry at me for getting pregnant. He'd been adamant about not having children for six years. But then the IUD fell out; I was sure it was a sign that I was meant to have a child.

"It's raining," I say. A weak bolt flashes to the southeast. "See that one?"

Jack acknowledges the flash with a grumble.

I understand his desire for freedom. I know that he believes when you're young, you have plenty of energy to do whatever you want. When you're older and your energy is lower, there's plenty of time to work. He believes in opposites. If everyone works during the day, we should work at night. If everyone works while young, we should work while old. So now we're working during the summer, saving money to live off of during the winter. When we move back to Spokane, we'll live in the green old-mare house where I miscarried. We'll cross-country ski every day and sit by the popping woodstove at night. And maybe I'll be pregnant by then.

Just like that, it's pouring outside. The distant strikes have petered out. I get up from the chair and note in the strike log the few I recall. Lisa Douglas complains about farm living. She pleads with her husband to move back to New York City. For some reason, she reminds me of my mother.

Jack lights a pinch of weed, offering me a hit. Declining, I get up to make tea.

At the doctor's office, a nurse inserted a catheter to gather a clean urine specimen to test for the presence of life. I cried the whole time I laid on the table. The nurse said, "I'm sorry, hon." Her kindness was comforting, but I knew the baby was gone before the test came back.

After the D&C, I needed bed rest. Jack let me know in no uncertain terms how he felt about waiting on me. He can be such a prick. Maybe he's right, he *won't* make a good father. It's been two and a half months since the miscarriage, and he's shown little sensitivity to my feelings. The doctor said to wait at least three months before getting pregnant again. I guess there's no harm in trying!

The lightning show, for what it was worth, is over. Jack turns off the transistor radio. We brush our teeth to the sound of rain pummeling the shutters. Jack switches off the gas light. I expect darkness to fold in on us, but instead we are surrounded by a blue glow. The eerie glow edges the shutters, runs along the railings, drips down the uprights, and lights up the night.

"Fucking-A!"

I follow Jack, climbing onto the picnic table where we sit side by side, mouths agape as every drop of water that runs along the shutter edges and down the rails glows blue. We sit cross-legged, shoulders touching, as if we're watching a movie, taking in the natural phenomenon, our minds completely blown. "What is it?"

"Saint Elmo's fire," Jack says. We watch the blue plasma trail along shutter edges, dripping streams of glowing water onto the catwalk. The luminosity runs along the railings and down posts in rivulets, spattering and spraying off sharp edges. Every droplet lights the tower like Christmas.

"Wow! What a show!"

Laughing, Jack says, "It's out of sight!" He strikes a match on the seat of his cutoffs and tips the flame to his pipe. He puffs and the skunky scent of weed fills the air.

"What causes the blue glow?"

"We're in a charged field from the thunderstorm. It happens at sea too, St. Elmo's fire surrounding masts and rigging and sharp edges."

"But what makes it glow?"

"Static electricity."

We watch until we're too tired to watch any longer. Then we strip and climb under the covers, tangling bare limbs together. We kiss a little, drifting off to the sound of blue rain sheeting off the shutters, streaming down to the ground, refreshing the forest all around.

Weather Report

Hell-hot
Muggy
Windy
Stormy
Pissing down rain
Stifling
Gloomy
Cold
Freezing
Foggy
Misty
Charged
Spitting

nine

Silence thrums on and on at six thousand feet. It's like the sky and trees and everything all around give off a sound. Silence can be pretty loud—lonely even—and at the same time, it can be peaceful. The telephone never rings, or rarely does. Once, it was used to report wildfires. Arizona said, "If you want to call home, you can." But, like I said, the phone barely ever works.

Some folks don't like telephones. My brother, for one. I can never get him to call me. And when I call my stepdad, I always feel like I must be polite first. I should say, "Hi, how are you? How's your girlfriend?" before I say, "May I borrow the truck?" or "Could you loan me money to pay medical bills?" I don't want to be polite, so I put off calling. Mostly, I write him letters these days.

But every child needs a father's help when leaving the nest. So here I am on the tower looking at a ringing telephone, imagining it's my stepdad calling. I feel a little storm brewing in my chest. "What, already?" I say, staring down the receiver without picking up. This is how it is when you're dull from isolation and worn out from the blasted heat.

Jack steps inside from the catwalk and bellows, "Answer it, for fuck's sake."

I shrug. "No one's calling us back, since we didn't call anyone."

We know the line is broken or crimped somewhere between here and where it hooks up with Ma Bell. We've seen how it's strung through the forest, draped over tree limbs down from the tower to the farmer's place. It's not a village, just a junction of two roads where the farmer has lived forever.

"Maybe Mom is sick," I say. "Or something has happened to my sister. She's been unsupervised since the divorce, you know." I jump up to grab the receiver. "Hello? Hello?" Nothing.

"Shit, it's static calling." Jack turns to the horizon, squinting hard.

"Doesn't look like a storm's building," I say, still holding the receiver in my hand. I put it to my ear and listen to the dial tone buzzing on and on.

"The sky's thickening. This could be bad, Nance."

I nod, staying focused on the big black thing, much like a pay phone, only we can dial without adding coins. When we first arrived, Arizona said, "When you call out, call collect. If the phone works, that is."

Jack is a bundle of overfiring nerves—not much different than when we married two years ago. But we could both use some connection with the outside world right about now. He's pulling at his mustache, standing straight and expectant as he stares at the receiver I'm holding. He reaches out his hand and waggles his fingers at me to give it to him.

I hand it over, knowing he'll hear the same dial tone that I hear, since it's electricity calling. I think of that sparky character the electric company uses in its advertisements: a lightning bolt cartoon who's always in a hurry. We are definitely not in a hurry. We are watchers of the sky and hills, shy and vulnerable escapists wishing for something tangible to manifest from the molecules, something we can hold onto. I wish we could clutch those molecules tight to our chests, then we wouldn't feel such fierce loneliness.

But these are my words, not Jack's. Jack never admits to feeling pain, but God, his mother just died. Man, he feels heavy to me right now. Everyone's so sorry, carrying on about the loss, including Squeak—his dad—who must be the saddest of all. And also the person who has changed the most from her death. All the way from saying: *Get a haircut; clean yourself up; don't do this and don't do that; go sweep the driveway; turn down your music,* to—*Is there anything I can do for you? No? You sure?*

Holy shit! Last fall, his dad handed him a few dollars to buy a snack pack from Kentucky Fried Chicken. Jack had swept and raked up all the pine needles from the front yard, driveway, and the roof of the house and garage. If I were there standing in Jack Sr.'s driveway right now, I would say, *Tell your son you don't blame him for his mother's death. The woman died of a brain aneurysm. Shit happens!*

The massive hemorrhage was caused by a bit of tissue growing in her heart, breaking off and traveling to her brain. The doctors theorized that the nub was from a bout of rheumatic fever she suffered as a child. My brother had rheumatic fever as a child. I wonder if he has a nodule in his heart that will break away some day. Anyway, it was no more Jack's fault than the hospital's. But Squeak needed someone to blame her death on, because his heart was broken in a hundred thousand pieces.

I always say I had nothing happen to me growing up: no broken bones, no mumps, no three-day measles, and no chicken pox. I did have the weeklong measles, though I barely felt sick. And, I did have other things happen to me, like my stepdad coming to my bedroom to molest me every chance he got. I so wish I'd known he wasn't my real father back then, just a stepdad abusing his adopted daughter. If I had known, it could have made a world of difference. I think it would have, anyway.

Here I am, standing by the phone, watching Jack's hazel eyes turn cartoonlike, a silly character about to run off a cliff. "Who would call and talk to us? Your dad? My mother?" I say.

I have a hard time calling Jack's father "Dad," though Squeak says I should. "I'm your dad too, now that you two are married."

My stepdad didn't want me to marry Jack, and because I went against his wishes, he's been giving me the cold shoulder ever since our wedding day. Squeak said to me once when I was crying about my stepdad not speaking to me, "You have me. I'm here for you. You can't get rid of me."

I sigh, remove the receiver from Jack's hand, and hang it up. "It's static electricity, like you said. And look, the horizon's as thick as a winter blanket."

During a lightning storm, it is best to sit in the green chair with the glass insulators cupping each of the legs. Either there or on the bed—just stay out from between two metal objects, such as the Osborne Firefinder and the gas stove. Lightning could arc between two metal objects and fry you like Southern chicken.

My mother says lightning will come through a broken windowpane. She grew up in the east with frequent thunderstorms bludgeoning her town. Now, whenever a storm's brewing, she runs around the house closing all the windows. When the wind comes up, she's beside herself with nerves. I think she passed that behavior onto me, because when the wind blows, I bite my fingernails with a vengeance. Right now, however, I'm feeling pretty excited by the storm building over Camas Prairie—huge thunderheads blooming like giant mushroom clouds.

Once, when I was a kid, the wind came up while we were picnicking in Comstock Park. Mom immediately headed for the car. Cars are supposed to be safe, with rubber tires insulating passengers from lightning. I followed, climbing into the back seat. She sat in the front, chain-smoking, a white haze curling around her head, filling the car.

I said, "You should stop smoking."

She said, "Mind your own business."

"It is my business. You could die."

She got grouchy as hell after that and wouldn't talk to me. Outside, the clouds blackened and thunder rumbled all around. We waited for Dick and my brother and sister to return from a friend's house so we could go home. Soon, rain started falling and Mom rolled up the windows. The car filled with smoke and I held my breath, rolling my window down to gulp fresh air. She snapped at me to close it. *Lightning, you know*—

That was after we'd eaten all the chicken and potato salad together as a family and Dick remembered his business friend lived nearby. We packed up the picnic in the trunk of the car and walked across the street to pay him, his wife, and his kid a visit. Right away, his daughter and I hit it off. We ran around the house, looking at all her neat stuff. The girl had just baked two loaves of bread with her mother and she gave me one. When we were getting ready to leave, I stood there holding the loaf of still-warm bread against my chest. My stepdad said, "What do you think you're doing?"

"She gave it to me," I said.

"Give it back," he said, and got that mean look on his face, the one that drills clear through a person, scaring them half to death.

I don't remember why Mom and I ended up in the car that day without my brother and sister, but there I was, getting the cold treatment from the back of my mother's head as the storm blackened the sky west of town. While growing up, a storm was always brewing, one that didn't require closing up windows.

Now, cumulonimbus clouds bloom into huge anvils over the prairie. Lightning flashes from cloud to cloud and, occasionally, cloud to ground. We wander around the tower, feeling uneasy, as if we're waiting for something bad to happen. We don't know whether to eat or read or twiddle our thumbs while we wait for the tempest to arrive. I pace the room, my gaze falling upon a cracked windowpane. I gasp, pointing it out to Jack. "Lightning could come through that crack. We better call Arizona and tell him."

"Go ahead!"

"I feel stupid calling and complaining about a cracked pane when the summer's nearly half over." I imagine pressing the handset button and saying nothing, or mumbling something incoherent like I did in high school English class one day. I was so happy to be called upon by Mr. Finner, but then nothing but gibberish came out of my mouth. I was horribly embarrassed. "Will you call?" I say. "The lightning could come inside and kill us dead."

Jack faces the pane and the prairie beyond, pulling at his mustache, sticking hairs in his mouth and chewing. A large multi-forked lightning bolt brightens the sky over Grangeville.

"Please?"

Finally, he picks up the radio handset and calls the district. Arizona laughs when he learns of the problem. "Sit on the bed," he says, "away from the broken pane."

"That's just it," Jack says. "It's next to the bed."

"When we pick up the trash next, we'll fix it. In the meantime, tape it up. Anything else?"

"Nope," Jack says, looking sheepish.

"Then enjoy the storm. Over and out."

Hissing, he hangs up the receiver. I feel responsible for his humiliation. But no time for remorse, as clouds now blot out the sky, bringing dusk on early. The prairie disappears as the storm stampedes toward us.

Multiple bolts, jagged and bright, sear the view. One after another, a flurry of strikes: too many to count and certainly too many to record in the strike log. I pull the log out from beneath a stack of papers anyway. Feeling as if I'm walking to the gallows, I carry the strike log over to the bed.

Jack climbs onto the bed next to me. The cat wriggles beneath the covers. "It'll be all right, Nancerella."

"We don't have tape," I whine. "It's coming so fast. We've never seen anything . . ."

I know that the rate the storm's building and the frequency of the bolts point to the worst storm we've had since we arrived on the tower. A transformer blows—an explosion of bright, sparking light illuminates the prairie. Then another transformer blows. Then, what appears to be a ball of lightning lifts off the ground high above the prairie, hovering there momentarily before settling back again. "Did you see that?"

"Yep, ball lightning. It's a natural phenomenon, though I've never seen it before. Lightning can go anywhere. And do anything."

"Great!" I laugh. "And we have a cracked windowpane."

Darkness falls and distant Grangeville disappears altogether. Zigzags of searing light blind us as the storm continues steadily onward, throwing out one jagged bolt after another. Despite seeing too many strikes to count or record, I still clutch the log to my chest. I feel Jack's fingers moving next to my leg, prodding the mattress. "What's wrong?"

"Shit! There're fucking metal springs in our mattress." He rips the narrow mattress out from beneath us—bedding, cat, and all—and tosses it onto the floor.

"Fuck!" I'm nearly overcome with nausea. I sit cross-legged on the hard plywood box that serves as a platform for the mattress, leaning close to Jack for protection. I know we're in danger. I begin biting my fingernails down to the quick.

In the darkness, each volley of lightning peppers the forest in a prairie-wide swatch, blinding us like car lights on a lonely highway. The strikes burst just seconds apart, charging the tower. At one point, treetops burst into flames. Between bolts we see the orange glow of fire blaze higher. It seems the entire forest is burning. I think of the jet engine roar that a firefighter once told me about. My fingers grip Jack's so tightly that I think I must be hurting him. "What will we do?" I say, loosening my grip. "We're going to be trapped."

"Grab the cat and head east," Jack says. "Camp out with the chick on Pilot Knob until they put out the fire. They may have to airlift us out. But it's rocky up higher. It'd be almost impossible for the fire to burn past the ridge."

"I'm scared." My heart races as I calculate how much time we'll need before we head down to the Scout. At the rate the fire is coming, I imagine we'll have to evacuate shortly.

"Jude," I call. She meows from beneath the bedcovers Jack threw on the floor. "Should I grab a few things? Toothbrushes, pillows, cat food? My camera?"

Another series of bolts tear the night open. For a moment, a patch of prairie becomes visible in the distance. The booming thunder crashes, echoing off nearby ridges. I close my eyes, resting them from the lightning's brilliance, the shape of the last bolt remaining emblazoned on my retinas. Another volley of strikes, and another swatch of trees flames up. We can easily see the orange blaze burning treetops downhill from us now.

"Grab the cat," Jack says. "Let's get out of here."

I turn and begin to move off the bed when I hear the rain start, huge pelting drops spattering the windows, whipping around the sides of the tower, shaking the shutters, drowning the forest. I turn to face the woods. The blazing evergreens are no longer visible. The lightning has slowed to a bolt here and another one there, with enough space between to relax a little.

Rain continues to drench the forest. My legs feel weak. We haul the mattress back onto the wooden box. Jude wiggles out of the bedding. I collapse, pulling the covers and the cat around me. The rain pours all through the night. By morning, there's no fire in sight.

We linger in bed this morning, worn out from the storm. The day looks fresh, and the sky is mostly blue. You'd never guess we had such a terrifying storm last night. As we spoon beneath the warm covers, I begin to think about writing an article for the *Idaho County Free Press*. A firsthand account of the storm that they can publish. I give Jack a squeeze and climb out of bed.

Coffee on, I sit down in the green chair with my tablet and ballpoint pen. I feel the need to get the facts down on paper, although my thinking is a bit scattered this morning from the anxiety produced by the storm. Besides describing what happened, I also start a grocery list, imagining a hot shower and three washers of dirty clothes tumbling at the laundromat. *The roads could be goose grease. I'll have to drive slowly.*

I press the pen to paper again, frowning at the whiff of BO rising from my armpits. Even though I'm wearing my cleanest dirty clothes, I stink to high heaven.

Jack has been off and on the radio since breakfast, assuring the district that we are fine. Arizona called it a Terrible Storm. We remain stunned by the booming thunder, blinding lightning flashes, and the hard rain that fell afterward. What luck to have a torrential rain extinguish the treetop fires. The rain fell heavier than we've seen so far. We're lucky the downpour came when it did. If it hadn't, we'd be waking up on Pilot Knob this morning.

Over the radio, I hear Arizona say, "Sorry about the mattress. We'll get you a new one, and we'll fix that cracked pane, pronto. Tell Nance to just walk on in the trailer and use the shower when she gets here. Over and out."

I finish the article and head out. Following the Elk City Wagon Road, I slow at what appears to be a slick corner. The road is good, but my mind isn't. Along with stir-crazy, the storm left me feeling shaken and vulnerable. I bump along, replaying last night's lightning and thunder as I try to avoid potholes filled with water. Ball lightning, trees flaming up, and torrential rain pouring down—it was a nightmare. Again, fear jumps in my chest.

The drive down the mountain is uneventful and soon I'm showered and walking along Grangeville's Main Street, the sun hell-hot, my blue halter top, cutoffs, and Dr. Scholl's wooden sandals keeping me as cool as can be expected. Cowboys smile and nod at me. I look away. I don't like their attention, catcalls, winks, hey sweethearts, one iota. I hurry, shortly turning into the newspaper building, ready to deliver my story about the terrible storm with the ball lightning hovering above the prairie. Even this morning, Jack insisted it was just another transformer blowing.

"Transformers don't hover like that," I said. "Transformers blow like M-80s."

The ball of light appeared large, even from twenty-five miles away. In the pitch blackness, it lifted off the ground and hovered there for a few moments, reminding me of Mother's story about ball lightning back home in Virginia. When she was a girl, a ball of lightning rolled in the front door and out the backdoor.

Lightning can do all sorts of strange things, even roll down the aisle of an airplane. They say that we have one in three thousand chances of getting hit. Anyway, I feel cocky standing at the newspaper counter—*well, if you can't outsmart a lightning storm, you can survive one.* And we survived one of the worst storms Grangeville, Idaho, has seen since who knows when.

I feel a little bit like Lois Lane when I set the handwritten article on the counter. "I wrote this about the storm last night. I'm one of the lookout attendants on Corral Hill."

The lady nods. "A cowboy was killed in the storm. Another got hit, but he survived."

"Oh," I say, and look down, feeling less sure of myself now. "I didn't know that. You can publish my firsthand account if you want."

"Thanks. I'll pass it on to the editor."

I nod and slip on my sunglasses. As I step out into the blazing sun, I pick up a free Tribune and head down the street to the laundromat.

The summer night is dense with humidity, its weight pressing in on us like heavy winter blankets. We lie naked on the twin bed, the orange-flowered sheet pushed down to the end of the mattress, our feet uncovered as we attempt to sleep. Out the mullioned windows we see no stars, just darkness as black as bear scat. I shift my weight away from Jack's body. His skin is hot and sticky and smells of salt and sweat. I know he's awake, so I nudge his shoulder.

"What?" he says.

"I can't sleep."

"Shit, me neither." Jack throws a heavy arm across me and nuzzles into my neck. "I'm so tired, my mind is set on you."

"Ha," I say, grateful for his whimsical attitude. His hand slides up my thigh. I grab hold, stopping it midway. I know the rules of lightning, having been raised in Spokane: muggy air, static, and freaky black skies mean business—as we have just experienced. And I know my own rules. "Not tonight," I say, returning his hand to the safe zone: my hip bone.

In my family, when a storm was brewing, we were ordered to leave the pool, to close all the windows, and to not use the telephone. Electricity could zip through the phone wires unexpectedly. Jack's family didn't have lightning rules. In fact, he ran outside whenever the sky grew stormy, like it is now. Yet, he stays in place next to me, squeezing my hip, and then once again, inches his fingers downward. I don't say anything, just grab onto his wrist and hold steady. He stops pushing and relaxes a little. Soon he snores lightly, his arm resting heavy across my body.

Talking to him when he's in a bad mood is like approaching an angry cat. His eyes turn dark and he takes on a frightening, predatory stance. When I said I had a right to say "no" whenever I wanted, he arched his back. I can choose to be the seductress or the nun. Unfortunately, if I choose the nun route, he punishes me. Sometimes, to keep the peace, I give in. But not tonight. I'm dripping in sweat and feeling out of sorts. The day in town wore me out.

Really, I'm a pushover. Even when I lived at home, my sister pleaded with me to bake cookies after I'd said "no." She promised to follow through, but never cleaned up, just ate gobs of cookie dough, then ran off to her room to play with her gerbils. I knew how it would turn out if I agreed. Everything would be a mess: the sink, the big pink mixing bowl, butter and chocolate everywhere, cookie dough smeared around her mouth by the time we were ready to bake the cookies.

"You finish," she'd say, and bolt from the room.

At some point, I started saying to her, "N . . . o . . . spells no, and that's what I mean—NO!" But with Jack, if I say "no," I get the silent treatment. Sometimes for days at a time.

His breathing has slowed to a soft inhale and exhale. The weight of his arm overheats me. Gently, I move it to the side as I lie there, imagining the space where my consciousness floats to when I cave in. The space between the big bubbles spreads like a web of shimmery light. I told a tea reader once about the giant bubbles that I drifted through when I engaged in unwanted sex. I explained the feeling of stretching and contracting as I drifted between the giant bubbles, untethered and unweighted, simple consciousness floating in space.

The tea reader said, "There is nothing to fear in the big bubble space."

I was surprised that she even knew about the big bubble space. Then I told her about my body lying on the bed, all its parts arranged at odd angles: a leg bone bent backward, an arm angled unnaturally to the side, all the while, Jack on top, dripping in sweat as he pounded into me. She said, "Uh-huh," all matter of fact, like she'd heard the same scenario a million times before. Somehow, that made me feel better.

Strange events, when you bring them up with people who understand, become as normal as homemade chocolate chip cookies. Perhaps leaving the body is natural. Yogis do it—that, and astral travel—things happen so easily for the spiritually adept. Like T. Lobsang Rampa meditating expansively after his third eye had been activated. I used to think that when you imagine you're somewhere else, you're just thinking about that place, but your consciousness actually goes to that place. Part of your spirit leaves your body and circles through the big bubbles, leaping across large expanses of time and space to end up far away. All in a split second.

Jack rolls over on his side, leaving a heated emptiness between us cooling as he snores. I try to relax my back and neck. Outside, the wind picks up, blowing from the east toward the prairie. I imagine furious, black thunderheads building over Grangeville and a wave of anxiety tightens my chest. For a moment, I think I might lose it.

Jack thinks I'm as crazy as a loon. He says so when I talk about the big bubbles, opening the third eye, or astral traveling. But loons are only birds with plaintive cries. Being called a *bird brain* is supposed to be insulting to a person who might consider a stay at Medical Lake, the insane asylum where a straitjacket—the same kind Houdini escaped from—is the norm.

Once my stepdad told Mom that he needed a shrink and called counsel in the living room. I was running through the room at the time, dressed in my favorite red skort—a skirt with shorts attached—and frilly peasant top, perfect for the hot summer sun. He grabbed my arm and ordered, "Sit down." So, I did, on the floor opposite where he sat on the couch, the well-dusted coffee table between us. The same coffee table my sister and I ran around and around as we danced to the record *Hall of the Mountain King* until we dropped to the floor, exhausted. Hearing about the hole in my stepdad's head that required a shrink also made me feel exhausted.

Mom worried her hands as he explained his need for a shrink. I didn't know what a shrink was, but then he said "counseling," and I agreed. Maybe if he saw one, he'd quit coming to my bedroom at night.

Jack mumbles something in his sleep. I turn toward him, spooning lightly, as it is way too muggy-hot to get any closer. Beyond him, a flash of cloud-to-cloud lightning sears the blackness. My heart scuttles, making a beeline for my bowels. "Jack," I whisper. He replies with a snore.

I pin my tired eyes on the sky, waiting out the distant rumble, anticipating the next flash. In a few minutes, I'll get up and close all the windows. I'll wake Jack and we'll have to throw the mattress on the floor again. I lean up on my elbow and watch for a bolt. Lightning ripples across the horizon, brightening the clouds to a pale pink. I rest back, waiting for a distant rumble. This goes on for a while, but the storm never comes close enough to matter. I close my eyes.

Remedies for Cramps

Aspirin
Midol
Tylenol
Codeine
Peppermint tea
Raspberry tea
Lemon & honey tea
Catnip tincture
Masturbation
Marijuana
Massage
Hot water bottle

ten

Terrible cramps awakened me before sunup this morning. My first thought—*Damn, I'm not pregnant.* Then my stomach started to churn, and I almost ran out onto the catwalk to barf over the railing. It never came to that, thank goodness. Now, after a day in bed and several doses of aspirin, I am down below sitting in the outhouse, my blue flashlight in hand. It's stinky as hell in here, so I prop the door open with my foot, letting the scent of twilight drift inside. Outside, scrapes and snaps interrupt the glooming. I listen hard, a habit I learned in grade school.

If I froze, I would be able to hear my stepdad's footsteps on the stairs. I guess I thought escape was possible, though once I heard him, I was too terrified to do anything but remain frozen in my bed. If I had been able to run, I know he would have caught me as I sped past. Laughing, he would have turned me around and pulled me to him, holding me tight against his body while he reached a hand inside my underpants. I obeyed because he threatened me not to tell. Though I don't recall what he said he would do to me if I did tell. In any event, I was too frightened to say anything to anyone about the molestations.

Bushes rustle outside the outhouse. I hold my breath. Though my hearing's acute, I can't tell which direction the noise is coming from. I finish and pull up my shorts, lowering the seat cover silently. I step outside, letting the door close behind me without a sound. There's a scampering noise. Twigs snap. My heart jumps. I'm practiced at playing dead—a spider folding its legs beneath itself when threatened. I stand statue-still, listening. All at once, Jude leaps out from behind the salal, scaring me half to death.

"You fink!" I shriek, grabbing my thumping heart.

Jude weaves between my ankles, meowing softly. I catch my breath, bending to pet her, feeling grateful that it wasn't a bear or worse, a chainsaw murderer.

I aim the flashlight in front of me and start up the brushy path toward the tower. I've feared chainsaw murderers ever since last summer when Jack and I had planned to go camping. I'd heard a rumor that some campers had been pulled from their tent during the night and sawed to pieces. Of course, this happened somewhere else, so Jack, his sister, and I drove to Idaho's Reeder Bay Campground on the upper Priest Lake and pitched our green tent in space number nine. Still, I lay awake that night, wedged between the two of them in my down mummy bag, holding my breath, listening for the chainsaw murderer, who was still at large. Jack assured me that my fear was unwarranted. My stomach tightened and my lungs burned while I held my breath listening. *What-ifs* raced through my mind when the sound of thudding feet hurtled toward the tent. I grabbed Jack's arm, whispering urgently, "What's that?"

"Fuck! You woke me up," he snapped.

"Listen," I said, as the sound came thudding back past the tent from the other direction.

"Just a bear," he said, and fell back asleep.

Just a bear, I think now as Jude darts ahead of me, leading me across the gravel parking lot to the base of the tower. We climb slowly. Forty-five feet is usually easy enough to run up, but to-night my thighs burn almost as hotly as when I climbed Gunsight Peak. I didn't say in my job application to Clearwater Ranger District that working for them as a fire lookout attendant meant that once a month I'd be out of commission. I hadn't factored in my painful periods. Good thing they hired two of us. When I reach the catwalk, I feel winded. I stand there for a moment, waiting to catch my breath. The night sky teems with stars, asteroids, distant suns, and a sliver of moon. A shooting star falls in a graceful arc. I think of waking Jack and telling him to come outside—the sky is amazing. The Milky Way, Big Dipper, Little Dipper, and every-thing else above shimmers like crazy. I want to tell Jack how badly I'm hurting. I want to ask him to comfort me. But he isn't good at comforting people, and right now, he's snoring like a chainsaw.

Jude rubs up against my legs and trills. "Come on," I whisper, and she follows me inside the cabin. I feel around for the aspirin bottle on the counter and shake out a couple pills, popping them in my mouth. Acidic and salty, they melt slowly on my tongue. I drop my shorts and pull off my tank top, shivering as I cross the room to the bed. Jack sleeps fast. Careful not to wake him, I settle in next to his warm body, realizing that my hormone-driven emo-tions have been all over the place today. I can do nothing about what the doctor calls PMS and very little for the pain—except aspirin, which helps a little. I know it's hard on my stomach, but I actually do like the taste of it.

I curl around Jack, grateful for his warmth. Jude jumps up on the foot of the bed, takes a few steps toward the head of the bed, and stretches out beside me. I'm sandwiched between the two of them, clinging to the thought that even though I'm forty-five feet in the air, I am safe.

I'm awakened before sunup the next morning with the bed shaking. My heart lurches. What now? When the quaking stops, I crawl out of bed and am about to head outside when Jack rolls onto his back.

"Why up so early?" he says, groaning as he stretches his bare arms over his head. He sits up, his eyes dropping to my breasts. He smiles a sexy smile, and says, "Come back to bed."

The tower shakes again and Jack's eyebrows narrow. "What the fuck!"

"I'll be right back," I say, grabbing a towel and wrapping it around me. I scamper across the chilly floor to the door. Outside, the catwalk is wet with dew. I tiptoe around to the prairie side and look over the railing. Down at the base of the tower, a giant moose scratches its backside against the support beams. It rubs its hairy hide back and forth and back and forth against the huge, creosote-treated timbers. The tower shudders. I turn and wave for Jack to join me. He's at my side in a flash and together we lean over the railing, watching the lumpy brute with the overly large head scratch its haunch on the beams. I've heard that moose can be dangerous. They'll paw a person to death just for the heck of it. Glad we are way up here and he's way down there as we take in his magnificence.

The sun rises over Pilot Knob, brightening the territory, and I don't feel frightened of this monster. Birds sing. Dew sparkles like a million tiny crystals, decorating bough and bush. The air smells sweet and of the coming day's warmth.

The moose continues to scratch his dusty haunch. We remain there, leaning over the shaking railing, Jack in his birthday suit, me in my towel, until the huge animal finishes its scratch and ambles away, crashing back through the underbrush into the forest. Back inside, we eat our breakfast of peanut butter toast and coffee and talk about animal sightings. We've seen plenty of wild animals since we've been together: buffalo in Yellowstone, coyote and racoons while camping, and tons of black bears. Jack waves an arm in the air, his biceps flexing, his naked chest rippling as he recites the story again about the black bear our friend caught leaving our bread truck camper after eating our garbage and all of the juicy navel oranges.

"Glad it was Michael who surprised the bear and not me," I chime in.

Jack laughs. "No harm done," he says, grabbing the binoculars. "Bears are fucking cool!"

"And dangerous!" I remind him.

Buck-naked, Jack walks out the door and circles the catwalk. Leaning over the railing on the prairie side where we spied the moose, he peruses the ground three stories below. He looks back at me, shaking his head. I know he's toying with me.

I pour another cup of coffee and tip it up, sipping as I watch my naked husband parade along the catwalk. I'm totally attracted to him. I continue to follow his movements around the catwalk, and when he returns to the cabin, he pulls me toward him. He's obviously ready for me. "I'm still on my period," I whisper.

He shrugs.

"We have to wait. My insides hurt," I say. "Besides, we're on the clock. Better check on the forest."

He groans and heads back outside, binoculars in hand—glowing naked in the sunlight.

I've wanted a child since I was sixteen and despite Jack's pronouncement that the Nelsons of his family always have boys first, I know I'll have a girl. He likes to argue this point, saying, "Take my cousin Bobby and me, both of us are firstborn. He and his wife had a boy first. You'll have a boy first too."

"Boy genetics may have ruled in your family," I say, "but I'm naming our first child Keri Marie—a name that came to me out of the ethers." Generally, people call "hearing things" schizoid, but Dr. Gilmore defines hearing things as psychic knowing. I receive messages from the other side, most likely from my ancestors and guides. Clairaudience, the ability to intuit through hearing rather than sight, means I'm gifted—not crazy.

Crazy invades Jack like a virus when he's mad. He turns blustery and mean; his face hardens and his eyes narrow. His lips pull back and he hisses like a cat. The sound always makes me jump. But right now, he seems lighthearted. I recall the advice Dr. Gilmore gave us before we married: *Take off your clothes and dance naked. Lose reserve. Love each other with abandon.*

My reserve comes and goes. I feel wary about who I let in close to me. I guess it's understandable, after what Dick did. And it wasn't just him. I seem to attract people who want to get me alone, touch me, and kiss me. Like the boy in high school who tried to kiss me in the greenroom beneath the stage. And another one who drove me to a remote spot after our date. When he turned the car into the quarry, headlights shining through the barren darkness, I sat straight up and said, "Where are you going?"

"The quarry," he said. "Are you scared?"

"Take me home!" I ordered. Thankfully, he did.

The Spokane doctor said it would take my body a while to heal from the miscarriage. Or maybe he just thought I was too young to have children. By the time I saw him—and unbeknownst to me—my body was already aborting the baby. The doctor didn't know this either, of course. What he said to me, however, raised my hackles: "Do you plan on putting the baby up for adoption?"

"No," I said. I imagine I frowned at him, or maybe it was the pain brought on by the early stages of miscarrying that had me furrowing my forehead. It's interesting how opinionated people can be around the subject of marriage and children. What do they know? It's not their life.

Finally, I dress and get the day going, wandering about the tower and straightening up after all that quaking. Jack is still searching the territory through the high-powered binoculars. He left crusts of toast on his plate, as usual. I take a bite and throw the rest outside for the chipmunks. Despite the period cramps, I grab my camera and step out on the catwalk, snapping a shot of him leaning against the railing.

Though small in stature, only five-foot-six, he's well-built. His beard has grown bushy, so much so that he looks like a hillbilly. I suggest he put a leg up on the railing, so "Little Jack" isn't in the photo. We talk about his jewels like they're a separate being living on the tower with us. I say things like, "Looks like Little Jack is happy to see me!" Of course, Little Jack is always happy to see me. And he lets me know each morning by getting pushy. Since nakedness is one of our freedoms living here in the middle of nowhere, I'm an easy target for said poking.

I once knit Jack a cock-warmer as a joke. Before we were married, I camped with him at Luby Bay campground. At home, in my Browne's Addition apartment in Spokane, I'd pulled out the orange yarn left over from a childhood project and knit a little bag with a drawstring at the top. We were stoned on Maui Wowie the night I gave him my knitted creation. He got up on his knees in the pup tent and tied it on, waggling Little Jack as he modeled the orange sock. We started giggling and he fell against me, knocking me down on our shared sleeping bag. We were laughing tears when we heard a noise outside the tent: snapping twigs and snuffling sounds. Surprisingly, I wasn't afraid. Too stoned, I guess. I remember closing my eyes and seeing repeating patterns of the huckleberries we'd picked earlier that day: green leaves and purple berries echoing an Escher painting, which I discovered later to be Jack's favorite artist. As the black bear roamed the campground surrounding us that night, we went back to our uncontrolled giggles, which eventually led to making love in the pup tent.

Weirdly, the minute I met Jack, I knew he would be the father of my child. I haven't changed my mind about this, but some days he can be a real asshole around the idea of having children. Still, I love him so much I could never leave him. You can't take a meant-to-be-a-lifetime away from someone when it's written in the stars, can you? I don't think so.

Laughing, I take another photo of my naked husband prancing along the catwalk. This time he's looking out toward Buffalo Hump. Beyond him the forest languishes in the morning sun, along with miles of dry hills and valleys and the heat-streaming prairie. In the far distance, the mill in Lewiston belches out giant plumes of steam, which, if the wind is right, scents the air like rotting eggs clear to the tower.

"Give me that," he says. I hand him the camera and he turns the lens until I come into focus. I flash him a grin, knowing how the shot will look: me with my bangs cut too short and dark circles under my eyes. He snaps the photo and advances the film. I touch my hair where the beautician hacked off my bangs. Hell, it's summer and with all this heat making us sweat like pigs, short hair's cooler. Then I recognize that knowing feeling; we'll have company soon.

"Better get dressed," I say. "Company's coming."

In no time at all, we hear the hum of a BMW crawling up the last steep grade to the parking area. Our friend, Syl, climbs off the black bike, takes off his helmet, and stands there looking up at the tower. "Fuck," he hollers, "I found you!"

Jack is dressed and down four flights of stairs faster than I can say, "Boo!"

I watch over the railing as they hug and slap each other's backs. I scramble down the stairs, overhearing bits of the story on my way. "I got lost, so I stopped, climbed off my bike, and put my hands to my mouth and bellowed: Jack! Nancy! . . . Jaaackk!"

Of course, we never heard him calling us. But the idea of him standing there on the dusty road, heat and trees looming all around, hands to his mouth and yelling for us made us laugh like crazy. Really, it's amazing that he found us at all, since he only had a vague idea of where the tower was located.

I step up to receive a giant bear hug and am happier than happy to have loneliness temporarily step away, that feeling of loneliness I've begun to realize scares me more than some dangerous monster lurking in the dark.

Syl wanders around in the woods a bit, takes in the area down by the weather station, then climbs slowly back up top. He drinks a glass of water and checks out the view. "Incredible," he says, turning to us. And we all start to laugh again.

We decide to head down to the stream to refill the bladder bag. Syl says something about the stairs and how they must tire us out, and I say, "Makes us strong. We run up them." Syl grins, nodding.

Wind gusts scuff dust from the road and a chill penetrates the shade. The sky, though mostly blue, is turning milky with high clouds that move quickly across the prairie, casting stampeding shadows across the ground below. It's still comfortably warm outside, though we decide on soup for dinner. It's easy and, well, it's all we have.

After we eat, we smoke a joint. Jack shares his guitar, which Syl happily grabs from him. He strums and serenades us with the only song he knows: "With a Little Help from My Friends."

As evening draws down like a window shade, we light the gas lamp and continue to talk long after darkness sets in. We discuss the meaning of life, the high school wrestling team, the nerdy math teacher who acted as the wrestling coach, and the pranks wrestlers played on each other—like hiding a teammate's shorts that they always wore over their tights.

We are all pretty stoned and a little drunk by the time we turn in. Syl insists on sleeping on the catwalk and I am relieved that Jack and I will have our privacy, as much as the bank of windows affords us, that is, as there are no blinds.

I'm restless and still a bit crampy. I toss and turn in my T-shirt and shorts, achy with each wind gust that shudders the tower.

Lucky for us, no rain or lightning is expected to entertain our guest who is now settled into his sleeping bag out on the catwalk. Of course, he'd be invited in to share the small cabin if a storm did roll in. I'm glad one isn't expected tonight, as I wouldn't get much sleep with another man sleeping in the cabin with us.

The men are still asleep when I crawl out of bed in the morning. I slip on a sweatshirt and shoes and step silently out the door and down the stairs. I dreamed last night about the dirt basement at my stepdad's first office on Division Street. The tower steps are the same type of open-at-the-back wooden stairs. At the office, they led down past shadowy, web-strewn dirt walls. At the bottom of the stairs, dusty shelves squared up under a bare lightbulb dangling on a black wire from the ceiling. Around to the left, a vacant, tiny room with a workbench—the science lab. That room is where the molesting first started—Dick told me to be quiet, to hold still, and to not tell anyone our secret. I was six years old the first time he pulled me against him from behind and slid his hand down my pants.

I've heard that the way an abuser gains a victim's confidence is called "grooming." It's like someone is getting you ready for something special. Only, what happens after you've begun to trust the groomer is not special. What it is instead is horrific and can cause a lifetime of emotional problems.

Molesting continued in the basement at his second office, the one a block off Sprague Avenue. I was older then—but not by much. The touching went on at home too: in my bedroom, in our basement rec room, and more subtly, in my parents' bed with my mother and sister curled beneath the covers next to us.

It happened early in the morning and late at night. It happened at other times of the day too, like when he sent me purposely to the basement to polish his shoes before he and Mom went out dancing. I was in high school by then and we'd moved into a different house in a different part of town. As soon as I saw him coming down the stairs, reaching his hands toward my waist, I backed away. I used evasive tactics: dodging his reaching hands, putting objects between us, or bolting past him and running upstairs to my room. Of course, that only made him laugh. Or angry, as I was supposed to do what he said no matter what.

People like Dick go to prison, but no one ever found out what he did. Not until I told Dr. Gilmore. I've tried to talk to my sister about his inappropriateness, but her usual response is: "But he's such a nice person. He helps so many people. He wouldn't . . ."

But he did do it. And he did it again and again.

Sometimes in my dreams, I pummel him, pounding his face until I'm crying and gasping for air. I wake exhausted with my heart in my throat. The dreams have been going on ever since I left home. I hate him for what he did. And I'm super pissed off at him too, which breaks me apart inside. I don't know how to contain my fury at times. Perhaps I do need help getting over this.

As I head to the outhouse, my breathing quickens. I've upset myself thinking about Dick. The morning is chilly but fresh. I hold the outhouse door open with my foot. When I'm finished, I'll take the weather stats, and then maybe the guys will be up, and we can have breakfast.

I think about all the times I've lashed out at Jack when he pushes me to have sex, saying it's my duty as his wife. I have the right to say no, but if I do say no, I know what's coming. He'll pout and give me the silent treatment. I take it until I can't any longer. Then, I cave. Yes, I have given in plenty of times, having sex when I didn't want it, lying there on the bed like a broken doll while he humps away. I can see that he hates my passiveness, but forcing me is gross and wrong!

Sometimes I wonder if that's why I have a mass in my abdomen. Maybe my body is trying to protect itself, building up tissue around my female organs to hide them from the abuser—imagined or not.

I finish in the outhouse and, with hands fisted, stride down to the weather station. The numbers on the instruments blur with my tears. Above me, the flag snaps in the wind. I look up at the tower and see Syl and Jack moving about the cabin. They step outside together. Jack lifts the high-powered binoculars to the territory. Once finished, he hands them to Syl, who takes a look around, then focuses on me. "Hey, Nance," he yells, pointing the binoculars in my direction. I wave, turning quickly away from his gaze to finish gathering the weather stats.

I wipe my eyes with the edge of my T-shirt and start back toward the tower. When I arrive up top, I've pulled myself together. I smile at Syl as I wash up, readying to cook breakfast.

He nods, saying, "My sleeping mat blew off the catwalk in the night. It was windy and cold, and it turned into a kite. It wasn't expensive. So, no worries."

"Good, then," I say, filling the coffee pot with water. "We can look for it later if you want. But right now, I'm going to make us something to eat."

I light the burner and put the coffee on. "You guys hungry? I'm craving a grilled cheese sandwich. Want one?"

"Won't turn it down," Syl says. "It'll keep me going on the road."

Jack concentrates on rolling a joint, mumbling something about Syl staying longer.

"Nah! I just wanted to see what you two were up to. Pretty cool place to spend the summer."

"It's a trip!" I say, buttering bread, sandwiching slices of cheese between.

I like Jack's former wrestling partner. After we graduated from high school, Jack and I stopped by his family home one day to visit. This was after I had dyed my hair red while staying at the campground with Jack. Syl was the one who said, "Ah, geez, Nance. You look like a hooker."

Even though I'd laughed, his comment got my dander up. I'm not a hooker. Jack's the only person I've ever had sex with. And the molesting I experienced—though I was sexualized as a young girl—never included penetration. Some people don't realize the damage covert abuse causes. Kissing, fondling, and fingers touching privates . . . all of it secret and terribly harmful. Abuse should never be minimized.

Maybe everyone has a cross to bear. Like you're sick or a family member is mentally off or there's a suicide hidden in the closet, something that is off-limits to speak about. I think about it a lot, this cross that's so heavy to carry around all the time.

While I check the sandwiches for the perfect grilled color, I listen to Syl playing the "one song" he says he knows. It's pretty. I turn the sandwiches over, browning them on the other side, getting out plates while Syl sings and strums the guitar. He has a nice voice. Then Jack lights up the first joint of the day and hands it to his friend. Syl stops singing and lays the guitar on the bed. He takes the joint between his index finger and thumb and inhales.

Jack dulls his sadness with weed, as his cross to bear is pretty heavy—losing his mother and growing up with a super critical father. *What a bummer!* I watch him narrow his eyes, smile in a stoned way. The two friends seem happy catching up. They turn to me and comment on how good the sandwiches smell. Jude is interested too. She circles my feet, meowing loudly like she did for the shrimp Squeak fed her when we stayed with him after Jack's mother died.

We'd flown home from our honeymoon road trip, leaving our bread truck at the Texas airport while we were away for the funeral. Jude stayed with Squeak in Spokane until we returned a month later. It was weird not to have her riding along with us. But really, the remainder of the trip was a bummer, the two of us going through the motions, heading back home through Texas, New Mexico, on into Arizona, past the Grand Canyon—which should have been thrilling, but was just one more windy, cold stop to get through before heading north through Utah. Then, finally, Idaho, which meant we were nearly back to our life, only devoid of Gladys, which was going to be sadder than sad.

With the sandwiches served and the coffee poured, Syl grins across the table as he chews. He swallows and says, "Sure has been fun visiting you two on top of the world. What a life! You must be having a blast!"

"It's great," I say, smiling despite the weight growing in my stomach. That sour heaviness that arrives as company leaves. It's so seldom we see people that we're a little awkward with them at first. I think of the lookout on Hughes Ridge, and how he had trouble speaking to us at first. Then giddiness took over, and he acted almost like he was drunk being around people again. Though sometimes we feel the heaviness of loss even before they announce they must take off. We anticipate the hole they'll leave behind. I get up and begin clearing the table, knowing the end is near.

Wildflowers

Deerhorn
Lovely penstemon
Fireweed
Indian paintbrush
Johnny-jump-ups
Wild onion
Wild asters
Salmonberry
Nettles
Thistle
Camas lily
Phlox
Watercress
Marsh marigold
False buttercup
Wild rose
Syringa

eleven

Boys are mean and aggressive, I think. In grade school, the neighbor boy, who lived in the air force rental house behind ours, often chased me on his bike down C Street. He threw rocks, dirt clods, and wormy apples at my back as I rode past his house on the way to the library.

The air force brat furiously pursued me, standing up, pedaling so hard that he rocked side to side, chasing me nearly to Northwest Boulevard. I usually didn't get hurt, but he scared the living daylights out of me. By the time I reached the library, I was drained and breathless.

Once inside the library, I held back tears, keeping my face stony, hoping to remain invisible as my heart beat SOS. I checked out novels about kidnappings, abuse, and dangerous confinements. In the stories I read, the girls tried to escape, to run away. Sometimes they got away, sometimes they didn't. That's how I handled all the aggressive boys and men in my life—I took off running in the opposite direction, terrified they'd catch me and hurt me.

By high school, the kid next door watched me and my girlfriends over the fence. He was older, maybe college age. I could see the top of his head when he stood on his back steps peeking at us girls stretched out on beach towels, perfecting our tans. We oiled up with baby oil and sunbathed in our bikinis, gossiping about couples at school while listening to "Daydream" on the transistor radio. The disc jockey alerted us when it was time to turn over. That summer, I caught the neighbor peeking over the fence more than once. That's when I began to perfect my dirty look. Like my mother aways says, "If looks could kill . . ."

I turn to Jack, who's sitting on the bed rummaging through a baggy of marijuana, searching for a viable seed. He bites into one, reminding me of how he cracks pine nuts in the fall at his father's house. "Hungry?" I ask.

He grumbles something I can't make out.

I shrug and go back to crocheting, recalling the rodeo star who manages the local café in Grangeville. I stopped by the café one day when I was down to buy groceries. I asked if they might have a place for me come fall, if we stuck around, that is. The rodeo star's mother said, "Sure, come work for us when you're finished on the lookout tower." She said, "You can make donuts for the early crowd, and then serve breakfast. You'll wash dishes in soapy bleach water when the rush is over."

"No automatic dishwasher?" I know that bleach leaves my hands raw and cracked. Once the dishwasher at Hill's said, "Never, whatever you do, mix bleach with ammonia. If you do, you'll need the fire department to rescue you from the noxious gas cloud."

At twenty-one, I think I'm old enough to know better than to mix bleach and ammonia together. I give people dirty looks whenever they say something that insinuates stupidity. Again, my perfected dirty look comes in handy.

I set down the afghan I'm crocheting and walk to the door, adjusting my face in a nonplussed arrangement, when Jack looks up from his baggy of weed and raises his tongue to his upper lip.

I roll my eyes as I turn away, raising the binoculars to search beyond the haze, out past the prairie, clouds build on the horizon, puffy as carnival cotton candy. "Looks like rain's coming," I say to no one and make the rounds, checking the clear-cuts, the ridges, and the drainages for smokes. No fires to be had.

Back inside, I fix peanut-butter-and-pickle sandwiches and cut them diagonally, placing halves neatly on green Melmac plates. There's a bouquet of Indian paintbrush, Oregon grape, and wild asters sitting in the middle of the picnic table. I move it over a tad and petals drift to the green painted surface. "Lunch," I say.

Jack glowers as he gets up off the bed and wanders outside to pee.

I touch my chin to see if it is puckered, like he said I do when I'm unhappy. He once pointed out my puckered chin when I was feeling bummed about losing the baby. I was surprised by his perceptiveness but insulted by what seemed like criticism. Losing the baby was one of the saddest things I'd ever experienced.

Right now, my chin is smooth, despite feeling weary of the unhappiness written across his face. He takes a seat at the table and picks up his sandwich. He bites into it, crumbs collecting on his hillbilly beard. If his chin is puckered beneath, I'd never know it with all that hair.

When we left Spokane for our honeymoon road trip around the United States, my chin was most likely permanently puckered. I was half-sick from my stepdad's advances, dealing with stress headaches all the time. Once we started work at Hill's Resort, Jack would get up early and begin raking the resort grounds before the rest of the crew arrived. I slept late in the tent trailer, the catalytic heater practically asphyxiating me as I dreamed on and on about Dick coming after me, sometimes catching me in the basement of his office where he'd set up a table for me to work. In my dream, I'd manage to get the upper hand and pin him to the ground, clocking him in the face, over and over again.

In a book about dreams I once read, I learned that dreams work out problems in our lives, but this problem doesn't seem to be going away. I'm not sure what to do about the parcel of darkness I carry around with me. Perhaps a counselor could help, though everyone seems to think that counseling is for crazy people. I'm not crazy, but often my stepdad would make some offhanded comment about taking me to see a doctor at the nuthouse.

I finish my sandwich and again pick up the wool afghan I've been crocheting. Why I picked white, pink, green, and blue yarn, I'm not sure. I don't love them. And they definitely aren't the Aries palette: red, orange, and rust, and sometimes pink. Maybe they're baby colors. I shrug, imagining the throw covering me as I sleep. Maybe I'm making myself a cuddly blanket for when I feel so low I wish I were dead.

I talked to Jack about seeing a counselor, but he said the same thing, "Crazy people need shrinks."

Once Dick said, "You're just like your schizophrenic aunt." That was right after he interrogated me until I broke down crying: *Where were you? What were you doing? Who were you with? What were you wearing? Who's filling your head with these subversive ideas?* That day, I cried so hard that snot dripped from my nose. If I were crazy, it was because he made me so. I knew all the Clearasil in the world wouldn't stop the humongous zit that would erupt on my chin or cheek after a bout of emotional abuse like that.

During one punishing argument, my girlfriends waited for me outside in the idling Mustang. The four of us carpooled to school each morning and, on that particular day, my mascara ran beneath my eyes, giving me a Twiggy look. Once I moved away from home, I went *au naturel.* No hair rollers. No curling irons. No hairspray. No brassiere. No lipstick. No eyeliner. No mascara. And no accusing stepfather interrogating me daily. Just a well-scrubbed girl smelling occasionally of dark beer and sporadically of weed. And on rare occasions, Wild Rose Eau de Toilette.

Where was Mom during these arguments? Chain-smoking Winstons at the kitchen table? Snubbing out butts in the ashtray, trying to shut the yelling out? Occasionally, we find cigarette butts in the gravel parking area below, probably from sightseers visiting the tower. Don't people know that more forest fires are started by man than by lightning strikes? It's mostly cigarette butts tossed out car windows that start fires. Sometimes campfires. Sometimes firecrackers. Sometimes sparks from automobiles and sometimes other weird events: like burning debris falling from the sky.

"What's that sound?" Jack says.

I hear a distant roar that becomes louder by the second. We run out onto the catwalk, whirling around until we find the origin of the roar. Two air force jets soaring in formation, speeding toward us. They dip and curve in unison, covering vast territory in seconds. They're green and sleek and winged like swallows. They follow the terrain up and down, plunging in and rising over ridges far below, tracing the lay of the land. As they tip to corner, closing in on the tower, the sound of the jet engines becomes deafening. We cover our ears with our hands and whoop. Just as quickly as the jets arrive, they grow smaller in the distance, following the forest south where within seconds they disappear completely.

"Fuckin'-A!" Jack says.

"Holy shit!" I shriek, searching the empty horizon, the jets' roar fading along with our excitement. We wander back inside our lonesome cabin.

It rained in the night and this morning our view of the territory is one milky bath. Jack says it'll burn off by noon and then the temperatures will climb into the nineties again. I shrug and continue sweeping the floor. Crumbs and twigs and dead flies collect in the dustpan. Jack doesn't "clean house." And he doesn't wash clothes. He couldn't fold a shirt if his life depended upon it. I wish his mother hadn't ironed his T-shirts and jeans and waited on him hand and foot. It's not fair to me, as now he expects the same kind of attention from his wife. Though I must say, he is good at other things, like dealing with the forest service, brewing beer, and being a virile lover.

Some USFS dudes are coming up to the tower today to install our new windowpane. And they're bringing along a new "spring-less" mattress. I recall the horror we felt the night of the terrible storm when we discovered metal coils layered between sheets of mattress batting. "Sheez!"

Jack's out on the catwalk perusing the territory through the heavy black binoculars. He calls to me, "Dust lifting off the road down below."

I know it won't be long now before a truck turns into the parking area. I put the broom and dustpan away and step outside. From where we stand on the catwalk, we see the green truck grinding up the last bit of rutted road, bouncing into potholes as it pulls in next to the bread truck. Two dudes wearing yellow hard hats, jeans, and T-shirts step out of the cab.

Hard hats are made of plastic and cause a person's head to sweat like crazy. Although I'm not wearing a hard hat, I'm already sweating like a pig, and the day is just beginning to heat up. It's supposed to be even hotter by the end of next week.

One of the men swings around and looks up at us leaning over the railing forty-five feet above. "We got your glass," he hollers. "Okay if we come up?"

"Come ahead," Jack hollers.

The first guy grabs a toolbox and the windowpane from the back of the truck. The other guy leaves his hard hat in the truck bed and wrangles the mattress on top of his head. He hauls it around the base of the tower to the stairs. I lean over the railing, curious as to how he'll maneuver the four switchbacks. It's just a twin mattress, but it flops over his head like a fish out of water.

I feel shy today. I'm always worrying about how people see me: plain or pretty, articulate or stupid, graceful or bumbling. Bumbling is usually where I land, or bitchy, as Jack likes to say. I think of myself as assertive, not bitchy. I practice asking for what I want and need because I didn't get to do that while growing up. But right now, I need to settle down. It would be easier to do that if these freaks weren't interrupting my peace.

"Sorry we're late," the first guy says as he pokes his head up through the trapdoor. He smiles a wide grin. "We goofed off on the way here," he said. "Then bozo made a wrong turn. But you'll both be happy. We brought your mail!"

"Mail?" I say, excited to see the envelope from my mom. Nothing from my stepdad, of course. I haven't heard from him since we left Spokane, not even when I wrote to tell him about the mass in my belly, the possibly cancerous one that may need surgery come fall. I rip the envelope open. Mom and her new beau, Charlie, are coming for a visit Thursday. I fold the letter back inside the envelope and put it aside to read more closely once the men are gone.

One flight down, I hear the second guy groaning.

"Hey man, need a hand?" Jack calls out. He hurries down the stairs to help wrangle the mattress up the last flight.

The two men carry the mattress into the cabin. Now the cabin is full-up with four people and two mattresses. I step outside and watch the milkiness burning off the forest in waves of heat. Off to the west, heat streams up from the prairie. I think about offering the two guys a slice of honey bread and a cup of coffee, but the coffee is cold, so I'd have to make a new pot. The longer I think about it, the less I feel like doing anything and decide not to be the "hostess with the mostess" today. I don't want them hanging around the tower any longer than necessary anyway.

Jack pulls the old mattress out the door and tosses it over the railing. It hits the ground with a thump and a cloud of dust puffs skyward. Jack's method of getting the mattress down to the ground startles me. Then I laugh, turning to the new windowpane and the fresh putty the taller guy smooths. I watch him wipe his hands on a rag. He looks up at me and says, "Arizona will bring up a can of green paint so you can touch up the window grills."

"Okay," I say. "I need paint for the cupboards too. I told him the last time he was here. I guess he didn't pass that along."

The guy just shrugs.

"Huh!" I say, biting my lip as I recall the conversation—*Someone used flat paint over green enamel and now it's peeling. Who would do such a stupid thing?*

Arizona laughed and shrugged his big shoulders. *Working for the USFS don't make 'em geniuses like us.*

The guys gather their tools and head down. I make up the bed and take a seat, rereading Mom's letter. Mom and her boyfriend are coming to visit on Thursday. That's just two days off. And they're bringing chicken—Mom's favorite recipe we all die for. And potato salad—another dish we die for. I know how to make it just like Mom does. I recall a scene that embarrasses me still. When I was a kid and she'd go out of town, I worked hard to make food as delicious as she did. I wanted to be praised by my stepdad and told that I was beautiful—like he always did Mom. I even tried on her sundresses, which were far too big for me. I shake my head to disperse the memory.

Time has flown by today, which is unusual. I made up the new mattress, we hauled water, and I made a decent dinner for a change. Now we're sitting on the catwalk, staring out at a darkening sky. Jack and I are good at trying to outdo each other by spotting the first star or meteor zipping across the sky. Once I was told that if you look directly at a faint star, you can't see it, but if you look to the side of it, you can see it. I don't know why this is true—but it seems to work.

As I stare up at the sky, my mind flashes back to the thin T-shirt I wore around those two dudes today. Perhaps my nipples beneath were like stars they couldn't look directly at. I feel a little embarrassed now. Was I dressed like a floozy?

To keep my mind from going further south, I realize that tonight I will sleep on a lightning-safe mattress. The USFS guys looked sheepish and apologized for the springs. "It was a bad storm, right?" one of them said.

"Yes," I said, realizing he was staring at my chest.

Then he stepped close enough that I could smell his BO. I took a step backward.

"I saw your article in the paper," he said. "Too bad about that cowboy." His eyes lowered, taking my chest in as he pretended to study the mattress behind me.

I crossed my arms over my chest. "Yes, too bad," I said, and turned and walked outside.

Jack points out a shooting star, startling me. I turn just in time to catch the tail end of its freefall. We decide to turn in, get up, and go inside to brush our teeth. We climb in bed and fall like stars into a deep sleep.

Mom's a lady raised in the South. She loves to wear fancy clothes with matching heels and stylish handbags. In her closet she keeps alligator totes, suede clutches, fancy beaded bags, black patent totes, and a number of shoulder bags. Now she's sitting on the catwalk dressed in white shorts and an orange sleeveless blouse. She's wearing jeweled sandals, Jackie O sunglasses, and a white fringed shawl draped over her shoulders. She looks pretty much out of place on Corral Hill.

Charlie, her new boyfriend, holds a tiny green forest service cup in one big hand and one of my freshly baked chocolate chip cookies in the other. Mom declines the cookie, but she's loving the Lipton. "I'm so British," she says, "and so are you. The British are proper."

I shrug, unwrapping the present she brought me: a soft, fringed shawl identical to hers. I hold it to my face and breathe in its new-yarn scent.

"It's washable," she says, reaching to move my hair out of my face. "In case it gets dirty."

I step backward, laughing. I don't say that there's dust, soot, and grime everywhere we turn. In no time at all I'll be throwing the shawl in with Jack's jeans, dirty socks, and smelly T-shirts—an act totally against Mother's practicality. I wrap it around my shoulders and say, "Thanks. It's cool!"

Mom smiles. "It's lovely on you. Clean-looking."

Mom's good at sorting laundry, always washing whites together, not with reds like I've been known to do. On more than one occasion I've turned Jack's jockey shorts pink. Mom would never put jeans in the wash with paler colors, only with darks. Knits run on a gentle cycle. And she washes her underwear by hand. *They last much longer that way.*

I want to tell her how sad I *still* feel over losing the baby and about trying to get pregnant again. But we can't talk privately and who wants a stranger listening in on such a personal conversation? That's who Charlie is, after all, a stranger until he proves himself otherwise. I think I'm beginning to understand the power of disclosing feelings, when the time is right, that is. Ever since Dr. Gilmore and I talked about the abuse, I've worked hard to speak up. He said, "It's better to be intimate." I didn't understand what he meant at first, because I thought intimacy was sex, but now I guess I have another piece of the puzzle to ponder. Or rather, Jack and I do, although Jack thinks talking about emotional stuff is a *fucking waste of time.* He once said, "I don't have any problems; however, you do!"

"Right!" I said and turned away.

The other thing Dr. Gilmore told me was how to talk to each other about feelings without getting all bent out of shape. *Defended*, he called it. When I think of defended, I think of weapons, like the BB guns my family target-practiced with in my stepdad's five-foot-thick Styrofoam-walled basement the previous owner once used as cold storage for rich women's luxurious furs. Fur coats shed in the heat, just like cats and dogs, which I didn't know until my stepdad rented the east half of the building from the downsized fur company.

After I got my work permit in grade school, I worked at Dick's office until Jack and I got married. Once the business moved into the fur building, Mom was always decked out in mink, and my sister and I, rabbit. Now I'm wearing Dr. Scholl's and ripped cut-offs made from an old pair of Jack's jeans. Trashy? No, practical! And honestly, a better look for me! Though I'm sure my mother doesn't agree. I notice her checking out my outfit when she thinks I'm not looking. I want to say, "What?" but I don't.

Charlie is dismissive with Mom and full of bravado for himself. I don't like him, but at least he's available. The married guy she dated after Dick left her carried a pistol. That freaked me out, but Mother just shrugged when I questioned her about it. When I met her already-married date, I was rude, sarcastic, and smoldering with hostility. I pulled her aside, telling her to get rid of him. It wasn't long after that that they broke up, not because of the gun, but because she decided dating a married man was a bad idea.

Charlie follows Jack inside the cabin to check out the fire-finder. I remain seated next to Mom on the catwalk. Finally, I get up the courage to say, "We're hoping to get pregnant again."

Mother scoffs. "There's plenty of time for that," she says. Then she leans over and whispers in my ear, "Charlie wants to marry me."

I almost say, "Why the rush? There's plenty of time for that," but I only say, "Huh!"

Her white shawl flutters in the breeze, as does mine. Her big sunglasses reflect the landscape. Her hair's lighter than her natural brunette shade and cut very short. She looks better than the last time I saw her when all she could do was drink and weep because her husband had left her for some bleached-blond bimbo. Hopefully she isn't drinking herself stupid every night like her best friend warned us she was doing. And hopefully, Charlie won't hurt her like Dick did.

Charlie and Jack return from the tour of the cabin. I collect our empty teacups while Mom attempts to light a cigarette in the mountain breeze. Her manner is flamboyant, her laughter practiced as a movie star's. It's gross, really. All for the sake of Charlie, who steps close, holding the lit match cupped in his big hands. I'm beginning to hate him even harder. And, before long, she will too, no doubt.

The thing is, you can't feel close to someone you have no history with. It makes sense that when Mom left our birth father and married our stepfather—whom we didn't know one iota—my brother and I balked at his orders. And there were the bare-bottomed spankings, and in my case, secret touching, to be angry about too. Plus, we were to call him "Dad" every day until one day we forgot our real father's face, or that a real father even existed. And as much as I try, I cannot conjure up Virgil's face.

Mom says she's working on becoming a real estate agent like Charlie.

Charlie smiles at her and says, "And you're doing a damn good job."

She smiles back and takes a puff of her cigarette, turning to look out over the prairie.

He takes her hand and suggests it's time to go inside and set out the delicious fried chicken and potato salad she's made. They move uncertainly around the catwalk to the door. Once inside, she takes a seat at the table. I set a jar lid before her to use as an ashtray. She rolls the tip around to knock off the ash, takes one last long drag, and rubs out the smoke.

While I set the table with green Melmac plates, cutlery, and a bouquet of Mom's favorite wildflowers—Indian paintbrush—Mom washes up at the Igloo cooler. We all take a seat at the picnic table, chowing down on an early dinner. Well, Jack and I chow down; Mom and Charlie eat like the wealthy. And, that's it! Finished with the meal, they pack up the leftovers in food containers and gather their things together, readying to leave the mountain.

I get a hug and a kiss on the cheek and Charlie shakes Jack's hand. They carefully head down the stairs to the green LeMans, my mother in her jeweled sandals, Charlie in his beige tennis shoes. We follow them slowly down forty-five feet to the ground. Mom, bless her Southern-belle heart, takes the path to the outhouse. When she reappears, she wears fresh red lipstick. She climbs into the passenger seat and they pull away, honking as they disappear around the bend, heading toward the orange stain of the coming sunset.

I stand there waving, tears welling in my eyes, until I can no longer see their car. I never got to tell her about the surgery the doc said I might need. Or about how lonely I feel away from home and how mad I am at Dick for destroying our family. She didn't say boo about her plans with Charlie, but no doubt he will be moving in soon. There's something about that dude that I just don't trust, but I can't quite put my finger on it. Maybe it's because he thinks he's in charge, which bugs the heck out of me. No man is in charge of a woman!

My chest begins to hurt, so I head back up to the cabin while Jack stays below to pick thimbleberries. I feel like a big hand grips my heart, squeezing it far too hard. I pick up the binoculars and try to fool my heart by pretending to check the view, but I can't pretend for long. Soon tears stream down my face, blotting out the dust that lifts between the trees from Mom's LeMans curving down the mountain.

A few days have passed since Mom and Charlie's visit. Too bad I didn't talk to Mom about the specialist I'm heading out to see in Lewiston today, but I couldn't bring myself to speak of it with Charlie there and all. Now, I'm driving the Scout down Elk City Wagon Road, heading toward Grangeville where I'll shower before heading west to Lewiston for my appointment with the ob-gyn.

I press lightly on the gas, gingerly navigating the muddy road downhill. It rained harder in the night than I realized. The road is slick. I grip the steering wheel tighter and think about learning to drive. My stepdad grew up on a farm where kids began driving when they were barely twelve. I guess that's why he was excited to let me drive Auntie Van's Chrysler New Yorker, the Model A Ford truck he bought on a whim, and the GMC work van. I didn't care much for any of them, but it was novel taking different vehicles out for a spin. Mother's Pontiac LeMans was the easiest to drive. But the '55 Chevy (also known as Baby Beulah) was my favorite and became the car I drove all through high school and after I moved away from home. I drove it until my brother returned from Nam and Dick decided to give *my* Chevy to him. Not long after that, my stepdad laughed as he told me that Bruce had dropped the Chevy's tranny in the middle of a Spokane intersection. That wouldn't have happened if he hadn't taken *my* car away.

I turn from driving lessons to the shower I'll soon take at Arizona's house. Hot water and soap are far more appealing than a specialist palpating the mass in my belly. If I think about the mass, I feel like I'm going to throw up, so instead I think about sharing rides back and forth to high school with my girlfriends. One day, when the others had stayed home sick, I told Shelly, my best friend at the time, about the party Jack and I went to down by the railroad tracks.

Gary, our artist friend, had invited us to a pot party. I knew my stepdad would never allow me to go to a party in the bad part of town, so I lied, saying I was going to dinner at Jack's house. When we got to the party at Gary's friend's house, his friend led us through a cloud of pot smoke and booming Pink Floyd to the kitchen. He gave us each a beer and then showed us to a tiny bedroom. It was tidy with a polished wooden bed frame and pink chenille bedspread. He shut out the loud rock 'n' roll and said, with a flourish of his hands, a few words pronouncing us man and wife. "I'm an ordained minister," he said. "Feel free to consummate your marriage now," and left us alone in the prim pink room.

Nothing happened that night, nor any other time, even though we'd heavy petted at Suicide Pond, in the family room, and behind the shelves in the pottery room in Ferris's art building. Jack wanted me, I knew that. But other than kissing, I was too frozen inside from the forbidden touching to desire more. Jack was just going to have to wait, though I was tempted by the idea of marriage.

The morning I told my best friend about the party I was sure she would support me. I repeated the story of how Gary's friend had married us at the party, saying that we could sleep together now. She said, "That guy sounds weird. I wouldn't do that if I were you." She looked at me so sternly that I drove the rest of the way to school without saying another word to her. That was the beginning of the end of our friendship.

As I leave the forest and pass a clear-cut abloom in purple fireweed, I lift my hand to shade my eyes from the bright sunshine. My heart lifts with the beauty of the territory, but at the same time I remain vigilant, gripping the steering wheel tightly, surveying the territory for deer that could leap out in front of me.

The rain last night turned Elk City Wagon Road to goose grease. I creep along, the Scout sliding sideways here and there. I slow the jeep further, thinking I have things under control, when I round a corner and the Scout spins out, careening nose first into the ditch.

Freaked out but uninjured, I climb out, slipping through the mud to the front tires. It's the first time I've used four-wheel drive, but somehow, I figure out how to lock in the front hubs. I climb back in the driver's seat and back easily out of the ditch. I'm so impressed by both the Scout's tractor-like quality and my mechanical ability that I burst into laughter. *You do know what you're doing, Nancy!*

Jack and I have driven in all kinds of conditions: raging blizzards, washed-out roads, and mud so thick a tractor had to pull the bread truck out with a chain. Once, a dust storm blowing across the Palouse entirely obscured the highway. At the time, we were driving some rattletrap that we'd scraped together a hundred bucks to buy. I remember holding my breath and praying as Jack careened through the whirling cloud of dust, unable to see oncoming traffic until it was nearly in front of us. He likes living dangerously, which includes buying the cheapest vehicles on the road. Though the Scout cost five hundred dollars—a veritable fortune.

We lived in our bread truck at Priest Lake, and if the apocalypse ever happens like some people think it will, we'll live in it again. Some people suggest buying property out in the boonies and hoarding food and weapons. I can't wrap my mind around a scenario like that, though we agreed to buy the hundred-pound bag of soy protein from Jack's neighbor. Actually, I don't really believe in things like World War III and alien invasions. Most bad stuff happens at home. Sure, there are feuds and standoffs, especially in Idaho, but the whole country going to hell in a handbasket seems unlikely.

I creep around the corner at the turnoff, rocking the Scout onto the steep logging road. There's a truck downhill from me and I realize that if it hadn't rained in the night, I'd be eating his dust all the way to the highway. I hang back, inching around hairpin turns. What good does it do to worry about the world falling apart when I have a mass in my belly? Sure, we can buy a piece of land just in case, but for now, all I can think about is a hot shower at Arizona's and then the hour-and-a-half drive to see the doctor in Lewiston. My stomach jumps at the thought of being examined by a stranger.

At last, I hit the highway and push the pedal to the metal, speeding around the logging truck, heading west past fields of camas and bleached prairie grass. The window is down, whipping my dirty hair around my face. I stop at Arizona's for a shower, and by eleven, sit on the exam table dressed in only a cotton shift that opens in the back. While waiting for the specialist, I look around the huge room that smells of antiseptic. The nurse, who ushered me into the makeshift exam room stacked with boxes and supplies, says they had to fit me in, apologizing for having my exam in the storage room.

The light is low. A stainless-steel tray stands next to the exam table and is arranged with frightening-looking stainless-steel instruments. I wipe my sweaty palms on the gown, then proceed to twist my well-scrubbed hands together until my fingers hurt.

The doctor finally arrives. He's small and curt with gentle eyes that peer out from behind wire-rimmed glasses. He introduces himself and I give him a squeak of a hello. He has me lie back and begins the exam. As he feels my abdomen, he looks thoughtful. "Yes," he says, "there's a mass near your ovary about the size of an egg."

I watch him closely, recalling the other doctor's speculation that the mass was the size of a lemon or small orange. I tell him this.

He says, "Perhaps closer to a small orange."

I recall the oranges in my Christmas stocking, fruit my brother and I rolled on the kitchen table until the insides turned to juice. I was a kid then, and in a way, still am. Right now, I'd rather be looking across the table at my brother with soft, pulpy juice sweetening my mouth than discussing the size of the mass in my belly.

I want to be pregnant again. I want to hold a baby in my arms. I want to nurse my infant. Loving a child is what my heart wants most.

The doctor continues to palpate.

"Ouch!" I say.

"Sorry," he says. His face is sun-withered, his glasses polished, short, curly, graying hair on top. I get up the courage to ask what is worrying me. "Is it cancer?"

"We won't know until we do exploratory surgery." He snaps off his gloves and tosses them in the trash. "You can sit up now."

I explain tower life, saying, "The season isn't over until September or October." I hear my voice break. I hope I can corral the tears until later.

"You're young. You can wait until fire season is over."

As I wing along the highway heading home, I think of Jack tending the forest, watching heat rise in wavering streams, lifting through the heat-crisped trees like smoke. The air is thirsty. Animals gather around smaller and smaller water holes: range cattle, deer, moose, and coyotes. Yellow leaves swirl along the highway as I speed past, driving through the hundred-plus heat, home to the lookout. We will be there until the clouds roll in this fall, until the view disappears, until the chill sends the chipmunks inside their dens to warm their fattened summer bodies against each other.

Two hours later, I'm back on the tower looking at the firefinder sighted on a distant smoke. It's thin and blue, visible to the naked eye—a tree probably hit by lightning in the last storm. I haven't mapped all the ridges and drainages yet, so I can't say exactly where it is. My stomach sinks at the thought of Jack being asked for coordinates that we haven't gridded yet.

The radio rattles and Jack picks up. I'm suddenly feeling so nervous that I crave driving down the dark highway, rolling through the night, stars bright above, not knowing what is in store for me come this fall. But the firefighters are only checking in, having easily found the smoke, and are presently working on putting it out. I take a deep breath and a cold guzzle of the beer Jack hands me.

He suggests we play a few hands of cards, but I feel too tired to concentrate. We crawl into bed, snuggling together. I sigh, unable to get the doctor's visit out of my head. While I sat on the exam table, K-Y jelly smeared between my thighs, the doctor sat on a stool at my knees, carefully writing his findings on my chart. When he finally looked up, he peered over his glasses and spoke slowly. "Probably not cancer. You're too young for that."

Smokey Bear holds a shovel and frowns. The arrow is in the red zone, indicating high fire danger. It's so hot out we could explode. Rather, the forest could explode, tinder igniting a firestorm. My handwashing dries in the blast-furnace heat almost as fast as I lay it over the catwalk rail. I collect T-shirts and underwear, keeping my eye on the browning forest to the west where the smoke is currently being fought.

We dab at our sweat and mist ourselves with spring water. As the sun lowers in the west, the rays shine straightaway into the tower and the heat worsens. Even with sunglasses, the glare gives us headaches. I wish I had wicker shades to lower, shutting out the sun. I imagine tacking a sheet over the west windows and immediately grow nervous imagining the sheet blocking our view.

We drink glasses of boiled water between binocular rounds and iced tea with tiny cubes frozen in the tiny freezer compartment. The tiny ice cubes melt almost instantaneously, the tea turning lukewarm, only slightly refreshing us.

The cat is a rag draped over the edge of the bed. Jack is naked out on the catwalk. I can't see his parts from where I'm standing at the counter, washing another batch of underwear in the washtub, but I'm sure it's an oversight on his part. He likes to entice me whenever he can. Earlier this morning when I didn't want to have sex, he made *the face* at me and said, "You know I'm in charge."

I rolled my eyes at him. No one's in charge at six thousand feet except for our boss, Arizona. And he's hardly ever around to enforce the rules. Sun, rain, fog, and lightning storms . . . now, they're in charge. And since Jack and I are both employees hired at the same GS rating, we're actually equals. And if anyone asks, yes, I am a women's libber. I want to earn as much as any man without having to sit on someone's lap for a paycheck!

I'd say I'm more of the Rosie the Riveter type—roll up my sleeves and get the work done. Last summer, I rebuilt the truck's carburetor. When I told Jack that I could fix it, he bolted outside, returning promptly with a greasy, gasoline-smelling contraption nestled in his blackened hands. I proceeded to rebuild the malfunctioning carburetor.

When one of Jack's friends discovered that I knew how to rebuild carburetors, he asked me to work on his old truck, which coughed and sputtered and conked out all the time. I said no, because I didn't want to get greasy that day, not because I couldn't do it. My mechanical ability came to me early on, partially from working on Baby Beulah, the Chevy taken from me around the same time Dick changed the locks on our family home. Really, I think he's been trying to oust me from the family ever since I turned sixteen. I wonder if said ousting is because I'm his stepchild. Or perhaps it's because of the abuse. If he makes me out to be the guilty one, he will be off scot-free.

With all this heat, there'll be no mechanical jobs for me today. I hate the smell of gasoline, especially when the weather is hot. As I wash another batch of laundry, I recall Mom calling mechanics "grease monkeys." Once, we pulled into a service station when Mom's car died on Wellesley Avenue. In grade school still, I shadowed my mother, holding tightly to her skirt from behind. Men were sitting around in their greasy coveralls, smoking up the dirty room stacked with stinky tires. The girlie calendar on the wall made me blush. Mom pulled me closer, whether it was for her own comfort or mine, I'm not sure. The men smirked as my mother told them what the problem was. I guess they fixed it and we got on our way.

I lay out the last batch of wet laundry and toss the dirty wash water over the railing. There's a pause, then a splash, as it hits the ground. I put away our clean clothes in the drawers beneath the bed. Jude opens one eye and studies me sleepily. I laugh, wishing I was the one draped over the bed like a limp rag instead of her. But, I'm on duty. I step out onto the catwalk and squint at the heat-wavering territory. The fire is out, thank goodness. Jack hails me from the other side of the tower. I ignore him.

Later, he pulls on his cutoffs and we wander down the road to the stream. I squat down, sinking the black bag beneath the icy spring, letting water seep in through the screw-top opening. The cold water feels divine.

While the bag fills, I look over at Jack. He checks out the mess the cows have made of our watering hole. The whole marsh is mashed with hoofprints: marsh marigolds, false buttercups, watercress, and cow pies. "Ugh, giardia." I stand up and wipe my hands on my shorts.

Cold water splashes off the bag as Jack lifts it onto his back. He can carry a full bag of water. I can only carry a couple of gallons of icy stream water that burbles up through the shadowed woods. He points out a patch of nettles farther upstream. "My Aunt Annie's immune to nettles," Jack says.

"I saw the tall nettles when we visited her in Hanover on our honeymoon road trip. But why is she immune?"

"Because she drinks the water where the nettles grow."

"We drink the water where nettles grow and I still get stung. Big red welts that hurt like hell. Did you know that Indians threw themselves in nettle patches as a spiritual passage?"

"You're fucking with me."

"Nope. And they were naked. It was a way of honoring Great Spirit, I guess." I give Jack a playful push. "Want to get spiritual?"

He nearly loses his balance but catches himself with a solid wrestler's stance—feet planted again in the mud, he hisses, "Fuck, what did you do that for?"

"It was a joke. No harm done."

"Go ahead and try to move me," he says, his expression easing. "You can't knock me off balance."

"You're right," I say, pushing lightly. "I can't budge you."

We laugh easily, but I know stir-crazy can just as easily go south and take the fun along with it. I kiss him. He grabs my breasts and gives me his sexy look. We kiss again, deeper this time. I step back, splashing him. He splashes me back. We hold each other's eyes for a moment, then laugh. *Sex later, perhaps?*

We walk shoulder to shoulder out of the woods and begin the steep climb back uphill in the oppressive heat. I take his hand. He holds on tightly.

When I first went out with Jack, he invited me to get naked with him down in the basement. I said, "No!" He suggested that we lie on top of the covers together in my brother's empty bedroom. Again, I said, "No!"

"We won't do anything," he promised. "Just lie together naked."

My heart raced. We'd be far enough away from the front door that if my scarily intuitive stepfather came home early to catch me doing something wrong, I'd hear the garage door open, and we'd throw on our clothes and run upstairs. We'd be sitting on the sofa in the family room when my parents walked in. Of course, I'd still be caught and in big trouble, but not the serious trouble I'd be in if I were caught naked in bed with my boyfriend—even though we'd just been lying there doing nothing.

After careful consideration and mounting sexual tension, I took his hand, letting him lead me downstairs to my brother's bedroom. We stripped and lay together on the bed. We were there for only a minute, perhaps two, when I couldn't take the stress of being caught any longer. I jumped up, dressing quickly. I sent him home.

We trudge up the last curve of road to the tower. Jack leans a hand against a huge creosote-soaked beam to catch his breath. I bend down and pull a few weeds growing along the edge of the concrete pad at the base of the stairs. Flies buzz around us as they always do at this elevation. A hot breeze rustles the treetops. I turn at a sound in the brush—perhaps a garter snake or a quail—but see nothing.

As I start up the steps, I hear rocks scattering. Again, I search the brush. Nothing. At the top of the stairs, I catch my breath. Soon Jack pops through the trapdoor, lugging the bag the last few feet into the cabin. I help him peel it off his back and together we pour the water into the galvanized cooler. I hold a pot under the spigot and fill it three-quarters-full. I put the pot on the stove to boil a fresh batch of drinking water.

By the time I start dinner, the sun has dropped low in the west, turning the prairie peachy-yellow. The patchwork fields become dark squares edged in buttery light. Inside the tower, the glare intensifies. We slip on our sunglasses. Yellow jackets find the hamburger I stir in the fry pan. One crawls from the spatula into the pan and sits on the meat eating hungrily. Another one crawls along my hand. I'm surprised by how *one with nature* I've become. I hardly notice the yellow jackets until one suddenly stings me. I yelp.

Jack comes to my rescue, cursing the insect for hurting me. He closes up the tower windows while I smooth calendula cream on the sting. He swats the remaining yellow jackets with a flyswatter. "Take that," he hisses, killing all the remaining wasps in the tower.

We eat in silence, Jack smiling over at me. I smile back. He isn't always this careful with me. He missed me while I was in Lewiston, I guess. And he's sorry about the mass, though he doesn't say so directly. I know he could just as easily grouch or hiss at me for complaining about the pain, but he doesn't, thank goodness.

An orange glow lights the prairie and the fresh smell of dry grass carries on a warm wind. I relax as we wash our dinner dishes. Afterward, he suggests we play gin rummy. We match suits and make runs until the sun sinks in the west. Cards returned to the shelf, we brush our teeth, spitting over the railing, white foam splatting the ground far below. Even though it's late, twilight lingers. We climb into bed and turn into each other's arms, kissing deeply. Jude curls up at our feet. An owl hoots in the forest. The only other sound is our lovemaking.

Stores

Tomato soup
Cream of mushroom soup
Cream of celery soup
Canned chili
Soda crackers
Canned clams
Smoked oysters
Tuna
Little smokies
Olives
Pickles
Onions
Tomato sauce
Coffee
Tea
Coors
Wonder bread
Salt
Honey
Butter

twelve

"Yo, Nance," a voice calls out. The tower shakes with each heavy bootstep.

Jack and I hurry out onto the catwalk and peer over the railing, surprised to see my brother's grinning face peering up from the first landing. For some reason, out here in the middle of nowhere, his presence seems weird.

"Bruce?"

He hikes the rest of the stairs and, winded, steps out onto the catwalk, looking around vigilantly, as if he's on patrol in Nam. He grabs the railing and leans against it to catch his breath.

"For fuck's sake!" Jack says and reaches for his hand, shaking it heartily. "Glad to see you, man."

"Far out!" I wrap my arms around his massive girth and hug him tightly. "You're here!"

He returns the love, burying me in a suffocating bear hug, mumbling something about staying with us for a while. There's a vague reference to needing to lie low, then a smirk, then loud hacks into his fist.

Jack and I look at each other and shrug. We see in each other's eyes that we're not sure what he means by "lie low," but don't ask for clarification. I can see from Jack's stance that though he's open to my brother being here, we're thinking the same thing: there's no room in our sixteen-by-sixteen-foot cabin for an extra body, especially one as large as my brother's.

"Great," Jack says.

"But where will he sleep?"

"I'll camp in the woods," Bruce says. "I brought my gear."

Jack and I catch each other's eyes, hesitating only for a moment. "Okay," we say simultaneously.

And just like that, Bruce turns, taking the tower stairs down to the ground agilely despite his new girth. I watch from the catwalk as he slings his backpack over his shoulder and heads down the road, disappearing into the woods.

He's not the same man who joined the marines in 1966 at eighteen. I feel connected to him and happy he's home again, but there's a distance between us now that wasn't there before. Something quiet and shadowed, perhaps the horror story he'll tell us one day when he's ready, and we are as well.

It's another hot one out. I brush away a fly and turn back to the cabin where it is time to copy down the weather report. We gulp down water. Jack checks the forest. I work on the ridge graph. We drink more water.

Bruce stays in the woods all day. When he comes out later, I'm standing on the catwalk, high-powered binoculars surveying the territory. He waves at me. I wave back, knowing he'll be fine sleeping in the woods. Good, even, given so many returning vets take to the woods for comfort—and sanity. It's quiet and safe, a hermitage of sorts.

At dinner, Bruce sits with us at the picnic table looking relaxed. We eat cream of mushroom soup and slices of buttered Wonder bread—which we explain is one of our standard meals. There's an awkwardness at the table. It's as if no one knows what to talk about. Certainly not Nam.

I study my brother across the table. His hair is curlier than mine. And redder. He wears it cut close to the scalp, military style, though it's grown out a bit since he's been back from Vietnam, making the curl more obvious. His beard, which is bright red in patches, burgeons around his plump, freckled face. He finishes his soup and lights up a cigarette. Jack hands him a beer and the two of them go outside to commiserate.

I clear the table and wash the dishes—of course I do, I'm the woman. And Mom always made me clean up after Bruce. Jack's mother never let Jack do anything around the house either.

I turn from where I stack clean dishes on the dish towel. Bruce got more of our Irish heritage. I have a smattering of freckles across my nose, but he's completely covered. Mom says we're Irish, English, Scottish, and Welsh. Oh, and there's a little bit of German in there too, which might explain Bruce's hairy body. Pennsylvania Dutch—which also happens to be Jack's mother's heritage—shoofly pie, hot bacon dressing, hard salted pretzels, cabbage, and sausage.

Outside, the two of them sit side by side on the catwalk. I pace, feeling discombobulated by my brother's presence. He's been at large for such a long time, hardly staying in touch with the family after he was discharged from the marines. We worried a lot, not knowing his whereabouts or even if he was okay. That's why I felt so shocked to see him standing here on the tower stairs. And relieved. The other part, well, there's just a level of discomfort between us because of the way we were raised.

I know how it will go: shortly, I'll be scolding him even though he's older by three years. My sister does the same with me, scolding me even though she's four years younger. Come to think of it, we all scold each other. They say you treat the ones you love most the harshest. I think we treat each other the way we've been treated. I look toward the woods, imagining Bruce's campsite: a small tent and fire ring. We'll have to tell him he can't build a campfire with the fire danger and all.

My stepdad told me that Bruce got an honorable discharge for medical reasons—alcoholism and obesity—which is much better than a dishonorable discharge, which would have happened if he hadn't volunteered for Nam after he went AWOL from Camp Lejeune. He couldn't handle being ordered around and then ridiculed by his drill sergeant: "Give me a hundred, Private Sponge."

I imagine that after being continuously put down at home for not being a man, boot camp pushed him over the edge. I overheard him tell our stepdad once that he'd enlisted in the marines to prove he was a man. I think we both left home to get away from Dick's emotional abuse, and in my case, sexual.

After two stints in Nam, he arrived back in Spokane from his station at Bangor. He proceeded to tear around in *my* '55 Chevy, flying into rages, slapping people across the face, drinking too much, getting into bar fights and thrown out on the street. We were shocked that his once-five-foot-eight frame carrying a lean 175 pounds now donned bulky farmer overalls and double-extra-large T-shirts.

Mother's fear of obesity could be likened to her fear of the wind. I think her fear comes from my grandmother being heavy. She's dead now from the strokes that paralyzed her left side, but Mom hasn't forgotten Grandma's excess weight and remains vigilant around not gaining an extra ounce, despite her prowess as a cook. I wonder how she views my brother's obesity.

It's odd to be so afraid of fat, especially when Mom's so thin. In the photos of her when she was pregnant with my little sister, she appears anorexic in her pin curls, plaid shirt, and pedal pushers, which she says she wouldn't be caught dead in nowadays.

Since obesity is Mother's *numero-uno* fear, she pulls every ounce of skin and fat off the chicken and pares lard from steaks and roasts before sticking them in the oven. Roasting is my favorite way to make chicken. When Mother makes her to-die-for Southern-style chicken, she breads the skinless pieces in salt-and-peppered flour and pours a cup of melted butter over the top. Pouring on the butter surely cancels out her thorough elimination of fatty skin, but the result is delicious beyond belief.

Mom's chicken just happens to be Bruce's favorite meal. He regularly requests it for his birthday dinner, which just passed. He just missed sharing his favorite meal with Mom and Charlie. Bummer! He could have eaten his fill.

The following afternoon, Bruce stands in the tower doorway, a .22 rifle balanced in his right hand. He shows it to me, saying how he's polished the gunstock and filed down the hammer to a hair trigger. He sets it in the corner behind the door. Jack hands him a home brew, which I hope doesn't loosen his light hold on his marine killer-instinct. A wave of nervousness washes over me. Feeling unsettled, I go back to cutting butterscotch brownies from the baking pan.

The men wander out on the catwalk and take seats facing the prairie. I follow them with a plate of sweets. Jack doesn't waste any time rolling a bomber. He claims the bomber is his own invention—a nice fat joint that will get the two of them wasted. Jack passes it my way. I wave it away. "No thanks. Someone needs to tend the forest, you know. We are on the clock, remember?"

I head back inside to make dinner. Even if I wanted to, I don't feel like getting high around my brother. The last time we smoked together, we were living in Spokane. Bruce was still enlisted then and home on leave. Somehow it got back to the corps that we'd smoked pot together and soon we were treading a fine line between possibly going to jail and staying below the radar. We called my stepfather's attorney and asked for his advice. Of course, Dick had already found out what we were up to and proceeded to go berserk. "See," he said. "Proof that you can't be trusted."

In the meantime, Jack buried the goods in the woods where he rode his trail bike often. He knew the nuances of the trails and hid his stash in an abandoned apple orchard. Nothing ever came of it, except for Dick's satisfied declaration that he now had proof that I really was a *crumb-bum*. All I could do was argue that we hadn't really done anything wrong, it was just that we didn't want to get Bruce in trouble with the corps. And furthermore, when he took me to see the Chief of Narcotics, I was sick from smoking a cigarette . . . not weed. Believe me!

It's clear to me that Nam took it out of my brother. It's a horrible war, complete with Agent Orange, napalm, gooks, monsoons, and jungle rot. "Rot," Bruce says, "ate away my feet inside my leather boots. No matter what you do, you can't get rid of it. There's no way to keep dry while wading through rice paddies."

I imagine swampy rice paddies and the wet, steamy jungle rigged with landmines. I think the stress of war turned Bruce's personality explosive. Once, when I still lived at home, he was home on leave and said, "Never wake me in the night. I sleep on the floor with a knife under my pillow. I could kill you in an instant."

"Come and get it," I say, and serve up canned chili and saltines. Bruce denies the offering at first—a hand lifted, a *no thank you* shyness written in his eyes.

"Go on," I say, "there's plenty. I opened two cans."

He mumbles his thanks and takes the proffered bowl.

After dinner, he heads back into the dusky woods. We don't follow him—just give him the freedom to do whatever he needs to do. We hear the scrape of a shovel every once in a while, but nothing more.

Late the next morning, Bruce hikes up the stairs and says he's heading down to town. I remind him it's a fifty-mile round trip. He shrugs. My stomach tightens. He may never come back, that's the way he is. I want to convince him to stay but know deep in my gut that he needs his freedom. I force a smile and say, "See you later."

I think about Mom saying that our birth father beat Bruce. I was only two at the time—Bruce was five. I wanted to know if he'd ever hurt her, or me, for that matter. She shook her head. "He loved you very much." I didn't tell her this, but since my stepfather isn't speaking to me, I'm thinking maybe I'll see if I can find my real father someday. I don't even have a picture of him . . . but I imagine I must look like him.

The silence is final with Bruce gone from the mountain: no shoveling, no hacking, no cigarette smoke, just heat lightning flickering across the horizon. Jack is stoned, tipsy, and pissed at me for turning down his sexual advances once again. I think—although maybe I'm wrong—that twice a day is too much sex for one person. I mean, I'm not conceiving again until the mass is gone. And sometimes, the mass hurts during sex. Besides, I'm too worried about my brother right now to give Jack anything more than a goodnight hug. Bruce is probably sitting in a bar in Grangeville swilling beer or bourbon, my flesh and blood downtrodden by two dads and a stupid war. *Fuck!*

Once, I asked Bruce if he could remember our birth father and he said he didn't. That's nearly all we said to each other that day, sitting next to each other at the table, time stretching out in a long, awkward silence. I finally looked at him and said, "I love you; you know that, don't you?"

He smiled a little. That was after the shrapnel injured his head and arm, after he recovered from losing his whole battalion in a deadly shelling. He healed, so to speak, from his wounds. And received the Purple Heart for his valor. But he'll never be the same, which saddens me terribly.

"Why are they sending you back?" I'd said.

We were silent again, our hearts swollen as roadkill. He smiled that smile that always seemed to say he found something I had said amusing, but he wasn't giving up what it was. I thought it meant he couldn't say how *bummed* he felt. Or maybe how uncomfortable he was with my prying. Or that he had to get back, that's all there was to it. Back to the bunkers, to the Asian piss-beer. Back to the gooks, rifles, snipers, explosives, helicopters, and napalm, for God's sake. Back to the booze. Back to being struck again.

Later that afternoon, Jack calls in a potential smoke. The plume is far out on the prairie and, as it turns out, the smoke is from a manufacturing plant. Still, we are on edge. Fire danger is extremely high. We've been scanning the territory constantly. As the day draws to a close, I begin to worry whether my brother will make it back tonight or not.

Jack says, "Fuck, he can take care of himself. He's been to war, you know."

"I know." And I do, but it's becoming clearer and clearer to me that what he survived in Nam was more shocking than we may ever know. "He's always scratching at the shrapnel," I say. "I want to ask him about it, but clearly, he doesn't want to talk about what happened over there."

"Leave him the fuck alone."

I give Jack a challenging look, staring intensely at him for a few moments, but like all good warriors, I decide to retreat. I drop my eyes to the catwalk.

Bruce is different than before he went to war: antsy, bolting easily, close-lipped, a vagabond at the mercy of the wind. He's no longer the guy who bought me a necklace for no reason at all or bragged to his buddies about his pretty sister, carrying my picture in his wallet during his two stints in Nam.

He's been here for three days now. I think about when he first returned from Nam and slapped me across the face, angry because I was dressed like a hippie. Hippies were protesting the war, so to him I was a war protestor. He expected to be honored for serving his country, but that didn't happen. The soldiers returned home to angry war protestors. Because I started dressing like a hippie once I graduated high school, he thought I was burning flags along with the others.

I argued that I wasn't a war protestor, but still, he backed me into a corner by the washer and dryer and, as fast as a snake, snapped out his palm, striking me across the face. I cried and cried, my fat, bloodied lip stinging. I wasn't being political. I just wanted to get away from how I'd been raised, just like Bruce.

I sigh, wondering now how long he'll stay with us. Or maybe he won't come back from town tonight. Then the tower shakes and I hear his boots on the stairs and a sense of relief washes over me. I feel giddy, like when my cat returned home. He pops up onto the catwalk and lumbers inside the cabin with a bag of food. He drops the bag on the counter. "Ciao!" he says.

"Wow man, thanks. How'd you get to town and back?"

"Hitchhiked." He grins mischievously, saying no more.

I nod, wanting to say something like *it's dangerous to hitchhike,* but I don't. Really, he should be the one protecting me, not me, him. He's the trained killer. I remember him holding my hand and taking me for walks in the woods at our new step-grandparents' house when I was only four. The ground was spongy with thick moss and gave as we walked. It frightened me enough to make me cry. I'm not sure why, perhaps I imagined falling through to the center of the earth. Or farther, all the way to China. "It's a long walk," I say.

"We walked miles through the jungle every day on patrol, you know."

"Right," I say. But no, I don't know. It isn't clear to me what happened to him over there. But really, I'm not sure that I want to know.

He unpacked the bag. Hot dogs, potato chips, beer, bread, and eggs.

"Far out!" I laugh. "We're going to have a feast."

I'm not okay with our birth father hurting him. If we ever meet, I'll tell him so. Even though he never hurt me according to my mother, as a kid I was as jumpy as a beaten dog—probably from being around Bruce when he was struck. And there is the questionable behavior of our stepfather too. I don't know if he sexually abused my brother or not. Someday, I will ask Bruce about it.

Bruce shuffles his feet, grinning down at me.

"Glad you're back." I want to ask him where he stayed last night but keep my mouth shut. After all, he has been dealing with snipers, jungle critters, foxholes, helicopters, rice paddies, and incoming. If he gets in trouble, he knows how to kill someone with his bare hands. He knows where to sleep, how to survive on little food, and how to outrun the enemy.

He says, "The cows are in the stream."

"Yeah," I say. "We're boiling the water."

He takes a seat in the green chair, wiggling a foot as he lights a cigarette. He smokes in short bursts, nervous as a cat.

Mom is a fiend for Winstons and Dick occasionally smokes a pipe packed with vanilla-flavored tobacco. Grandpa loved his Camels. I'm the only one in the family who doesn't smoke. I finish writing in the log, recording weather from the forecast earlier, noting the smokestack we called in by mistake and how there's little else that's urgent to record today.

Flies circle near the ceiling above the firefinder, a continuous, lazy loop in the center of the room. It's going to be another hot one. I hear a distant plane. Some days, that is all we hear. Then there are days when people wander up the road to the tower, committing to the fifty-six stairs to pay us a visit, moving tentatively around the catwalk once they're standing at forty-five feet above the ground. It's nerve wracking to have unexpected visitors. And they seem nerve-wracked too. But it is mostly always good to have company.

"I need the outhouse," I say, and head down to the ground. As I cross the road, I can see the path leading into the woods and a glimpse of Bruce's camp. I want to sneak into his campsite and see how he has it set up. I should have done that when he was away in town. I hurry to the outhouse, opening the door to the dark, hot stink. My worry turns to spiders climbing through the hole from beneath the seat. I become a vigilant warrior scoping out webs and tangled flies.

I'm dying for a bath and have come up with a scheme I think will work. In the meadow across from the watering hole, we'll dig a bathtub-sized hole in the path of the stream that trickles downhill. I'll line the hole with a black plastic bag. Once the bag fills with water, I'll strip and climb in. It'll be icy cold, yes, but a bath that I can submerge myself in and wash away the sticky sweat from this godawful heat will feel divine.

My brother hasn't wiped the smirk off his face since I explained my idea. He waits on the road, his back turned to me. It appears as if he's on patrol, hanging silently at the edge of the jungle of pine and fir, his .22 rifle pointed at the ground. My brother, the marine who can survive in the jungle, probably has already guessed that Jack and I are going off half-cocked.

I strip and climb in the icy water that has now risen past my knees. My legs ache from the cold. Watching the silty stream spill into the bag is a joyous experience. I'm going to have a bath. Then, all at once, the bag begins collapsing around me. The soggy earth surrounding the top of the bag crumbles, making me shriek as the hole that I hoped would contain my plastic bathtub becomes a sodden mess. Jack laughs and points at the muddy bag plastered to my skin.

"Fuck," I say, brushing away bits of black silt from my goose-bump-covered torso. As the wet earth continues to collapse around me, Jack offers a hand and pulls me to high ground. I'm shrieking and swearing as I climb out, covered in detritus and shivering from the icy dip. I dry off and hurriedly dress.

We walk along a narrow deer path up the incline to the road where my brother stands guard. Bruce falls in behind us, the gun with the hair trigger pointing supposedly at the ground behind me. I feel grouchy as hell and swing about, saying, "It's got a hair trigger, do you mind? Point it elsewhere!"

"No worries." He snickers.

"I'm walking in front of you, okay. Point it at the ground."

My brother gives me a look. "I risked my life in Vietnam for the past couple of years. I think I know what I'm doing." He lowers the gun and steps off the path.

"Right! Fuck!" I wrap the towel around my neck and follow Jack to the stream. Jack turns away from the brother-sister act, squatting down to refill the bladder bag with water.

My brother waits on the road in the blazing sun. He's pissed at me now. All I want is a real bath, and I consider a trip down to Grangeville, after all. I recall Arizona saying, "The doors are unlocked, just go on in and help yourself whenever you want." But I can't leave my brother alone with Jack. If I do, I'll come back to two drunken, stoned idiots. I decide that when he's ready to go for good, I'll drive him down to Grangeville, take a shower, and do some grocery shopping before carrying on with tower life.

Jack presses the bladder bag beneath the water's surface to fill. Bruce stands nearby, his gun pointed at the ground, eyes narrow and squinting, sweating as he watches the jungle for snipers. Jack needs a hand lifting the bladder bag onto his back. Bruce hands me the rifle, which I take begrudgingly. He easily hefts the weighty bladder bag onto his own back. I remember him saying that in Nam, he carried a seventy-pound radio pack on his back while slithering snakelike on his belly through the jungle. He takes back the rifle and, together, we trudge uphill through the relentless heat.

Back up top, I start dinner. We'll have the hot dogs Bruce brought us from town. He also bought buns, chips, and beer. While I cook, Jack and Bruce drink cold Coors, chatting easily, happily, even. Bruce says he'll walk to town the next day and get something stronger to drink: *You know what I mean?*

I suggest we drive down together so I can get a bath and groceries.

He shrugs, sipping his beer.

"We can talk about it in the morning," I say, serving dinner. "Thanks for the hot dogs."

Nodding, he takes a seat at the picnic table. Outside on the horizon, white, puffy cumulonimbus clouds pile up. The sky begins to turn pale peach. A warm glow lights the cabin as we eat. I get up and put on my sunglasses. A chipmunk skitters inside, stands on its hind feet, and begs for crumbs. Bruce laughs and throws him a morsel of hot dog bun. The chipmunk grabs it, clutching it between his tiny hands, eating quickly, then skittering away.

We finish our meal in silence. Bruce has clammed up, which now seems to be rubbing off on Jack. When at war, I guess, top-secret messages are coded. Bruce was worthy of capture, as he could break codes. The atrocities in his head remain, but he gives away nothing. I can only imagine gunfire, explosions, rumbling bombers, helicopter blades chopping steamy air, and all his buddies cut down. Blood and more blood.

Mom said that my brother was dying on the battlefield while his friends lay next to him, either dead or bleeding out. Maybe I was naïve writing him, describing my silly teen escapades: lake visits to the grandparents' house, the car radio playing Beatles songs, drinking pop and eating donuts after school, going out with friends for French fries and pizza—our normal activities were nothing but kid stuff to soldiers fighting in a war. Maybe my stepdad was right. "Don't tell the soldiers (I wrote to soldiers other than my brother) about the fun things you're doing. It'll just make them sad."

I guess compared to my brother's days threatened by incoming or steamy nights stalked by Vietcong, I've had it easy. Or maybe not—at least in the jungle, everyone knows who the enemy is. Whereas in my own personal war, the enemy remained secret. I couldn't tell anyone what was happening in my bedroom, the basement, and other places where I was captured. Still, even though I've been away from home for three years now, I still imagine how to protect myself if I am attacked by a potential rapist. I'd use my fists as a weapon to clobber a chin, nose, throat, or eyes. My rage would give me superhuman strength. The pounding would be violent like it is in my dreams—punching and punching and punching until my assailant ceased to move. I don't know how to fix the fear that remains inside me. Hopefully, someday, I can.

After breakfast the next morning, Bruce and I chat while I wash dishes and he dries. I tell him about our wedding presents stored in Mom's new basement. He says her new house is okay but doesn't feel like home. I tell him that she bought it with the money she got in the divorce.

"Do you know that Dick actually told Mom he no longer loved her," I say. "That's why she started drinking so much. She's broken-hearted."

"Uh," he said, shuffling around the cabin. We take seats at the table. I refill our coffee cups.

"What's with those floozy getups she wears, and she's dating a married man?" Bruce shakes his head. "That's fucked up."

"She got rid of the married guy." I recall the last time we all gathered at her house for a barbecue before heading off to

Grangeville. Mom came out from her bedroom dressed in a skirt with a matching bra and flimsy coverup. "Just put something on, for God's sake," Bruce said. "You're our mother."

"Good thing she dumped the married guy. But now Charlie wants to marry her," I say. "She better not say yes. I don't trust him."

I change the subject back to the cedar chest in Mom's basement. "I didn't register for one color of towels, so we got a mishmash of colors. Jack's mom and dad gave us a waffle iron. We got a pressure-cooker and a set of stoneware. I didn't bring any of our gifts up here, you know. Except the hibachi. I didn't want things getting wrecked here in the wilderness. I mean, one day, my yellow bowl fell off the railing and, amazingly, it didn't break when it hit the ground. Can you believe it?"

Bruce laughs, jiggling his foot continuously, smoking the cigarette cupped inside his hand to conceal the burning tip. I'm not sure he's even listening, as he has a far-off look on his face. Still, I go on, hoping he'll come back. "I have a complete set of Revere Ware. A copper fondue with six long forks. They're for stabbing hunks of French bread to dip in melted cheese. Too bad you couldn't make it to the wedding."

Bruce makes a scoffing noise. "Dad wouldn't have wanted me there, anyway. He doesn't trust me."

"Sure he does," I say, though I know Bruce is right.

"No, he doesn't. And when I call, he acts like he doesn't want to talk to me."

"He doesn't call me, either. The way he's acting right now makes me furious. I mean, we're his kids. Pay attention to us."

Bruce gets up from the picnic bench. "I think I'll go for a walk."

I watch his girth sidle along the catwalk toward the stairs, worrying that I caused him to leave. "Come back later for dinner."

"Uh-huh," he grunts. The tower shakes as he descends the stairs.

When Bruce worked for our stepdad, he goofed off, some- times breaking things—though, not intentionally. He was still in high school then. I get why he was a screw-off. He was young and not particularly efficient. Plus, Dick put him down all the time. He was nervous he'd do something wrong. War has changed him and our stepfather doesn't know him now. Nor do I, for that mat- ter. We should try harder to understand him. Hopefully, he'll open up someday.

The sun dips lower in the sky, beginning the late afternoon super-heating of the cabin. I wipe sweat from my face with my shirttail. I want something salty, potato chips or peanuts, but we ate all the chips and nuts, and we're out of beef jerky.

Salt tablets were Dick's solution to heat prostration, which means a suffering body reclines flat on the floor or on a bed. Mom used to do just that on humid afternoons. She had heatstroke once, which means it could be dangerous if it happened again. Here on the tower, when the sun lowers in the sky and lines up with the tower windows late in the afternoon, rays pound inside, roasting us like pigs. Resting helps; drinking lots of water does too. I step out onto the catwalk where a slight breeze feels re- freshing. Sighing, I raise the binoculars to the crisping forest and carefully peruse the territory.

I always resisted taking the salt pills that Dick ordered us to swallow on hot summer afternoons. He said they were necessary to avoid heatstroke. Then, there were vitamin fads he engaged in that had me burping up fish oil all morning at school. I refused to take my vitamins one morning, which pissed him off. He called me a baby and insisted I take them. To keep the peace, I gagged them down.

The afternoon passes like a *Gone With the Wind* scene. The for- est, dangerously dry, has us vigilantly searching for smokes.

Fortunately, there haven't been any lightning strikes lately. But now, dark gray clouds pile up on the horizon. Though I don't see any anvils, an ominous feeling washes over me.

I start dinner and soon the smell of frying hamburger draws yellow jackets inside. Jack comes back from a walk with an idea he says will stop us from going crazy on Corral Hill. He slaps away the wasps, cursing loudly. "We can excavate the garbage dump down by Elk City Wagon Road where the hotel and horse barn used to be. Miners rested their horses overnight while they ate a hot meal and got a good night of sleep at the hotel."

"You mean dig up the ground?" I say, feeling baffled.

"Sure, why not?"

"I don't know, it sounds like a dirty job."

Bruce shows up last minute, and soon the three of us are sitting on the catwalk with plates of "Mom's goulash" in our laps. I look over at my brother. He's lighting up a cigarette, having already finished his meal. He grins at me. I know he feels safe here with us. I smile, my heart filled with happiness.

We watch the clouds build in the distance. Lightning flashes cloud to cloud, pinking up their insides as the sky darkens. We hear distant rumbles and I suggest to Bruce that if a storm blows in during the night, he should come up top.

After a while, the storm clearly takes an southeastward route. Another tower will watch the fireworks tonight instead of us. We begin losing light and call it good. Bruce says goodnight and heads down to his campsite. We head back inside.

The next day, while leaning against the railing searching for fires, I breathe in the scent of warm evergreen pitch. Everything is tinder-dry, causing the forest to smell like incense—almost like the frankincense we burnt last Christmas. We bought it thinking it must have special powers, otherwise, why would the wise men have gifted it to Jesus? When there were no obvious miracles, we shrugged our shoulders and went back to wrapping gifts.

Squeak thinks incense is for dives. He says our friend Slow Bull lives in a dive—because we came home after a visit smelling of patchouli. "Actually, no, he doesn't live in a dive," I said. "He's staying with a friend who rents a nice apartment in Browne's Addition. It's furnished with Jaipur rugs and thick down pillows. Incense burned while we sat on the pillows and he told us all about his trip to India. He loves to travel."

Jack grabs his guitar and wanders out on the catwalk. He takes a seat in the shade and begins strumming "Stairway to Heaven." I used to think heaven was a place we went to when we died, but now I know our spirits move on, traveling through time and space forever. Or until reincarnating, that is. I believe Jack and I have been together before. That's why we hooked up so easily. It was like we saw each other and said, "Oh, at last, there you are." But it isn't always the good stuff that brings people back together. Bad karma can draw people together too; sometimes difficult things need to be righted in the current lifetime. I wonder what Jack and I are working out. Perhaps we have power issues to come to terms with. Seems likely, since we've been fighting ever since my brother showed up. I told Jack that he was spending too much time getting stoned with Bruce. He said he wasn't and that is why he yelled at me last night. I was upset about it, waking in the night several times feeling bummed. But Jack should be keeping fire watch, not sitting around with my brother getting high. They got stoned after lunch today, and now Bruce is back in the woods, probably sleeping it off while Jack strums away, higher than a kite. I guess that leaves fire watch to me.

My brother has trouble with booze. Perhaps Jack does too. And, what if there's a smoke? I need Jack's help. I'm constantly monitoring the black thunderheads building on the horizon, perusing the territory for fire, aware still of the missed fire early on. We've gone days without rain. The parched ground's as dry as a desert. What does he think he's doing, getting stoned during dangerous fire conditions?

August is always the hottest month. Things were easier on the mountain in June and July. Cool mornings, the two of us rising at sunup, making a pot of coffee, excited to start the day. We'd eat eggs and toast, and sometimes there was cream for our coffee from the local farmer. We arrived at Corral Hill with most everything we needed, but with Bruce here, we're going through stores more quickly than usual. I haven't been down to Grangeville since I drove to see the doctor in Lewiston. I wander inside, sit down, and make a grocery list, thinking I'll head down to Grangeville first thing in the morning.

"We're almost out of RyKrisp," I mutter, my stomach growling as the list grows. "And we're low on peanut butter. There are no pickles, or milk, or butter. Of course, beer, olives, and jerky."

I finish the note and grab the binoculars. Back out on the catwalk, I take in the enlarged territory through the two circular lenses. I can see Idaho and Montana from my vantage point. Montana has a lookout manned by a hippie couple who talk after dark sometimes. They say "Wow man" and "Far fuckin' out" every other word. One night, while sitting on the picnic bench talking to them on the radio, the guy said, "How the fuck are you, old man? How's the old lady?"

Jack's hackles went up. I squeezed his knee in the dark and he cooled it, mostly, though not entirely. So, I ran my hand up his thigh. He turned to me, grinning, and said back to the guy, "Fuckin' out of sight. Yep, old man, out of sight!"

But it wasn't totally true. That is, we don't exactly feel *fucking great* these days. Isolation drones on and on. If you're a recluse, then it's the perfect place to live. Plenty of time for the mind to drift. Memories sift up from the subconscious and flutter about like nuthatches, foraging as they move through the trees. Once memories are loosened, they can easily become an obsession. The memory of my brother and me walking naked into the lake while our stepfather filmed us with his Kodak movie camera comes to mind. When I saw the home movie, I was mortified. I mean, who cares about our privacy? Go ahead and show the film Sunday night and let everyone watch the two of us wade buck naked into the lake, turn slowly around, and walk back to shore. *Click, click, click*: I can still hear the projector rolling in my head and smell hot film, the bright lightbulb blinding.

Everyone was watching, I mean everyone: aunts, uncles, grandparents, and cousins too. I don't remember who was there for sure, because, like I said, I was a child, maybe four or five years old. Poor Bruce was seven or eight. Anyway, we were embarrassed beyond belief; you could see it in our faces. I shake my head and wander back outside.

Jack stops playing and sits staring into space. His mouth pinches together in a slim line. He looks bummed, but I say nothing, just lean against the railing and close my eyes, resting them from the glare. Soon, hubby gets up from the chair and heads inside. I open my eyes again, turning just in time to see him step on the picnic bench, then to the table next to the bed. He shoves open the attic trapdoor where he stores his home brew. I turn back to the territory, knowing he will take down several bottles and put them in the refrigerator, keeping one out to drink warm. We are lucky; some towers have no refrigeration, but we have a propane refrigerator. I don't really understand how heat can make something cold, but it works. He climbs down and does exactly what I'm thinking. Then he hollers, "I'll bottle the new batch of beer tonight."

"Whatever," I say, and decide to make dinner. Bruce will be stopping to eat, even though he says *no thanks* to dinner every time I invite him. I usually convince him to sit down with us, no matter what. After dinner, the men will retire to the catwalk and watch the pink and mauves of sunset gather, tinting the brilliant white cumulus to pale rose clouds, sometimes edging it in a searing backlight of orange. The curvature of the earth is emphasized— dark at the center of the horizon where the flash of green can be seen when the sun goes down. I've never seen it myself, nor has anyone I know, but I hear that it happens. I usually watch for it if the skies are clear.

Jack returns to the catwalk and takes a seat in the camp chair. He guzzles the green beer and sets the bottle on the deck. Positioning his guitar, he begins to play a lilting Beatles refrain, and I can tell that his demeanor has changed.

Back inside, I open my Fannie Farmer cookbook from grade school, which includes a Lazy Daisy Chocolate Cake recipe, calling for flour, sugar, butter, cocoa, eggs, milk, and vanilla. The butter and milk are running low. If I don't go to town tomorrow, Jack could make a trip down to the farmer's house and buy some cream to shake until it turns to butter. He's good at shaking things up. I laugh a little to myself.

I remember Mom buying cream for whipping. She ordered groceries delivered to our house. One day, she asked me to write a check out to the delivery boy, since she wouldn't be there when he arrived. I remember he came around to the backdoor. I opened the sliding patio door to this handsome football hunk. The boy stepped inside, set the bags on the kitchen table, and handed me the receipt. I stammered, giggling, unable to write the check as my mother instructed.

Although Jack and I were already going together, I still got heart flutters over cute guys. Even now, I'm a bit of a flirt, desiring other men at times, though I'd never follow through like my stepdad did. According to Mom, he was a real skirt-chaser. Why am I not surprised?

If I show interest in other men, Jack gets pissed. Can't say that I blame him, as I get pissed when he flirts with other women. But I don't change my stance, widen my feet, and push my pelvis forward like Jack does. I can see I'm in for trouble when he starts smoothing his mustache, and especially when he crosses his arms over his chest, his tanned biceps bulging from beneath the white Hanes T-shirt he always wears. Sexy. God, he's a sexy man. But impossible to live with some days.

The day the firefighters came to visit, he got furious when I flirted with the handsome one. What do you call it, a double standard? I mean, it's all right when he flirts with a chick, but I'm to remain uninspired. If I were to say, "When we lived in the green old-mare house, you put your arm around a crying girl at a party and comforted her, remember?" he'd just growl at me. I was so furious that day, I could have killed him. She showed up at a party across the street and then wandered over to our house. When I returned from the party, she and Jack sat side by side on the front steps, his arm draped over her shoulders, soothing her crying jag.

Jack returns to the cabin in his flip-flops. Weirdly, I notice how dirty his feet are. Then I check out my feet, realizing we both need baths. A film of dirt is smeared across each of our toes. We are unable to go to town together, and the next time down is my turn, so he'll have to stay dirty or wash in the stream. Maybe I'll suggest he take the Dr. Bronner's peppermint soap and haul his ass down the road. He's usually mad about something, so it doesn't matter if I upset him further. He acts as though life is out to get him: jaw clenched, eyes narrowed, hands fisted. *Fuck him*, I think and step past him, taking out the last of the butter.

I whip up the Lazy Daisy Chocolate Cake and light the oven, sliding the pan inside. Shortly, the tower smells heavenly, like sugar and butter and chocolate. The scent revives me. Even the yellow jackets revive and begin buzzing around, settling on the mixing bowl and then on the stove. I recall the last sting. Once the hurt went away, I was back to ignoring the yellow jackets. I have to hand it to Jack; he was sweet as sugar after I got stung— for about five minutes. Then he went after the poor yellow jacket and killed the fucker. I wish he'd be like that all the time, cooing and kissing me when I'm sad or hurting. Like he did with that crying girl. I could use a little comforting right now, after all, my womb remains empty—which breaks my heart.

That night, after dinner and dessert, Bruce helps Jack bottle the second batch of beer. They are drinking the cold ones he slipped into the fridge earlier. Bruce mumbles something about the root beer we bottled when we lived on Hoffman Street. I say, "I remember not being allowed to help, because I was too young. I was mad!"

"We found a bottle of it after we moved to Audubon Street."

"Mom dumped it out. She thought it was bad."

"Probably was fine. Why wouldn't it be?"

"Now I want root beer," I say, laughing lightly.

The light is leaving the sky. What was pink and mauve has faded to gray, but the heat remains. The men continue to work, finishing up bottling and storing away the new batch in the attic.

"Lucky we had home brew this summer. We would have had to make a heck of a lot more trips to town if we didn't."

Bruce guffaws, takes a drink of beer, and lights another cigarette. I step outside. Too much smoke and the smell of beer makes me feel nauseous. I drink in the evening freshness, the dewy smell of forest and prairie. There's a name for that scent, I think.

The next day, Bruce announces he's leaving the mountain shortly. I try to convince him that I'll drive him to Grangeville. He shakes his head, staring down at his shuffling feet.

I'm a little surprised he's leaving already, since he seemed to be comfortably settled in his campsite. "I'm so glad you came for a visit."

We hug and say goodbye. He slips on his backpack and takes the stairs swiftly to the ground. We follow him as he walks off down the road. I tear up, waving and hollering *goodbye*. I stand there watching him near the main road where he'll turn to the right onto Elk City Wagon Road and disappear.

Jack takes my hand in his and squeezes it. Bruce turns and waves one last time and rounds the bend. We walk back up the dusty road, me wiping my nose on my already-dirty T-shirt the whole way. Near the top, Jack wraps an arm around my shoulder and gives me a hug. *Ah*, I think, turning to him. "Thanks."

When we round the corner, we decide to follow Bruce's path into the woods and gasp. As we stand in the clearing, we see that he dug out a bunker, ten feet across and four feet deep, complete with a sleeping shelf. I imagine him lying on that bench and watching the stars come out at night, spying them between the sheets of plywood he found somewhere in the woods and placed over the top of his underground room as a makeshift roof. I wonder if he felt lonely. Did he have war flashbacks? Would he ever heal from losing all his buddies?

"Shit," I say. "He was still living in the jungle."

"It's a bunker," Jack says.

I've heard about guys returning from Nam, wandering into the woods, hardly seen or heard from ever again. I could see from Bruce's bunker that this was a definite possibility—probably the woods are a little like living in the jungle in Nam. He could have stayed here the rest of the summer if it hadn't been an imposition on us. Though really, if he had, it would have been doubly hard for me to do my job.

The survival manual I read last summer taught us how to live off the land. I learned how to catch fish and rabbits when lost in the woods. It also explained how to create sleeping situations that would keep a person warm and dry. Sleeping off the ground is important in retaining one's body heat. And for avoiding bites from critters that wander about in the night.

In Nam, the men slept underground, inside bunkers dug into the jungle floor. Seems like it would have been super wet inside one of those holes, especially during the monsoon season. The rest of the time, I don't really know. Guess I'm not sure about the holes or the monsoons or anything else about Nam. I'll have to ask Bruce sometime, if I ever get up the nerve to ask him about the war. If he ever wants to talk about it. If I ever want to hear about it, that is.

We tried to live off the land when we worked at Priest Lake, camping on the mainland or taking Squeak's motorboat, *Mellow Yellow*, over to the island to set up our tent. We'd fish for our dinners. It was easy to survive during the summer. Lots of silvers to catch and huckleberries to gather. Although, the survival manual says you'll die if you only eat lean meat. It's the fat in your diet that'll keep you from starving to death. Berries are fatty, believe it or not. That's why bears put on so much weight before they hibernate.

After we wrap our heads around the fact of Bruce digging a twelve-foot bunker in the forest floor, we head back up top. Birds of prey lift on warm air currents, soaring in wide circles. I point out to Jack two eagles flying over Baldy. I've heard if you're caught with an eagle feather, you could go to jail. You could also go to jail if you're caught with pot. You could be locked behind bars for burning a flag. If you protest the war and get overly rowdy—jail. If you go AWOL like my brother did—jail.

Who could blame my brother for running away from boot camp, after being harangued constantly by a red-faced drill sergeant? And all those miles of running and sit-ups and tire-drills and wall-climbs had to be exhausting. And the slithering along the ground with a heavy pack on his back, sweat-drenched and dead tired, had to be grueling. I imagine my brother probably shouted back: *Yes, sir!* But probably not loud enough to avoid additional push-ups.

Then there was our stepdad's constant belittling: *Your zipper's down, where's your hankie, your grades are too low, don't talk back, you're not a man—you're just a big crybaby.*

Once, Jack and I watched a movie about aliens with ships that spun through space like gyroscopes. The spacemen had big eyes, which I can still see when I close my own. Aliens and Dick's eyes watch me. Sometimes they hover nearby in my dreams. I blink, telling him—and the aliens—to go away, just leave me alone. But it rarely works. Dick just stands there saying things like: *You're a crumb-bum, you're undependable, you don't love God, and you don't love your mother and me.*

Then he calls me "Nasty" and laughs. I guess he thinks it is a play on words or something. It's not! And it's not funny how he jokes with me, then turns serious when I laugh. "Don't laugh, I mean it," he says, exchanging his teasing face for his most ornery face. It's a mindfuck. A landmine fuck, just like Nam.

He implies that I'm subversive, like I'll go bomb something or blackmail someone or burn the flag and get hauled off to jail. Well, I'm not a rebel, not in that sense. I'm an artist, yes, and I do look at things differently than other people. Like the guy who hosted an art talk one night at the Washington State University annex. The presenter called himself an activist.

"Activism at its finest," the artist said, and showed us his pencil drawings of dissidents. His sketches showed people rebelling against authority. Dissention is on the rise because of the Vietnam War, which hopefully is coming to an end soon. The war protestors are beginning to turn violent. As are the police. Protestors and students are being killed. It is terrifying!

Bruce told me that war protestors insult GIs. He wanted to be respected when he returned from Nam, not ignored, blamed, or sworn at. When he first came home, he started to tell me what it was like over there in the jungle. I put my hand up, unwilling to hear any horror stories at that point. When I watched him scratch at the shrapnel that remained buried in his head and arm—*severely injured* the officers who came to the house had said—I just felt sad. He was in the hospital for a long time before they sent him home on R&R.

He earned the Purple Heart for valiantly serving our country. I guess what he did was valiant, but it's a real bummer getting "decorated" for surviving a mass slaughter. Mom told me later that Bruce almost died from his injuries. I mean, we were on the other end, waiting and wondering, praying that nothing bad had happened in the jungle, especially when we hadn't heard from him in such a long time. But something did happen. When the men in uniform came to our door, our hearts leapt into our throats. We thought we'd lost him for sure.

I always wanted to say more to my stepdad about the way he'd treated Bruce, but his arguments twisted my mind and left me unable to sort out my thoughts. At the same time, he harassed me about dating Jack, the books I read (too much sex), and the music I liked to listen to. Bruce and I were beaten down by him, not encouraged, supported, or educated on how to live as adults in this world. Both of us continue to suffer from Dick's abuse.

I know I need counseling, but only crazy people need their minds examined, right? The time Dick said he needed a shrink, Mother and I just nodded, our faces somber. I don't remember what the problem was. I did know the problem I was having with him—all those unwanted visits to my bedroom in the middle of the night or early Sunday mornings.

When he said he loved me, perhaps he meant it differently than most parents. When he called me Nasty or claimed I smelled when we passed the meat processing plant, my heart fell to the ground like a slaughtered steer. Or maybe like a victim of shrapnel, like my brother lying on the ground next to his buddies bleeding out.

I'd like to make my stepdad understand how I felt when he abused me, but how do you bring up a topic like that? Perhaps by saying: Do you know that I was terrified to be alone with you? Do you know that I almost ran away from home because you were touching me every chance you got? Do you remember that girl, the daughter of your friend who ran away? She called all of her parents' friends, including you, and asked for money so she could eat while living on the street. You said she was a bad girl. Perhaps she wasn't. Perhaps she was being abused at home like me. Guilty people try to cover their tracks. Guilty people should pay.

Well, anyway, today cumulus clouds pile up on the horizon. Ravens play to the west, circling and diving, twirling and flipping upside down like stunt planes. Like Dick filming out the window of his airplane, turning the running movie camera in a circle, pretending he was rolling the plane. We all gasped when we watched that movie, thinking he really was a stunt pilot. Fool us twice . . .

Jack comes in from outside, looking bored without Bruce around to shoot the breeze. He says he's going to dig up a dumpsite down at the turnoff later. "Do you want to come?"

"That's a great idea." I'm being sarcastic, of course, because if I do excavate an old dump, I'll be cleaning dirt out from under my fingernails for the rest of the evening and the seat of my pants will be filthy.

He says he wants to see if what Arizona says is true, that garbage pits contain relics from covered wagon days. "Middens were dug around the hotel and livery stable."

"Middens?"

"Garbage pits," he says. "We could find some groovy stuff buried there. Wanna try it?"

I shrugged. "I can't imagine a hotel in the middle of nowhere."

"It's still fifty miles to Elk City. Not only a hotel, but a stable for horses and a farrier. Travelers ate a meal and rested their horses overnight at Corral Station."

"How do you know where to dig? I mean—"

"We'll just pick a spot," he says. "We're already dirty. It'll be fun."

"It sounds tiring," I say.

"You'll like it, Nancerella. You'll see."

I give up trying to shift Jack's decision and get busy copying down the weather forecast. No storms expected, and the nights are cooling. The snow level is dropping.

We go through our day as usual, scanning the territory often, finishing up the day by checking the location of the last smoke, making sure it remained cold. Fires can reignite, especially if they are burning underground. It's a little like unresolved feelings that have been stuffed away forever, erupting unexpectedly.

When we're off the clock, we wander down the road to the clearing near the watering hole. The cows have left their prints in the soggy mud, but nearer to the road, everything is dry. Beyond the spot where the ground rises slightly to the east is the turnoff to Elk City Wagon Road. Turn left and the road continues uphill to the north, then it turns off, winding its way south again toward Elk City. Arizona told me that miners headed there in droves to work in the gold fields. He said, "Elk City was a hopping town."

Jack carries a shovel. I bring an empty coffee can for keepsakes, if we find anything worth keeping, that is. At the bottom of the road, we choose a spot that's mounded higher than the land around it. Perhaps it will prove to be one of Corral Station's middens.

Jack begins to break ground, tossing several shovelfuls of dry dirt to the side. His face is tense, to task. I sit on the ground, legs spread wide, scraping the earth in front of me with a stick. I rifle through each pile of loosened dirt, finding nothing. I'm surprised, however, by the amazing fervor I suddenly have for digging a hole.

I think of my brother digging out his bunker. I want to chalk my fervor up to the bad case of cabin fever—but perhaps digging in the earth is enjoyable, in and of itself. Like gardening. I recall thinking I could plant vegetables on the mountaintop . . . silly ol' me. How would I have hauled water to my garden bed? What seeds would have grown fast enough to harvest? It could have worked by the stream, I suppose. Watercress is growing there. Perhaps spinach would have sprouted, or lettuce.

I smile at Jack. Even though it was a blast to have company, my brother was distracting. But just the act of doing something besides our regular lookout chores seems to have lifted the pall from our shoulders.

The sun is lower now, but still, it's warm on my back. The days are growing shorter; our season manning the lookout will end soon. Despite the daytime heat, when the sun goes behind a cloud there's a chill in the air that makes me shiver. In the distance, hillsides are dotted with reds and yellows. I swear I smell distant snow.

I hit something hard with my stick. Poking around, I pry a milk-glass canning jar lid loose from the ground. Brushing away the dirt, I shout, "Look what I found." When I hold it up for Jack to see, the sun shines through its milky whiteness, refracting pinkish light on my hand.

"Far out," he says, tossing a bit of broken ceramic crockery in the coffee can. The chip tings loudly as it lands.

I pull the chip back out and examine it. "Cool," I say. "Flow Blue pattern. Mom used to collect whole pieces of this pottery. Pretty."

I place it back in the can and continue digging. I discover a tiny bottle turned a faint purple color from its time spent beneath the ground. Jack finds a brown whiskey bottle, a pint that he sniffs, wrinkling his nose.

"Smell like whiskey?" I ask.

"Nope, like dirt and something rotten."

"Bummer," I say, climbing to my feet. I brush off my jeans. They're stained brown at the knees and I'm sure the seat is too. My hands feel dry and my fingernails are edged with grime. Jack's white T-shirt is smeared with dirt where he wiped his hands after each sifting. The whole excavation project keeps us entertained for over an hour, long enough for the chill in the air to intensify and the sky to turn a shade of dusky pink. My stomach growls. "I'm going up top," I say.

"Let's leave the hole open, come back tomorrow, and excavate again."

"Maybe," I say, feeling a bit more energized now, but unsure that I'll want to dig again. Jack is obviously happy about our discoveries. He could be pacing the catwalk right now and pulling at his beard. Instead, he's smiling and making eye contact with me.

"Hungry?" I ask, smiling back.

He nods.

Back on the tower, I light the gas light and we strip off our dirt-covered jeans. We pile them in the corner behind the green chair. We have several loads of laundry to take to town. I've been washing some of our clothes in the dish tub, but it's nearly impossible to wash jeans by hand. All our jeans are dirty, so we pull on shorts despite the chill in the air. Jack's teeth chatter. I throw the afghan over my shoulders and put water on to heat so we can scrub our hands.

Fire season fizzles by the end of September or early October, which makes me feel apprehensive in a way. I'm used to the daily routine of living forty-five feet in the air on a six-thousand-foot mountain. The storms are enlivening, and yes, sometimes frightening. Spotting a fire brings a rush of adrenaline. But I'm also excited to get back to civilization, to see our friends and family— plus switching on the bathroom light and stepping into a hot shower whenever I feel like it sounds divine.

We wash our hands in a washbasin. It takes a second washing with another squirt of Dr. Bronner's to get all the dirt out from around our cuticles and beneath our fingernails. Once washed and dried, I reheat leftovers while Jack checks the forest, scanning the territory through heavy black binoculars.

Back inside, he opens the last two aged beers and we sit down at the picnic table. We eat like it's our last meal, foraging from the Melmac plate arranged with sliced apples and cheese, green olives, and seeds. The best part of our dinner is the leftover chili we'd dip crackers in, if we had any. I will put canned chili on the grocery list next to RyKrisp.

After the dishes are washed and drying on the not-so-clean dish towel, I mix up some sourdough bread while Jack plays the guitar. Tomorrow, I'll drive to town to do the wash and grocery shop. For a second, I imagine I'll see Bruce in town. If I do, I'll give him a ride back up the mountain. But I know he's probably back in Spokane by now, surprising Mom and my sister with his smiling, freckled face.

Nature Experiences

Bear encounters
Standing inside a dust devil
Daring lightning
Fighting wildfire
Tripping on Amanita Muscaria
Scaling mountains
Awed by St. Elmo's fire
Dazzled by aurora borealis
Swimming in swift current
Braving windstorms
Driving through dust storms
Gazing at meteor showers
Surviving terrible storms

thirteen

As summer drags on, I become more and more aware of the pain in my belly. Intercourse puts pressure on the lemon-sized intruder and hurts like crazy, which leaves us both disappointed: Jack, of course, because he wants frequent sex. And me, already disappointed that my lust is nothing compared to what it was in high school, feeling protective of my body.

We were so hot for each other back in high school, so hot that we'd find out-of-the-way places to make love. I remember slipping out the backdoor after dinner while the adults retired to the family room to watch Lawrence Welk dance with "the pretty girls." We'd find a shadowy area near the edge of the pines where we'd make love in the hot night air.

Outside, the dusky yard snapped with sprinklers, dampening the perimeter and wafting the scent of wet beauty bark into the still night. We laid in the summer grass, staring up at first stars, turning to secretly kiss while Lawrence's melodies floated out through the screen door. The pleasure of it all was too seductive to pass up. We kept our naughty secret safe—high school sweethearts making love right beneath our parents' noses.

We didn't use birth control until I was eighteen. Prior to the pill, I trusted Jack, who said pulling out would keep me from getting pregnant. Really, it's a miracle I didn't get knocked up in high school. Or maybe it's my condition that prevented it. Maybe the first pregnancy was a fluke . . . because now I don't seem to be a bit fertile.

I've been imagining lately that something is drastically wrong inside. Even though the doctor in Lewiston said I'm too young to have cancer, I'm not sure he knows what he's talking about. Some days, I worry so much that it is hard for me to stay focused on fire watch. Maybe my stepfather was right when he said, "You're crazy like your aunt." Yes, I've heard about the electroshock treatments she had after feeding my cousins garbage. Somehow, I could understand my aunt's thinking; they'd already eaten the fresh food and survived it. Obviously, the leftovers in the garbage can were safer than the untested food in the refrigerator.

We pulled up in front of their house in our white station wagon after driving across multiple states from Washington to Arizona, a swamp cooler powered by a car battery spitting icy water from the back to keep us cool. We kids were at each other's throats while Mom calmly filed her fingernails in the front seat, claiming the sunburn on her thighs was from the sun magnified through the windshield. In my mind's eye, I can still see the station wagon pulling into my aunt's driveway, myself climbing out of the car to greet her and my cousins. I saw with my own eyes the sunlit dinner table where I imagine my wide-eyed cousins chewed on chicken bones from the garbage pail, getting the last bit of cartilage off the knobby ends.

Mom always feared tainted food. "Eating too close to the bone will make you sick," she said. "Undercooked pork will give you trichinosis. Potato salad, salmonella. Too much fried fat will leave you with the heaves." The jelly donuts I loved so much brought a no-no finger wag. Her terror around getting fat made us kids fearful too. And, of course, *never imbibe too much alcohol.* Mother doesn't follow her own rule on that one.

"Sit here," she said last summer, pointing at the chair next to her. She sipped bourbon and water and drew on her Winston, smoke trailing from her nostrils. A terrycloth apron was wrapped around her waist, her misery palpable as she relayed her story: *Your father loves a woman with bleached blond hair who lives in a god-damned trailer out by the airfield.*

One thing I know for sure, I escaped just before the rug got pulled out from beneath my mother's jeweled sandals.

Now Jack and I are eating fried eggs for dinner. I got stung again while cooking dinner. The pain isn't too bad. I hold out my palm to show Jack. He responds by showing me his old-man hands, holding a wrinkled palm up to mine.

"You win," I say.

"And you thought my hands would be so much larger than yours."

"Yes, when we first met, we compared hands." I press my palm to his, the same way we did that day we "parked" in his mother's car. Where our palms and fingers touched, they matched in size. "Exactly the same!" I smile. "On our first date," I say, "I wore flats to the winter dance so I wouldn't be taller than you."

He laughs. "I'm a squatty body."

"You took me to Suicide afterward," I say, recalling petting turning heavy and soon I was down to my slip. It was cold, a skiff of snow covering the ground, and Suicide Pond was frozen over. The windows steamed up and Jack slid his old-man hand inside my slip.

"You said you had Roman hands and Russian fingers, which made me laugh." I take a bite of eggs and chew slowly.

"One of my best pickup lines," Jack says.

"Right! But I wasn't ready for sex. I remember asking you to take me home."

I dressed quickly and we drove through the frozen night, circling the inky pond, headlights throwing long shadows across the snow-covered basalt, the heater blowing loudly. Jack said, "The pond is bottomless, a vast underground system of lava tubes. I know a place out at Deep Creek Canyon where icy air sifts through cracks in the basalt midsummer. We'll go there to cool off some scorching hot day in August."

I remember nodding in that dark car, the heater clearing the windows in frosty rounds. I was head over heels for Jack. I knew he was the one for me.

We drove slowly south, studded tires clacking up the hill where we lived just two blocks away from each other. He kissed me goodnight and I walked inside, my panties damp.

My parents were waiting inside the door. Mother took one look at me and said, "What happened?"

"Nothing," I said, touching my disheveled hair. I ran upstairs to my bedroom and changed out of my fancy clothes and into my shorty nightgown. I touched my stomach. I wanted a baby worse than anything that night.

Wind whistles steadily around the tower. Clinking guy wires and rattling shutters accompany our dinner cleanup. A baby is on my mind, but I know the discussion is off-limits until the mass is dealt with. I turn to the window, taking in the evening sky. Not a cloud in sight, not even on the horizon. I wish for a new natural phenomenon to break the monotony of these dull days. The full moon isn't far off. A Hunter's Moon, or is it the Dying Grass Moon? It is crispy-dry out there. Dangerous. Ominous.

Time creeps along like a woolly caterpillar. Whole days seem like weeks. It's only four in the afternoon, but it feels like it should be dinnertime. Jack climbs on the table and takes down a couple of green home brews from the attic, jumps down, and puts them in the fridge. I flip through Dr. Gilmore's book, *ESP: Extra Spiritual Power*. I stop at the chapter on marriage. Jack's and my hippie wedding party gathered in the woods at Riverside State Park where we stood barefoot in the grass, reading the vows Dr. Gilmore had written for us. I wore baby blue tulle with a white lace overskirt, the dress I'd designed while still in high school. The dress Mom scolded me for sketching when she looked through my sketchbook. Why was she snooping in my sketchbook, anyway?

A family friend took photos, which didn't turn out well. He warned me he wasn't a professional photographer. "That's all right," I'd said, laughing. He'd said, "Then, yes, I'll take pictures at your wedding." Then, as usual, he held his forearm to mine to compare our tans. He was always the tanner of the two of us. We both laughed. "You win," I said.

For the wedding, Jack wore a rented baby blue tux. Many of the photos are slightly blurred. Hardly any of them capture the crowd. But at least they remind us of our hippie wedding in Riverside State Park.

"Our hippie wedding," I mumble, recalling how I'd slept at my parents' house the night before our ceremony. I tossed and turned long into the night, frightened of sleeping in the same house as Dick. I hadn't realized how much living away from home in my own locked apartment had quieted my terror.

I look up as Jack wanders past on the catwalk, heading for the west side of the cabin, perusing the dry forest through the binoculars. Sighing, I turn back to *ESP*.

Our friend Michael was ripped on acid May 23, 1970, our sunny wedding day in Spokane, Washington. He dipped the silver goblet in the stream and ran back to Dr. Gilmore, handing it to him. Dr. Gilmore blessed the water and held up the silver goblet, reaching it toward us, his face not giving away the fact that the goblet was half-full of sand.

I took the goblet from him, noticing the sand, and for a split-second, didn't know what to do. Then we both sipped the stream sediment-water while mosquitos nailed every square inch of our exposed skin. Despite their intrusion, we felt giddy kneeling to wash each other's feet like Jesus did at the last supper: a sign of love and respect for each other.

In the wedding crowd, the men wore dress suits, and the women wore lace dresses with matching high heels that sank into the grass. Jack and I wore sandals. We left them at the side of the meadow next to our friend Mac. Mac sat on the ground with one arm flung over his panting Saint Bernard, who lay stretched out next to him, drooling.

Before the wedding, Mother said, "Your father almost didn't come to your wedding."

"Are you kidding?" I said, feeling surprised. "Why not?"

"He's furious at you for not asking him to give you away."

Her words echoed in my head as we turned to the line of greeters who hugged and kissed our mosquito-bitten cheeks, congratulating us enthusiastically. I looked around the crowd. There was my stepfather giving me his steely stare from where he stood in the back. *Why would I have asked him to give me away? I didn't belong to him. Besides, all he has ever done is abuse me.*

Everyone seemed happy at our wedding except for our parents. No matter what they thought of the esoteric nonsense implied in the vows he'd written for us, they properly appreciated Dr. Gilmore's efforts at officiating the ceremony. They gave him a fifty-dollar bill, which we stuffed inside a handmade earthenware pot that I'd turned on the wheel in art class. We also gave him a handmade candle we'd molded in beach sand at Priest Lake. The candle was from the same batch as the candle that caught my apartment on fire, torching the curtains and wall overlooking

Pacific Street. We reminded him that the candle was only for show. We didn't want him catching his house on fire too.

I'm still embarrassed by how drunk I got on my wedding night. My friends filled and refilled the wedding goblet with red wine each time I turned away to talk to someone. Later, by the light of the bonfire, we stood up, ready to start up the hill and head for the hotel on Sunset Highway. My Gibson Girl hairdo had come loose. My face was smudged with dirt. I had stickers in my wedding clothes and a mighty case of spins. Jack pushed and shoved me from behind, heaving me uphill to the car.

After a short drive, we stumbled into the hotel lobby, the night clerks staring unabashedly at my dishevelment. I ignored them, leaning drunkenly against the check-in desk. Finally, key in hand, we stepped into the elevator and headed for our room. Inside, I flopped down on the bed and stared up at the wildly spinning ceiling. I held very still, keeping my eyes open so my stomach would remain settled. I didn't want to barf on our wedding night, that was for sure. Somehow, I managed to keep it together.

The following day, Michael told us that after we left the park, the police showed up at the bonfire. Amazingly, they let everyone continue celebrating, because it was a wedding party.

Jack stumbles inside, binoculars heavy around his neck. I can see in his face that he is feeling pissy as a rat's ass. I try to cheer him up, but finally, feeling exasperated by the effort, say, "Holy moly, would you just knock it off?"

"It's too fucking hot," he says, squinting against the brilliant rays of setting sun. "I'm burning up."

I open my mouth to say something mean and decide against it. I get up from the green chair and walk outside. It is equally hot inside as it is outside. And the air is muggy. In the distance, the sky is clouding up. The smell of distant rain and sound of faint rumbling makes my stomach jump. Leaning against the railing, I study the mass of charcoal-bottomed clouds, their huge white tops popping like corn above the prairie. They'll most likely be saying hello to us later.

A gust of wind blows my hair in my eyes. I brush it aside, recalling the stories Mom told us kids about ball lightning rolling through the front door of her childhood home, tumbling down the hall and continuing out the backdoor.

I return to the cabin, thinking about ball lightning, my eyes settling on the glass insulators cradling the bottom of the green chair's legs. Even though I'm impatient to be done with this job, I'm so glad we got to see the ball of lightning hover above the prairie. Now I have a story to tell my eventual children.

Jack lingers near the stove. I step past him and once again take a seat in the green chair. I might sit here during the coming storm, riding it out separate from Jack for a change. All that closeness making love last night and now Mr. Grumpypants is a rumble of bad vibes. I could call him over and slide a hand up his cutoffs. Sometimes I do that to keep the peace, even if I'm not horny. It takes very little to make his eyes roll up in his head and his lips pucker into a kiss.

But tonight, there's no easy fix. Jack barks something about dinner, his hands fisting and his face darkening stormily. I think of his dad barking at Gladys. *The apple doesn't fall far from the tree.*

"Not sure what to fix for dinner," I say, thinking of Squeak riding Jack's ass over his many inadequacies. "Soup?"

Jack shrugs.

I smile. I guess wielding a grouchy upper hand with me comes from growing up with his critical father. It was like that for my brother too. I will never forget the terrible fight Dick and Bruce had right before he joined the marines. The worst thing anyone can do to a young man is laugh at his burgeoning manhood.

My brother one-upped our stepdad with Nam. *See, I'll prove to you I'm a man.* And now Jack one-ups me. It's like he gathers his own shame and arcs it like a lightning bolt, the power—or lack thereof—traveling underground, coming up in key places: trees, fence posts, power poles, an enemy, and a loved one.

I watch him messing around in the so-called kitchen. Maybe he has decided on something to cook for dinner. Fat chance! I lean around the firefinder and see him lighting a burner under a pot of coffee. I bite my tongue against the Bible verse I'm conjuring: *Love is not blind, not poisonous, not whatever* . . . I never remember it precisely. But it is in our wedding vows Dr. Gilmore wrote.

I open *ESP* again, looking for the verse, touching my tongue to my chipped front tooth. It happened one night at Priest Lake. Jack insisted I go to the bar with him and his friends, even though I wanted to stay home with Jude, who was about to have her kittens. She had them while we were drinking Stingers at Elkins bar, right in the middle of my new down sleeping bag. When I discovered the mess, I was so angry that I swung around and slapped Jack in the face. He punched me back, chipping my tooth.

Then there was the half nelson he put me in and the return heel I planted to his shoulder, leaving a massive bruise. I fought back when he tried to force himself on me one hot summer night after the wedding. I'm wondering if this marriage is really filled with the love Dr. Gilmore describes in *ESP*, or did I marry an abuser like my stepfather?

Pisspot (usually his word for me) pours me a cup of coffee.

"Cool," I say, my face expressionless.

"Check it out," he says, nodding toward the prairie.

I turn in the direction he indicates. A thin column of smoke rises skyward. I bolt from the green chair and within seconds have the crosshairs lined up on the wildfire. I feel a new inner strength take hold of me as I call headquarters. My voice is unnaturally strong on the radio as I relay the smoke's coordinates. After I report the location to the USFS, I go back to my chair and continue flipping through the book to the part about *love not being insolent or rash*. I'm no longer concentrating on what Dr. Gilmore suggests in *ESP*; instead I'm recalling reading *Goldfinger* in high school, or was it *From Russia with Love*? I left the book open on my bed, leaving a sex scene in plain sight while I ran off to get something to eat in the kitchen. On my way back upstairs, my stepdad came out of my bedroom, book in hand. In a loud voice, he accused me of being kinky. I'd only heard the word used to describe sexy boots, so I didn't know what he meant. I was pretty naïve still, having only learned about sexual intercourse in health class at fourteen. I could only assume he meant the sex scene I was reading wasn't appropriate for my age. But he had been teaching me about sex ever since I was six. My conclusion: he was the kinky one. Would he ever admit that? Maybe it will take a shrink to figure this one out.

The wind picks up. Anvil clouds blossom colossally over the prairie. Jack grows more nervous by the minute. He tips up his cup of coffee, finishing it off in rapid gulps. He moves quickly to the mirror and leans in close. I know what's coming next. He'll pinch the sides of his nose, getting out the worms (his word) from the clogged pores. I clear my throat. He turns just as the radio screeches, "Corral Hill, *scratch, scratch*... Clearwater Ranger, *scratch*, District. Come in."

I jump up to answer. Between staticky information, I piece together that a fire crew is on its way. The radio goes silent. I replace the handset and grab the binoculars. I stride out onto the catwalk, walk to the west side, and check the smoke. It hasn't increased in volume, which is good, as the fire is nearby. *We could probably walk to it*, I think. *Or ride the motorcycle there, a pickaxe strapped to the back.*

I catch a whiff of burning wood on a gust of wind. Dust makes my eyes water. Tears stream down my face. If I were standing in front of the forest service building right now, I'd see a hazy Smokey Bear holding his shovel, the arrow pointing to the red zone. We get through our days hoping the world is a safe place, but we know it really isn't. I wipe my eyes with the back of my hand.

Now I feel nervous. I need to go down to the outhouse and a storm is coming. A large gust shakes the tower. No lightning in sight—that's a plus—but the weather has turned crazy. I yell to Jack, "I'll be right back. I need the outhouse."

The sun drops beneath the horizon and twilight moves in like a squatter. I'm about to close the door behind me when the wind grabs hold and bangs it shut. Startled, I start down the stairs just as an owl swoops close, flapping his huge wings at me. I scream, covering my face and head with my arms.

Jack runs outside. "What's wrong?"

"An owl swooped at me," I say, heart thumping.

"Are you hurt?"

"I'm okay," I push my hair out of my eyes. "It didn't peck me. Just scared me."

Jack laughs. "Glad you're all right."

"Me too," I laugh. "I gotta go! Be right back!"

I hurry down the stairs in the gusting wind. Owls portend death, at least that's what I've read. I think about Jack's mother dying; could an owl visit after the fact? We all die eventually, but then we continue on in our spirit bodies. So, no big deal! Right?

I've read about people who see the dead and tell stories of what they've seen. I met a woman once with startling blue eyes, almost the color of glacial water. As a nurse, she assisted in a surgery where the patient died. She said the patient was standing opposite her at the other end of the table, smiling. Her body was pronounced dead while the two of them stood there connected on the etheric plane.

I finish up in the outhouse and hurry up the path. In the dusky light, the lit tower looks inviting. The wind gusts are less charged now. An owl hoots. I look around, wondering if it sees me with its sharp vision. It will find a mouse or two to eat, no doubt, and leave me alone.

At the top of the stairs, I round the catwalk to the prairie side of the tower. The moon comes and goes between a fleet of dark clouds. It is nearly full. A few stray lightning bolts flash here and there. The storm seems to be moving to the south. Stars begin to sparkle: the dippers, the North Star, the Pleiades. I sigh! Everything is right again with the world.

Jack slaps his rummy hand down on the bed. "Gin!" he guffaws. "Ha! I won again." He marks down his score on the continual tally we began at the beginning of the season.

"Like father, like son," I say, recalling Jack's father winning weekly card games at the City Club. Sometimes, he bought us dinner afterward. I crane my neck to see the score. I'm not that far behind, but I know he likes to be the leader, so I say nothing.

"Squeak wins often," Jack says. "He memorizes the cards played and guesses what cards are in his opponent's hand."

"Is that what you do?"

Jack shrugs and says, "I watch." He hops off the bed and hurries out into the night, unzipping his fly on the way. A few minutes later, he leans in the door, looking like he's about to go apeshit. "Nance, get out here!"

"But we haven't finished playing . . ."

He waves a hand. "Fucking hurry up!"

I jump off the bed and run outside, heart pounding in my chest. "Is it Jude?"

Outside, a cool wind lifts my hair off my neck. Shivering, I wrap my arms around my torso. "Hey, what the fuck," I say, feeling angry now. "Where's Jude? What's wrong?"

Jack points behind me.

I whirl about to face swirls of pale green light moving across the sky. "What the hell?"

"Aurora borealis!" Jack whoops, taking my hand and dragging me around to the north side of the tower. We stand shivering, gasping at the large expanse of color—yellow and green swatches sweeping across the night sky.

"Let's watch from the picnic table," I say, my teeth chattering.

Back inside, I turn off the gas light while Jack pushes aside the binoculars, salt and pepper shakers, and my jade plant. He climbs on the picnic table. He reaches out a hand to draw me up beside him, where we settle in front of the gridded windows. We sit cross-legged, shoulder to shoulder, facing the north sky with its saturated color sliding west to east in undulating waves.

It's not the first time Jack and I have seen the aurora together. We used to stretch out on the warm sand at Priest Lake and witness the night sky late at night. Often, Jack would point excitedly and say, "Look there, between the clouds. See that patch of pale green?"

Squinting, I'd say, "I think so!" I snuggled deeper into the warm beach sand, breathing in the fishy lake air, reveling in the heat of the summer night.

Jack has always been tuned to the aurora, spying it often. He's an Aquarian, which rules electricity, lightning, shooting stars, and electromagnetism; that's what our astrologer friend, Alice, says, anyway. Guess that's why he saw the aurora and I didn't.

"Electromagnetic energy disrupts radio waves; that's why the radio's been staticky all day." A bright swatch of blue-green light ripples across the nighttime sky. "Fuck, my mind is blown!"

"Psychedelic," I say. "That smear of turquoise below the lime green . . . far out!"

As darkness deepens and the colors intensify, we lean against each other, facing the aurora like moviegoers. Jack says the lights aren't generally this bright so far south. The best viewing areas are in higher latitudes: Alaska, Canada, and sometimes other northern states.

The radio squawks. We make out other fire towers exclaiming over the phenomenon. One tower calls another to exchange expletives: "Far fuckin' out; *scratch, scratch*, northern frickin' lights; *scratch, scratch*, old lady's freakin' out!"

As the show goes on, we forget about possible fires burning in the district, about painful loneliness, and about our hunger for love, and our families who worry about our safety. All we can do is watch, mouths open, the staticky voices on the radio fading into the background.

We sleep next to a bank of windows, so we have a great view of the constellations, full moons, meteor showers, fireballs, lightning storms, and ball lightning. We've probably slept through other aurora events or didn't see them because the sky was completely overcast. Or, like Jack says, we're just too far south here in southern Idaho to see the northern lights.

"What exactly is the aurora?" I ask.

"After a solar storm, electromagnetic particles stream from the sun into our atmosphere. The particles align with magnetic north. That's why the color undulates in parallel sheets. Must have been a doozy of a solar storm to see lights so far from the pole."

We jump when the radio blasts again. The couple from a tower to the southwest giggle, "Whoa, man, you seeing this way the hell over there?"

"Fuckin' beautiful."

"*Scratch, scratch*, mind-blowin'."

"Bad reception," Jack says. "Over and out."

He climbs off the table and grabs his stash of pot and returns. In the darkness, he deftly rolls a joint and lights up. He takes a drag of weed, holding in the smoke as he speaks: "Boreas means wind."

"It's like a sky dragon," I say, staring at a band of color as wide as a cumulonimbus is tall.

"Sometimes, there's a crackling sound." Jack hands me the doobie, touching his thumb to mine while making the transfer. He snaps his fingers as I take a hit.

The rippling colors intensify, changing from green to yellow-green, to a swatch of yellow outlined in pink. I let out a stream of smoke while reveling in the shimmering color.

The female attendant from Pilot Knob calls through the darkness, her soft, doughy voice surprised when Jack picks up.

"Oh dear, I thought . . . a female-attendant-manned . . ."

He turns the radio handset over to me. "Hi," I say. "Enjoying the show?"

"Oh, yes," she says. "Pretty." Her soft voice sounds weak in the darkness. She clears her throat. "Can I ask . . . a personal question? Where do you pee? I mean, you live with a man!"

I chuckle. "In a Folgers can on the catwalk, where else?"

She gasps, then goes silent. Perhaps she is imagining the whole event, wandering naked into the night to squat over a coffee can in clear view of the opposite sex.

"We're married, you know," I say, thinking in my defense that it's dark out when I pee in the can.

She giggles. "It's embarrassing, is all."

A rail of green-blue particles snakes through the fading sheet of yellow-green. The radio screeches. "My goodness." And she's gone.

It's late when we finally climb in bed, reminiscing about a particular roll of color that swirled past, the one that spiraled, the one that shot out like a roman candle. And just as yellow-green seemed to be the dominant color, pale blue and pink increased in intensity. I muse over the natural phenomenon, running a hand down Jack's bare back, sighing over the wonder of the universe. In this moment, nothing bums me out.

"On the beach at Priest Lake," I muse, "I hardly saw any color. Well, not like tonight, anyway. Do you remember that couple Dr. Gilmore had us visit, the one with the crying baby?"

"Fuck, that's why I don't want children," Jack says, making an exhausted groan. "That baby never stopped bawling."

"Yeah, but do you remember what the couple said? Life is one experience after another happening on a spinning planet moving through space. Accepting everything without judgment is the only practice that makes a difference."

"Fuck," he says, his voice a whisper in the darkness. "Wonder how it's going for them?"

"Yeah, me too," I say as Jack turns on his side to embrace me. His body is warm. He runs a hand down my side. "I want you," he whispers, kissing my cheek, then my neck.

"Okay," I say, feeling electromagnetically charged. We kiss a while longer, then lapse into a stoned silence. "I don't think I can stay awake. I should never smoke pot, you know that."

"You're cute when you're stoned," Jack says.

I snap my fingers, imagining the aurora's sound. "Tell me about the snapping again."

He climbs on top of me, his scent musky, his body burning with heat. He nuzzles my ear, whispering, "Electromagnetic particles collide with atoms. Snap!"

"Oh," I say, and nudge him off. "Too heavy." He's right back on me. "Sorry, not tonight," I say, pushing him away again. "I'm too sleepy." I roll over onto my side.

"You said you wanted to. Sleepy's okay, you know." He pushes against my backside, a hand tightening over my hip.

"No, it's not." I move a little farther away, no longer hearing him as I drift through a twinkling universe, astral traveling through black space, stars and colored lights and tiny wisps of sparkling dust streaming past like flocks of birds.

Rain fell in the night. The catwalk is cold and wet beneath my bare feet. As I look out over the territory, the overcast sky hangs low. Cabin fever leans a little closer. I haven't been to town since the day after Bruce left. The drive should be fine if I take it slow. I return to the cabin and sit down at the picnic table to begin a grocery list.

"What are you doing?"

"Going to town for groceries."

"But it's my turn to leave," Jack whines.

"I'm going," I repeat, feeling my new assertiveness bolster me.

We're neither saints nor monks comfortable with so much silence. Still, we do the best we can, I guess; well, I do okay. Jack's been having a hard time lately. Pot and beer seem to quell his anxiety, while I have books, crocheting and knitting, and photography to keep me busy. I heard about this lookout attendant who manned the same tower every summer, year after year, for thirty years. He didn't go crazy. And everyone's heard about the famous writer who wrote and wrote and wrote during his stay on Desolation Peak. We are streaming consciousness, I guess, just long riffs of ongoing nonsense. That's where meditation comes in. Perhaps Jack could use some quiet time erasing the blackboard in his mind. Just like Dr. Gilmore taught us.

I write in my journal, jotting down dreams, worries, and complaints. It's not that interesting, I mean, who would want to read my inner grappling around losing the baby, my stepdad's abuse, Mom's depression, my ruined friendships with girlfriends, and my immature strivings for independence and individuality? No one!

What I really want is to feel okay about being unique. As I read about altered states of consciousness, clairvoyance, magic, and psychic thinking, I realize that that is who I am. I've heard that being telepathic got some women in trouble in history; they were considered witches and burned at the stake. Well, that was then, not now. I'm not a witch, but I do have ESP—extrasensory perception. I hear that some people see pictures in their mind's eye of things that are going to happen. That has happened to me, now and then. And I've seen ghosts, which some people find frightening, but I do not.

Dr. Gilmore thinks Jesus used sleight of hand to multiply bread and fish. His magic tricks caused people to bow down and kiss his feet. He wanted people to know the power of the Heavenly Father. It was magic that convinced everyone that He was the son of God. The church deacons didn't like Dr. Gilmore's line of thinking and told him to knock it off or he'd be out of a job. So, he did.

There's nothing wrong with having a theory. Who could prove it right or wrong otherwise? Jesus is nowhere to be seen. I'm disappointed that Dr. Gilmore gave in to the Man.

Being psychic can be useful. When I *know* someone's coming up the road before I hear or see them, or when I pull over before the logging truck rounds the corner as it speeds toward me from the opposite direction, I know that's a gift. Jack has witnessed this phenomenon on a few occasions and each time looks at me like I'm some sort of freak.

"How'd you do that?"

"I don't know. I just seem to know things," I say and smile. But I don't know things when I try to think them up, only when they come to me unbidden. Like I didn't know ahead of time that I'd lose that baby or that my parents would divorce. But right now, I know I'll drive to town with a grocery list stuffed in my jean pocket and buy enough food to fill four bags. And I know I'll check out the bookstore—the lady there's always happy to talk to me about psychic phenomenon. And talking to anyone other than Jack will be a blast. Maybe I'll run into Nan on Main Street, and we can have tea together. I'll buy eight hanks of yarn for the green-and-gold sweater that I'll knit next. And of course, Jack wants a six-pack and a pound of beef jerky—the staple of his

Caveman Diet. But those are ordinary things. Maybe something will happen on my way there and back that I will consider prescient.

I grab my purse and suggest Jack be vigilant as Smokey the Bear while I'm gone. "Even with a sprinkling of rain last night, the forest is tinder-dry. A wildfire could start easily."

"Yeah, yeah! Don't worry; just buy me a six-pack," Jack says. "Then everything will be all right."

Loaded up and freshly showered, I feel good about my day in town. I'm halfway home when the gears grind and sprays of dust and rock shoot out behind the wheels. Breaking, I shove the stick in first, and let out the clutch again. The rig fishtails as I attempt to start uphill, gravel peppering the underside of the jeep. I double-clutch—like we do with the bread truck—and give the Scout gas . . . *bang, grind, clunk.* The jeep lurches forward and dies.

I hit the steering wheel hard with my fists. "Dammit!"

Outside, a tiny whirlwind of dust rolls past. The day is scorching hot. Cicadas buzz a high-pitched drone. Inside the cab, bags of groceries begin to warm up. I can smell the oranges, the brown paper meat wrapping, the not-crisp-for-long celery. Wiping sweat from my face, I look around, trying to decide what to do next. I could call the tower from the farmer's house. Jack could ride down the mountain and pick me up on his motorcycle. If the tower phone works, that is.

Our friend, Slow Bull, says that if he needs his sister to call him, she will. "But I have to really need her," he says, his eyes darkly fixed on mine. *Try it!* I hear him saying.

I picture Jack and send a brainwave: *Jack, I've broken down!* I think hard. *I'm at the junction of Elk City Wagon Road and the turnoff to the farmer's place. Come and get me.*

I sit there for a few minutes, wondering why bad stuff always happens to me. "Fuck!" I pull on the emergency brake and climb out of the rig. My clean cutoffs and halter top are dust-streaked already. As I step aside to shut the door, my right foot slips from my Dr. Scholl's sandal, landing on a rock in the powdery road. Hopping around, I grit my teeth against the sharp pain. The white stripe crossing my instep is dusted tan. Sore foot returned to the sandal, I stand there, a hand shading my eyes, peering through the blinding sunlight toward the farmer's house.

Sweat runs between my breasts. I press my palm against my chest, absorbing the moisture with my halter top. A lot of good that shower did me. I'm already filthy. Holding back tears, I start toward the farmhouse.

Next to the two-story farmhouse, a vegetable garden grows lush and green. Beyond the house, range cattle rest in the shade of tall poplar trees. A chicken squawks and flutters its wings as it runs out into the road and back into the front yard. Beyond the yard, I see the farmer crossing the field toward me. My gut tightens. I try to think up the words I'll say to him: *Rig broke down*—

"Problem?" he calls out.

"Clutch," I say, attempting to speak over the squawking chickens. I raise my voice, saying, "Clutch broke. That's what I figure, anyway."

I'm pretty good with cars. I received my highest score in mechanics on my SAT. Everyone, including me, felt disappointed. My stepdad thought my scores would reflect what he wanted me to do in life: secretarial work. I wanted my scores to show how good I was at art. Mechanics? What was I supposed to do with that? Work in a garage with what my mother called grease monkeys?

The farmer wipes his hands on his overalls before tipping his sweat-stained cowboy hat in acknowledgement. "Clutch, you say?"

"Yes, sir. I can't get it in gear." I bite my thumbnail, thinking I know how it works: the transmission gears line up when you push in the clutch. We double-clutched the truck, because it takes longer for the gears to stop spinning in the old Ford. It took some getting used to, but once I had the rhythm down—push in the clutch, take it out of gear, push it in again, shift into the desired gear and let it out again—it wasn't that hard. The Scout's a four-wheel drive vehicle with hubs to turn on both front wheels. Even so, four-wheel drive will only work with a functioning clutch.

"Not hurt, are you?" the farmer asks, walking beside me up the road toward where my rig bakes in the sun.

"I'm fine," I say, and wipe sweat from my face with my palm. "Thanks for asking."

"That's good," he says, his BO hovering on cruel. "We'll just roll it off the road. Then I'll drive you home."

"You don't have to do that," I say. "I can call my husband. He'll come get me on the motorcycle."

The farmer didn't answer, just climbed into the rig and rolled it backward, parking it along the edge of the road near his fence line. He steps out and slams the door hard enough to shake dust off the sides of the Scout. Pointing up the road, he says, "There's your problem."

I turn and look. Transmission fluid stains the beige dirt in a long red streak. "No wonder it won't shift. No transmission fluid."

He waves a hand at me to follow him.

Inside the farmhouse, the cool kitchen smells of coffee and bleach. He offers me a glass of cold well water and I gulp it down. He points to the telephone on the kitchen counter. "Go ahead. Call hubby."

I dial carefully, praying the phone will ring and Jack will answer. "Hello?"

The farmer's truck squeaks and rumbles, the cab smelling of exhaust and BO. Bags of groceries sit between us, paper rustling as the vehicle rocks over potholes, bumping along the washboard.

In the back, covered with a tarp, rest two baskets of clean, folded laundry. My once-clean feet are now covered in powdery dust, as are my sandals.

"The phone rarely works," I say. "Just twice since we've been on the tower."

"How's it goin' up there? You likin' it?"

"It's okay. Gets lonely at times. The whole idea of having a phone is to call home. But the line's broken somewhere between the tower and where it hooks up to Ma Bell."

The farmer nods, making a gruff noise in his throat. "They can't fix it?"

"Arizona said the crew traced the wire through the woods. They fixed a break and thought the line was good to go. Now the crew is busy putting out spot fires. No time to follow the phone line through the woods a second time."

The truck rumbles on, rocking around the corner, turning right onto Elk City Wagon Road. I pull at a torn cuticle on my thumbnail. A sharp sting and a tiny spot of blood pools in the quick. I suck on it as I study the landscape like I'm interested in one more clear-cut. I'm not, but I don't know what else to say to the farmer.

"You like the vegetables we send?"

"Yes, we love them," I say. "And Jack can't get enough of that raw milk. He licks his lips over the cream!"

"Wife's idea. Too much for us to eat," the farmer says, then is silent for several grinding miles. Finally, he swings the rig onto the side road approaching the tower. We bounce past the spring where range cattle have left messy hoofprints in the mud edging the water source. I sit forward, looking at the churned-up mess. "We have cattle in our drinking water."

"Bad news," the farmer says, clearing his throat. "They won't leave it alone, now."

"Right! We've been boiling it."

At the top of Corral Hill, the farmer pulls in beside the bread truck and turns off the engine. We step out of the truck and Jack greets us, grabbing the farmer's hand and shaking it enthusiastically. He runs around to my side of the truck and opens the door. I step into his arms and hug him tightly, so glad to be home.

Jack releases me and turns to the farmer. "Thanks," he says, "for bringing Nance home."

The farmer nods, grabs the laundry baskets from the back of the truck, and sets them at the bottom of the stairs.

"With the Scout out of service," Jack says, "the forest service will have to deliver our food."

"Not much to fix, I 'spect," the farmer says. "Just need a plug for the transmission fluid."

"Mind if it stays put at your place until I get the part?"

"Sure enough," the farmer says, lifting the groceries from my arms and starting up the stairs.

"Thanks for everything," I say, watching the men climbing the stairs. I turn away and hurry down the path to the outhouse.

Mountain Obscuration

Socked in
Low ceiling
Smoky sky
Dust storm
Haze
Virga
Fog
Mist
Milky sky
Drizzle
Soup
Whiteout

fourteen

They say *socked in* can make you crazy. When we woke this morning, cumulous clouds tucked around the lookout like batting in a giant's quilt. Even though it's only late August, I half expect the radio to buzz and our boss to warn us that soon he'll be bringing us down for the season. Shivering, I pull on the gray sweater I just finished knitting. Jack lights the stove, which whooshes out a flame, singeing his eyebrows. He turns to me with a startled look.

"Are you okay?" I say, swallowing a laugh.

"Yeah," he says, touching his burnt brows. He jumps to his feet and leans close to me, raising and lowering his newly torched eyebrows like Groucho Marx.

"Ooh, no eyelashes either. You're naked . . ." We both begin to laugh and hug each other briefly, then step back, assessing each other.

"No worries," Jack says, and we carry on with our morning ritual. Soon, the coffee is perking, and Jack is finished copying down the weather report.

Lately, it's been noticeably cooler at night; still, I'm not rattled by the low ceiling or the misty molecules parting long enough to give us a glimpse of forest before the territory turns opaque again.

The sparkling mist is beautiful, drifting and swirling all around. And there's a delicious smell of snow in the air, or perhaps the smell of damp laundry hanging out to dry.

It's nearing time for us to come down from the tower, which I want and don't want at the same time. I sip coffee, reflecting on how I've only been down to Grangeville a handful of times this fire season: the time the doctor discovered the mass and the coveted shower at our boss's doublewide, beforehand. I muse over how erotic the hot water felt running over my body after going a month without a shower. Then, there was the terrible storm and the appointment with the specialist in Lewiston—also a delicious shower in Grangeville, first. And a few more trips to Grangeville to pick up groceries, shower, and do laundry . . . the last trip being when the Scout broke down.

Jack rides down the mountain frequently, barreling along logging roads on his Bridgestone. He looks ominous in his rust-colored leather jacket and white helmet, black gloves, and sunglasses. For him, riding helps keep *crazy* at bay. I'll take the Scout down and grab a shower at Arizona's house as soon as Jack repairs the clutch. He's going to see if he can get the part the next time he's in town.

This mountain of isolation has been hard on Jack. One evening, recently, he went crazy. He paced like a caged animal, pulling at his beard. I pleaded with him to calm down, but he ranted that life wasn't worth living and threatened to jump off the tower. I was scared shitless.

It's all this blasted silence, day after day of nothingness, that's doing him in. Some days it rains all day, other days we sit inside icy, white clouds. And then there are those days when it's so blistering hot with clear, endless skies and a continuous buzz of cicadas that we want to pull our dank hair out. Then there are the windstorms that shake the forty-five-foot tower, howling and rattling around the shutters day and night, and of course, thunder-storms rumbling and flashing all through the night.

I've gotten used to the storms and feel pretty calm most days. Maybe Jack's craziness quiets me—one of us must keep our wits. I tell him that calmness is a choice. The evening he went crazy, I suggested he drink a cold beer—unfortunately, the attic stores needed further fermenting. And the beer from the grocery store was gone. He chewed his mustache and paced, claiming again his intention to jump.

"Why not talk to someone," I said, waving my hand toward the telephone. "How about calling Hill's Resort?"

"The phone never works," he said, and continued pacing.

"It did when the Scout broke down," I said. "It's worth a try." I stared at the black phone mounted at the base of the firefinder, knowing full well that when I picked up the receiver it would be dead.

The possibility engaged Jack's curiosity long enough for him to stop pacing and stare at the big black thing. But he didn't pick up the receiver, just fisted his hands and swung around, ready to bolt out the door.

"Wait," I said, and grabbed the receiver, bringing it to my ear. "A dial tone," I shrieked. I dialed Hill's Resort collect. Once I heard it ringing, I handed him the receiver. He made a noise in his throat but went along with the routine anyway. Then his face lit up, and I knew that someone had answered.

He sat on the floor, relaxing against the green firefinder cabinet, legs splayed out in front of him. He and our former boss, Lois, chatted long into the night.

I shift my position in the green leather chair and knit another row of seed stitches. These long days of silence make us stir-crazy: no visitors, no variation, not much to do besides knit and read, play cards, and strum the guitar. And for Jack, drink beer and smoke pot. If there is any weed or beer, that is.

Fog drifts past. A parting in the clouds lets a beam of warm sunshine through. I look around for my sunglasses, find them, and put them on.

We take turns leaving the lookout for an hour or two each day. Jack rides his motorcycle fast along mountain roads, sometimes stopping to shoot the breeze with our New York friends. Other days, he stays back, and I wander around photographing wild onions, tiger lilies, and Indian paintbrush while he surveys the territory. The forest remains dry, even though, clearly, the season is turning. Bright spots of orange-red foliage smudge the hillsides.

Really, it's a miracle we connected with the Hill's that night, since the phone wire loops over branches for fifteen miles or so, down the hill between the tower and the farmer's house. The phone has only worked three times—twice when we most needed it.

The fog burns off by afternoon, leaving the air laden with an icy chill from the cloud parked over us all morning. I check the territory through the bins. The larches are beginning to turn yellow and the huckleberry leaves are turning red.

Later, we fix a simple dinner of soup and crackers. After dinner, we play a few hands of gin rummy. Jack continues to win. Laughing manically each time he slaps down a rummy. I know he's never going to let me forget how he creamed me this summer.

Dusk comes early and a few stars appear in the gloaming. I sigh contentedly. I mean, if the Scout hadn't broken down, I could be in town tomorrow, taking a shower and washing the bedding. But really, I am happy staying put, watching fall begin its takeover like shadows at dusk. And I know I'll turn giddy when a snow flurry or two whitens the landscape.

Jack stands in the doorway and holds out a hand. He's a wild man these days, hair long, beard overgrown. Tomorrow, I'll suggest we shampoo over the railing. I take his hand and we wander outside, leaning against the rail to face the prairie. Amazingly, a shooting star zips across the expanse of western sky just as we show up at the railing. "Whoa," I exclaim. Jack just makes a noise in the back of his throat and squeezes my hand.

I can't wait to see the Milky Way shimmer and the Corn Moon rise in the west. He squeezes my hand again, so tightly this time that I know he fears falling if I were ever to let go.

The next morning, I boil water for tea, which happens around two hundred degrees at six thousand feet. Jack says that the atmospheric pressure lowers the boiling point. It's also what makes my yeast bread rise higher than when we lived in Spokane. I put the remainder of the day-old loaf in the oven to warm. I want Jack to smile like he did while talking to Lois Hill. Hopefully, food will cheer his mood. If he is pondering his mother's death, he'll be bummed for the rest of the day. If he's dealing with cabin fever again, I'm not sure what I'll do this time.

"*Darlink*," I say in my Zsa Zsa Gabor accent, "I make coffee now." I sweep my hands through the air as I swish over to the stove.

Jack shrugs. His lips press together in a thin, pinched line. Not even a twinkle crosses those hazel eyes of his.

"*Voila*," I say, striking a wooden match to light the burner. *It's your fault*, Jack Sr. had said. We'd just flown in from Texas, our honeymoon road trip temporarily on hold after the state patrol pulled us over and told us to phone home immediately. We'd found a phone booth in the next town and dialed Jack's father.

"You should have called sooner," his dad said. "It's your fault she's dead."

After a game of golf, Jack Sr. had arrived home to collect Gladys and take her to lunch at the country club. "Gladys, you ready? Let's go! We're late," he barked as he walked through the front door.

He told us later that it was then that he turned to the kitchen and saw his wife sprawled across the kitchen floor next to the refrigerator. "It was horrible," he said. She'd collapsed from a brain aneurysm at forty-five. She died a week later.

Whether he is bummed or not, I love Jack. The first time I saw him in the hallway at high school, I was walking between Mr. Finner's English class and Mr. Zollar's art class. I knew immediately that those hands would someday skim along my naked sides, curving around the small of my back to pull me close. I knew he would be the father of my child.

I wasn't naïve, though I was still a virgin. My stepdad's unwanted touch taught me to freeze like in the child's game, Hide and Seek. Though freezing provided some safety in the moment, making a habit of it became dangerous. If I felt threatened when a boy came on to me in high school, I couldn't move or say anything. I was frozen. When that guy took me below the stage and tried to kiss and fondle me, I froze momentarily. But thankfully, I snapped out of it, shoving him away. I turned and ran out of there, back up the stairs and outside into the fresh air.

Sometimes, even now, it's hard to know the difference between what I want and what is expected of me. I shake my head to clear my thoughts as I measure coffee into the basket of the aluminum percolator. I turn to where Jack sits on the bed, watching me. When our eyes meet, he touches his tongue to his upper lip. I smile. He smiles back. "It's not even noon yet," I say, turning back to light the flame beneath the coffee pot.

At seventeen, Jack took me to his friend's apartment in Browne's Addition. His friend waited in the kitchen while we climbed in bed together. The darkness of the apartment, the rumpled sheets, sneaking into bed while my parents were out drinking and dancing—all of it made my heart race out of control. The quarter-sized hickeys Jack left on my chest had my best friend, Dee, scolding me. She wanted to know if we *did it*. I said no, but it wasn't much longer after that that we did—I lost my virginity on the family room couch.

Just a crush is what parents say when their children are young and in love. His mother told me one day, "Find a different boy to marry, someone better than my son."

"But I love him," I argued.

She shook her head and continued clearing the kitchen table. "Jack will never make you a good husband."

Jack's parents fell for each other while they were in the army. They didn't back away from love. I pulled Jack's mother's army boots from the utility room closet the day Squeak cleared out her belongings. I admired the good leather, the brown laces, and the calf-high shaft. He said I could have them, but her feet were tiny. I attempted to pull them on and gave up, tossing them in the Goodwill box.

I can't help but recall her warning: *Find someone better.* If I'd left Spokane like I'd originally planned, graduating high school and studying art in Banff, Canada, I could be sketching in a design firm instead of watching for forest fires with my young husband. Yet here we are, tangled together beneath warm covers while icy clouds blanket the sky from here to the horizon. Yes, he has convinced me to make love while the coffee simmers and the day-old bread warms in the oven.

My desire for a child hasn't waned. I dream regularly that my belly's round and hard. I can't separate lust from my longing to feel the stirring of life in my womb again. I lost the baby while my hormones were full on, my jeans no longer buttoning, colostrum oozing from my nipples, the tiny flutter of life stirring deep in my pelvis. Losing our child broke my heart.

Even if we occasionally grab each other's wrists and argue about bringing a child into this terrible world, we will keep trying—ignoring the abyss where we disagree on this topic.

"I love you!" I whisper.

"I love you too," he says.

Clouds drift past our windows. Another day, another low ceiling—the shimmer of water droplets thinning occasionally, giving us a glimpse of the forest beyond the tower before the landscape disappears again. Jack's green sweater, the one his mother bought him at JCPenney, is tossed over the back of the green chair. The gray one I knitted is folded on top of the counter. It's a work-free day made for eating warm bread and drinking coffee with a bit of raw milk splashed in. If we want, we can linger beneath the quilt, the cat curled up at our feet, luxuriating in each other's arms for the rest of the day.

Instead, I get up and pull on my clothes. I pour coffee, setting a cup on the windowsill next to Jack. He grabs his guitar and strums and sings "Blackbird." Beyond him, the clouds thin and the western sky turns orange from a distant smoke. Maybe the fog will lift entirely and the smell, like snow melting in the woods, will mix with the scent of heated pitch and wildfire.

I take the warmed day-old bread from the oven. The sourdough starter that Mrs. Bard gave me, along with thorough kneading to elasticize the wheat gluten, keeps the bread from falling as it bakes. The Bards rented us the little green swaybacked house on 29th Avenue in Spokane the winter before we started this job. They live down the road in a farmhouse set on a few acres outside the city limits. Just like the Arnolds on *Green Acres*, only the Bards know what they're doing.

They say they love us like their own children and will be happy to rent to us again when we return from the tower. I recall Mr. Bard watching me across the table one day. "You have doe eyes," he said. I looked down, picking at my cuticles. "You draw his bath?" he asked.

I shake my head. "No, but I cook our meals."

I imagine being the old-fashioned wife Mr. Bard thought I was and shiver. I like being a women's libber . . . though it's a

conundrum, this wanting to care for another as well as the desire
to be strong, be independent, and say "no" to the Man. Besides,
Jack seems to think he is in charge of me. I hope I'll prove to him
otherwise someday.

I cut a slice of warm bread and butter it, setting a plate before
Jack. I take mine to the green chair where I curl my feet beneath
me and read T. Lobsang Rampa's book, *The Third Eye*. Rampa had
the unusual clairvoyant ability to tell when a person was harboring
emotions unsuited to monastic life. Dr. Gilmore taught us how
to see auras, or rather, he taught me. Jack isn't very talented psy-
chically; however, I took to it like range cattle to our mountain
stream.

I study the dark spots clustered around Jack's forehead. Is it
grief? Worry or some other malady? Jack thinks I'm crazy believ-
ing in this stuff. But it isn't a belief system. It is my way of being—
and it works; the logging trucks are proof. As are the visitors who
have yet to make it far enough up the mountain for us to see dust
billowing up from their vehicles—but I know they're coming anyway. Prescience, it's called.

The bread is dry but still sour, sweet, salty, and buttery, and
it's made with stone-ground flour—so it's nourishing. We visited
a mill on our honeymoon road trip. In a big barn with a section
built out over a stream, two big wheels of stone the size of a large,
round bed turned together, the wheat berries rolling between the
stones, grinding them into flour. The whole shebang was cranked
by the stream rushing past, far below the mill's rough-hewn floor.

As I sip my coffee, wondering what *my* aura looks like, I look
over at Jack. He takes a bite of warm bread and chews, leaning
back in his chair, watching me. He smiles. Apparently, the sour-
ass in him slunk off while making love. Perhaps he can see how
bright my aura is now. I think about asking him what color it is
and decide not to.

We finish our snack and I wash the FS green plastic cups and plates and leave them to drip-dry on the not-so-clean towel. I wipe my hands on my smudged jeans, smelling the familiar, dusty odor of dirty denim. The smell brings me back to the swaybacked house, the bed, the blood coursing between my legs the day I lost the fetus.

Jack gets out his stash of weed and rolls a bomber. This time, I join in.

Small brown birds whistle a thready reed, pecking at the huckleberries below the tower. There hasn't been enough rain this summer to make the berries plump, but they are abundant. I picked enough berries earlier to make a huckleberry crumble. I walk around the catwalk to where Jack stands observing the territory. There's a wildfire burning somewhere and a haze has milked the air as far as we can see. Jack hands me the binoculars. I take a long look at the sheets of virga streaming blue-black across the prairie, followed by distant clouds full of weather. It is hard to say what will come of it later, if anything. I hand him back the binoculars and head inside to put on a pot of coffee.

The tree down by the turnoff that was struck at the beginning of the season could have smoldered underground for months, but it didn't. Jack and Tom worked until it was cold. And all the other fires we saved the forest from this summer—we should pat ourselves on the back for taking good care of the land. It is turning autumn now, almost overnight, it seems. Finally, when I lie down at night, I sleep soundly—partly because it's cooler in the cabin, and partly because not as many thunderstorms wake us with their rolling, brontide thundering like a stampede of large animals.

One storm reminded us of a cheesy movie set, the rumbles and zigzags of lightning eerie and constant. The storm lit up the forest again and again, the flashes reminding me of when we danced at the Grotto to loud rock 'n' roll our senior year. The strobe flashed in the dark, cavernlike room in repeating bursts and made me feel like I might lose it. Like the day after the terrible storm, I felt crazed and my eyes stung from so many blinding bolts pounding the forest.

Inside, I push open the box that I've started packing with my favorite books: *The Herbalist*, T. Lobsang Rampa's *The Third Eye*, and *Psychic Discoveries Behind the Iron Curtain*. Next to go in is my four-pack of slim volumes on magic that Dr. Gilmore suggested I read—the set that teaches a person how to cast a circle, build a purifying flame, and other weird shit that I can't quite wrap my mind around even if I try. But Dr. Gilmore is super excited about the idea that Jesus was a magician. He is certain that that was how Jesus made wine from water, and multiplied bread and fish, and walked on the sea. Weird ideas, I know, but even so, I love Dr. Gilmore, because he helped me get up the courage to tell my mother about my stepdad's advances.

Jack walks in from the catwalk, the heavy bins swinging from his neck. Beyond him, the sky grows dark as distant virga moves closer. He makes a yummy noise, sniffing air that smells like sweet berries and brown sugar. Jack accepts the cup of coffee and serving of crisp I offer him. As I dish up a serving for myself, I begin to hear a loud thrumming.

We both turn at once. Outside, hail pelts the catwalk. It comes down hard, bouncing off the deck and back up in the air, peppering the windows. We watch as the hail falls even harder, so hard that it roars as it pummels the roof. Soon a fine coating of white covers the catwalk, trees, and ground all around. Our faces look eager and we've hardly touched our crisp. It's silly, but I feel thrilled that it has taken a new weather phenomenon to break us out of our doldrums.

Although it isn't time to *go down*, I know we will be fogged in on a regular basis from now on. A "low ceiling" is what my stepdad used to call it. As a pilot with a Cessna, he was quick to dispense weather information like he was preparing a flight plan. I don't remember exactly why his lung collapsed in the military and he was grounded, and he doesn't answer my letters now, so I can't ask him even if I wanted to. He does know it's possible that I'll need surgery, but still I've heard nothing—nada, nil—no answers back from the letters I've written. I don't like the hollow it leaves inside of me.

The hail slows and finally stops. The sun comes back out, lighting the cabin blindingly. The tower drips. We finish our crisp and sip coffee. Shivering, I reach for my gray sweater. What I like best about my new sweater is the seed stitch that runs from the center of my waist diagonally to each of my shoulders. The yarn has a thread of silver running through it. The sweater sparkles in the bright light.

I pull it on, thinking of Spokane and the pine needles that will soon be covering the driveway at Jack's dad's house. When we return home, Jack will have to rake the needles up, no doubt. We'll scuff through piles of dried maple leaves when we take our walks in Manito Park. And the frosty grass will crunch with our footsteps early mornings.

It feels scary to think about being back at home, since I'll be seeing the doctor about the mass once we are settled. It will also be a relief, in a way, to know for sure what has gone wrong inside. I mean, all the stupid fights that Jack and I have had could be partially caused by wacky hormones. We're like the weather in some ways, sometimes hot and sometimes cold, sometimes blindingly bright and, at other times, darker than dark. I turn to Jack, who's staring off in the distance. Perhaps he's also musing about what will happen when we get back home, or perhaps he has checked out for the afternoon.

But for now, we are still here. I get out the sourdough starter, which is bubbling from the cup of flour I stirred into it recently. I mix up a batch of bread and set it aside to rise. My psychic sense is acute right now, most likely peaking because the campers and explorers have gone home and the forest is silent, except for an occasional falling tree or skittering sound in the brush. In the silence, I seem to know what Jack is about to say before he speaks.

Yesterday, he said he had a thought. I said, "What's that?" Then he just stared off, so I said, "Jack, what was your thought?" He said, "What thought?" Then we both started laughing and couldn't stop. It was like we were stoned, though we weren't. The random moment turned things hilarious. Laughter is like crying hard or shouting out during an orgasm. It gets the chi moving, and boy-oh-boy—it can really rip through a person when unimpeded. It felt good to laugh.

Manning the tower has been the most exciting and most boring thing we've ever done. Yes, we made some mistakes, but we have improved, and improving has made our bosses happy. So maybe the mistakes were a bonus—a contrast—we were there, but now we're here. I have grown more confident, stronger on the radio, and I am better able to deal with the silence. Though, in the silence, my mind sorts through old memories regarding how I was raised. With the sorting, I figured out it wasn't my fault.

I push aside my plate and examine my garbage-pit-treasures arranged around the jade plant—a tiny bottle, a couple of milk glass canning jar lids, and several colorful chips of pottery. The Jade plant is doing well because of all the light in the cabin. I read somewhere that light makes people happy. So why do we have such devastating waves of sadness while living here in all this light? Perhaps because we're like children with our noses pressed against the windowpanes gazing at the frigid landscape. We can't wait for it to snow, but that's all we can do . . . just wait.

Jack carries the boxes I packed down to the truck. I like to get a jump on moving. That way I will have less to do when it really does come time to *go down*. That's what we call it now—when we *go down* from the tower. Or when we *come down*, that's the perspective from the ranger station or when Arizona *brings us down*, like he'll come up here and help us pack up. That would be cool, but it's not happening. We'll be driving out ourselves, me in the Scout, and Jack and Jude in our loaded bread truck. If the truck starts, that is.

The weather has turned warm today. I'm sweaty and pull off my sweater. Yellow jackets become erratic, bumping against the windowpanes, a few flying inside and back out. I step out onto the catwalk, staring out at the milky landscape, soaking up the heat. The buzzer goes off and I head back inside to punch down the dough. I split the dough in half and shape it into two logs, one each for the two oiled bread pans. I set the timer for another hour, letting the bread rise again before baking.

A couple of hours later, we are sitting at the picnic table scarfing down fresh buttered bread. "No big smears," I tell Jack. "That's all the butter we've got." Even with a thin coating, the bread is delicious beyond belief. I begin to think happiness can be ignited like the forest—just a tiny spark of something pleasurable will set off euphoria. I turn to Jack, smiling. He smiles back. He doesn't say, "What?" He just looks at me with loving eyes. I take in this love, realizing that life is worth living, every single moment of it, even if dusk is coming earlier now and, soon, snow will begin to fall.

Jack leaves the cabin to peruse the territory. I remain seated at the green picnic table, pen poised over a sheet of airmail paper. In the letter I feel compelled to write I will tell Dick how pissed I am at him. The letter could be fifteen pages long, listing all the times he touched me and where we were when it happened. I'll tell him how the molestations gave me sick headaches and how I ended up in the nurse's office at Finch Elementary, green with nausea. How I couldn't think straight and did poorly in grade school, then again in junior high, the sick headaches following me, sometimes causing me to throw up, once in the hall as I hurried for the girls' bathroom. I still remember how I carried my stack of textbooks against my chest and the vomit hurled over the top of them onto the floor. Projectile, they call it.

Then there were all those nights lying awake in my attic bedroom, terrified I'd hear his weighty footsteps on the stairs. "You owe me an apology," I write in heavy blue ink across the thin airmail paper. "A big one!"

Maybe it won't do any good; after all, he's dating someone with bleached blond hair. How does Mom know this? Has she ever seen the woman? I try to imagine where they met, perhaps at the bar where he'd stop for a drink after work. When I worked at the office, he'd say he needed to buy a pack of gum. He made me wait in the sun-heated car while he went in the bar for a pack. The wait always went long, which meant he was swilling a bourbon and water and, most likely, flirting with blondie.

In my letter, I say: *I'm not the bad one here. It's you who's sick, with all the fondling and drunken kisses you forced on me while I lay frozen in my childhood bed. I will no longer keep your damn secret.*

"Shit!" The last time he tried to get in my bed, I was in high school. Maybe being older gave me the guts to stand up to him—I don't know. But when he woke me with his liquored mouth pressed against mine, I screamed, shoving him hard, hitting and kicking at him and yelling, "Get out of my room."

That was the first time I fought back. And I've never had to since. I think screaming and fighting him made him realize how close he was to being caught. After all, my sister was asleep in the next room. My shouts could have awakened her. My stepbrother, not so easily, as he was asleep in his basement bedroom. My brother was in Vietnam and my mom was visiting her sick mother in Arizona. *Almost* the perfect setup.

The next day, while on our way somewhere in his fancy red car, he said—loud enough for my siblings sitting in the back seat to hear—"You had a terrible nightmare last night, Nance." Then he directed his next question at my siblings. "Did she wake you two with her screams?"

I heard a weak *no* and *nuh-uh* from the back seat. Furious, I turned to him and hissed, "It wasn't a dream, and you know it."

I wonder if he feared I'd tell. Well, I have told people! Dr. Gilmore, Mom, and Jack's friends know, but not the police. I am afraid to go to the police. I bet he'd use the "crazy" defense and the police would believe him. He can talk his way out of anything: speeding tickets, accounting discrepancies, cheating, and, no doubt, child abuse.

As I write these difficult words, my heart breaks: *Please, just be my father!* And if he writes back, my wish is that he'll say, *I'm so sorry, Nancy. How can I fix this?*

Then . . . we'll see!

But I don't say, "please write back." I don't do anything but cry big, gulpy sobs. I see his drilling eyes in my mind's eye threatening me not to tell. Those shaming, critical, icy-gray eyes. I wad the letter into a ball and throw it in the trash. I wipe my eyes with my hand and walk outside, staring out at the blurry, pine-scented forest. Jack stands with his back to me, the binoculars raised to the southeast forest. He doesn't turn around and I am glad.

In the night, I turn on my side and pull the covers up around my shoulders. I've been awake since the wee hours, listening to the howling wind, the pinging and creaking tower. I tighten my muscles against the shiver that runs down my back and curl closer to Jack.

Unlike Mom, I don't chain-smoke when the wind comes up. On stormy nights and other tense nights, like when we waited on dinner for Dick, Mom's eyebrows pinched together as she rubbed out one smoke after another in the glass ashtray. I can see her now, standing by the stove, wearing an expensive brown woolen dress that accentuated her curves, jewelry, and matching high heels. A drink sweated on the counter. As classy as she was, she was afraid of birds, the wind, of weight gain, and of driving at night. And maybe she was afraid of Dick, as well. Who knows.

Her friends claimed she was beautiful in all ways. I hope some of that beauty washed off on me, but I think not. Dick always insisted I was beautiful, though I don't feel glamorous at all. Especially now with my bad haircut and dirty fingernails. I remember one birthday when he strolled in late for our family party. He cleared his throat and blew his nose—I've now come to realize this as his giveaway. It is what he does when he is feeling guilty.

That night, Mom made stroganoff that I had requested especially for my birthday dinner: beef, egg noodles, and sour cream gravy. We all waited while dinner grew cold. I remember Mom's angry mouth pulling hard on her cigarette, smoke rolling from her nostrils like dragon fume, her dark eyes flashing. Tapping the ash into the ashtray, she rolled the tip to a glowing point, probably thinking: *Late for Nancy's special birthday dinner. I could kill him!*

Another gust shakes the tower. Jack snores on. I snuggle closer, pressing up against him to rob some of his warmth. I'll get the down sleeping bag from the truck tomorrow and open it over the top of our summer quilt. Another shudder and I tighten my grip on Jack's waist. Eventually, I fall back to sleep.

When I wake, I feel dizzy. I turn my head slowly to the side, feeling like my kid-self again. My mother took me to the doctor for dizzy spells. He shined a light inside my ears and up my nose and down my throat, saying, "Abundant mucus. Probably allergies." My mother blanched at the reference to mucus. She blanched at the mention of all body fluids. How about *fondling*? I guess she would have had a problem with that word too, if it had ever been spoken aloud in the house, that is. Anyway, nothing seemed to work to make the dizziness go away. Sometimes, it would get so bad that my head felt like it was tipped sideways, my ear nearly meeting my shoulder.

I turn over slowly so as not to disturb my equilibrium or my sleeping husband. Settled again, I close my eyes and doze a bit.

When I open my eyes later, I see Jack standing naked in front of the refrigerator, drinking milk from a pint bottle sent by the farmer. I lift my head carefully, settling it back on the pillow, saying, "I'm dizzy as crap."

Jack puts away the milk and turns to me. "I'm hungry, Nancerella."

"Will you make coffee?"

"Shit!" he shrugs. "Where is it?"

"In the cupboard next to the heater."

I push myself up to sitting, and slowly swing my legs over the side of the bed. The floor's icy cold. I curl my toes against the shock of it, grabbing hold of the firefinder to steady myself. Tentatively, I bend to pull on jeans. I slip on a sweater and shuffle across the chilly floor to the stove. Jack has the coffee pot apart, examining the grounds container, the stem, shrugging helplessly.

"Fill it to here with water," I say, realizing why it's so much easier to do the cooking myself. "Put the stem and basket inside the coffee pot and add five heaping spoonsful of coffee. Then light the burner and heat the pot on high."

Jack grumbles, fumbling with the equipment.

"Thanks," I say. "I need the outhouse."

Growing up, my siblings and I tried to be polite, sitting with our hands folded in our laps, heads bowed as Dick said grace. On my birthday, after he'd finished praying, Mom tipped up her drink and polished it off, setting it down with a loud clunk—the same way she slammed cupboards and drawers when she was angry.

Dick grinned sheepishly. He knew he was in the doghouse— late for my special dinner. Continuing to grin, he raised his glass and sang a little song off-key while we dished up plates of slippery egg noodles. "Hares eat groats and cows eat groats and little rams eat ivy . . ." Then he served himself stroganoff and passed the dish to my mother.

"She's a wonderful cook, kids. Beautiful too. Be sure to thank her for this fine meal."

We all murmured our appreciation and dug into one of our favorites.

I hold tightly to the railing as I slowly descend the stairs. It comes to me in a flash. He was late to my birthday party because he'd been at the bar—probably hanging out with that bleached blond. Our beautiful mother replaced by a barmaid!

I don't look down; just feel the stairs in my Dr. Scholl's sandals, drinking in the cold morning air as I descend. The crisp morning seems to clear out the cobwebs. One careful step at a time, I reach the ground to cross the road to the outhouse trail.

A while later, I'm back standing next to the hissing gas heater, sipping coffee and warming up. We're both wearing sweaters. Jack looks contemplative—though I know he's actually stoned.

He picks up his steaming cup of coffee and sips the hot brew. We lock eyes over our cups. He gives me a mischievous grin and touches the tip of his tongue to his upper lip.

I giggle. "We're on the job, you know," I say. "Besides, I'm still feeling dizzy. If you don't mind, I need you to take over for me today."

"It's foggy. We don't have to work today." He waggles his eyebrows.

I smile, knowing it's true, and an orgasm would be nice. "Doesn't matter," I say. "We're on the clock."

He shrugs, exchanging the cup of coffee for the joint he relights with a stick match drawn across the back of his jeans. He tokes the weed, filling the room with smoke, and hands the joint toward me.

I wave it away.

He studies me as he takes another puff, holding his breath, his scrutiny intensifying. "You have dark shadows under your eyes," he says, exhaling smoke along with his words. He dabs saliva on the glowing end, saving the roach for later. "Sorry you're not feeling well, Nancerella."

"Oh," I say, refilling my coffee cup. "Thanks. It's not as bad as it was when I first woke up."

Jack reaches inside his pocket and pulls out the Mickey Mouse pocket watch my sister gave him for his last birthday. He holds it to his ear, squints at it, and gives it a shake. He looks at me, turning the knob back and forth to wind it. "I found this in the truck when I took the boxes down. Mickey says it's time for the weather report."

I smile, tickled over the fondness he has for that watch. I open the logbook and take a seat at the picnic table, coffee steaming in the green FS cup before me, pencil poised to copy down the report: *Ninety percent chance of rain, wind gusts west to northwest 25 mph, temperature 48 degrees during the day, upper 30s at night. Snow level lowering to 7000'.*

I scribble down the forecast and click off the radio. Outside, clouds float past, drifting apart enough to make out the American flag clinging damply to the flagpole. We meant to get into the habit of taking it down each night and hoisting it up again the following morning, but the days passed quickly despite the slowness of the mountains. And now it is late September, and the flag ritual is completely forgotten. I take another sip of coffee. "I need to go down to the outhouse again."

Jack grunts as I step out into the cold. "Use your coffee can."

"Need the john," I say. I descend the steps to the outhouse, this time a little more quickly. Along the brushy path, I lean sideways to avoid being soaked by the dew-laden brush. Plum leaves glisten yellow, some fluttering to the ground before me. The huckleberry bushes burn bright orange. Salal and Oregon grape are speckled: orange, yellow, and green. The moist ground and scent of fog mix with the amazingly funky smell of the outhouse. Despite the lye we toss into the hole after each crap, the odor remains. I prop the door open, wedging a rock against it with my sandal. I hold my breath and sit forward on the wooden seat, watching for spiders.

A yellow jacket buzzes around a bunch of salal berries outside the door. I imagine loading up the truck and bumping down the mountain to Grangeville, rolling along the highway to Lewiston, turning east on I-90, and speeding home to Spokane. We'll stay with Squeak when we get back home. He loves Jude. And he misses Gladys like crazy, so having company will be good for him. Then, onto the green old-mare house. I recall our wedding gifts packed in the cedar chest stored beneath the stairwell at Mom's house, just waiting for us to set up housekeeping.

"My doctor," Mom wrote in her last letter, "is the best gyne-cologist in Spokane, actually in the state. And he's kind. Once he patted my arm and said—I'm sorry you're hurting so badly, MJ. His kindness meant so much to me."

It was after the divorce that she began drinking more heavily, losing weight, and crying herself to sleep at night. I don't criticize her about the drinking, as who am I to say she shouldn't drown her pain with bourbon. I partake in a beer and a sip of blackberry wine on occasion. And sometimes Southern Comfort or honey mead, especially while we lived in the truck at the resort. The ritual of an evening nip comforted me in a weird sort of way.

I finish up in the outhouse and head back up top, taking the four flights slowly. My thighs are strong but my energy is low. Back in the cabin, Jack plucks out "Good Day Sunshine" on the guitar. His face is wide with contentment—hazel eyes, liquid, mouth, two flat lines—not exactly a smile as much as a look of concentration and peace. I drop onto the bed and pull the afghan over me. Jude stands and stretches and curls up again, nuzzling tight against my feet.

I know not to interrupt Jack with my worries. I know not to say how terrified I am of having cancer. Or how much I worry about going under the knife. He doesn't like being pulled from his reverie, so I close my eyes and listen to the song. He has become a pretty good guitarist this summer.

The radio buzzes and Jack rouses himself from his euphoria. He stands, reaching to pick up the handset, but it's not for Corral Hill, it's another tower calling in. They are getting loads of hail over their way. Soon it will be Arizona saying, "Pack up, kids. We're bringing you down."

Jack sits back down and picks out "Let it Be" on his guitar while I continue to nurse my dizzy spell. I sit on the bed, propped up with both pillows, eyes shut against the whiteness of fog brightening the cabin.

In a book about healing I once read, blocked energy was suggested as a cause for dizziness. T. Lobsang Rampa would probably see it as a dark blob of energy spinning above my head. Then he'd do something mystical to clean my aura. My solution: lie still until the room stops spinning. Sometimes sleeping makes me recover more quickly. Sometimes it takes a couple of days to recover from a spell.

Once, when a dizzy spell came on, I was staying with a friend who gave me a remedy—a tincture of catnip. As I laid there motionless, I imagined I was dying. I felt terribly sad about dying, since I would never see my loved ones again. However, I knew with death, a release would come and there would be an end to my emotional pain. In that way, dying seemed like not such a bad idea. However, I didn't die. The catnip tincture just put me to sleep. When I woke again, I felt much better.

Jack sets the guitar down and gets up from the chair. He messes around in the kitchen. I can't see what he's doing as the firefinder is blocking my view. I do see the loaf of homemade bread drop onto the counter and then the refrigerator open and close.

"What are you making?"

"Grilled cheese sandwiches. Want one?"

"Yes, please."

I hear the process rather than see it—Jack placing two buttered slices of bread face down in the hot fry pan. I know he is slicing cheese as I hear the clunk of the knife hitting the cutting board. Soon, I smell the buttery bread toasting and cheddar cheese melting and my mouth waters.

This is an act of caring, I decide. Dr. Gilmore says caring for another starts with self-love, which is spiritual in nature, not sexual. It's necessary to learn to love the self, first—then you can truly love another. I can't wait to see the people I love. It will be amazing to be back home, to spend time with my sister and Mom and our many friends.

I fiddle with the fringe on the white afghan I crocheted from wool yarn. It keeps me warm as the fog thins and thickens, vaporous clouds creeping around the cabin, ghostlike, while Jack makes lunch. Soon, he brings me a perfectly browned grilled cheese sandwich cut diagonally and delivered on a green Melmac plate. I balance it on my stomach and, with cold fingers, pick up the warm sandwich, cheddar oozing in melty globs. I take a tiny bite and chew. The fog folds in and around the treetops, milky thick, but it's brighter now than when I hauled myself down to the outhouse earlier.

As a kid, when I said, "I'm dizzy," my stepdad would say, "Yes, you are." Which he thought was funny. I don't think sickness is a laughing matter, and it isn't a "Get Out of Jail Free" card. If you don't want to participate in life, just say so. In my growing-up-home, the only one with any power was Dick. Mom had migraines and I had terrible cramps. My brother had pleurisy and my sister, bouts of constipation. It's easy to make up stuff to get out of something you don't want to do, rebelling against a schedule, a responsibility, or a person. But sickness is also a way for the body to cope with the bad stuff that's happening.

As we eat our sandwiches, the sun breaks through the clouds and fills the tower with diamond-bright light. The sandwich is a miracle. The day suddenly seems miraculous too. Jack fixes me a cup of tea. He's being so nice, not complaining at all about my sickness adding additional responsibility to his day. That's the way it should be.

The heater pumps out hot air that smells of summer dust. The sun breaks past wisps of fog and shines inside. We decide Jack will take the motorcycle to town the following day and buy a plug at the junkyard for the Scout's transmission drain. He'll stop in at the forest service office and talk to Arizona, see about our responsibility for closing the tower for the season. And he'll stop at the farmer's house on the way back up the mountain to repair the Scout. The motorcycle will fit in the back of the Scout perfectly and, once tied down, will stay safe during the ride back up the mountain.

Jack sits on the bed next to me. We look into each other's eyes, meeting in our usual way—though he is hard to read right now. I wonder, *What if Arizona wants us to stay on with the forest service after the season? I know we could use the money, but the doctor I want to see practices in Spokane. There's always the doctor in Lewiston, I guess.*

I open my mouth to speak and close it again. I feel frightened and unsure. Of course, I could drive myself to Spokane to see Mother's doctor. We'd need an apartment in Grangeville. I'd miss the heck out of Jack if I stayed away for long, but they say absence makes the heart grow fonder. Maybe it would be good for us both.

"I didn't use to be brave," I say. "But this job has made me stronger." I think about the Scout breaking down and how competent I was in getting back home.

"In some ways, you're braver than me," Jack says.

"Maybe," I say. "But I'm lonely and want to go home." I look around the cabin, knowing I will miss tower life, but it's time to resolve this health issue and get on track with having a child.

Winter has arrived. Or at least fall, though already the snow levels have dropped and we can see a faint snowline on the higher hills. The tower is cold this morning. The hiss of the propane heater combines with the sound of the whistling tea kettle. I turn off the stove and make two cups of hot tea.

Jack wipes humidity from the window with the sleeve of his sweater. "Steamy," he says, turning to me. He raises his eyebrows and touches his tongue to his upper lip. "Got plans for the afternoon?"

"You're funny," I say, carrying the tea to the table.

"Why not? There's frost on the catwalk."

I take a seat and turn to look outside. A crystalline sheen whitens the deck, the rails, and beyond. "This December, let's not light candles on our Christmas tree."

"Why not?" Jack says, and takes a seat next to me. He rests his hand on my thigh. I place my hand on top of his.

"Fire," I say. "We should continue fire watch, even when we're back home." I nudge the plate of blond brownies toward him.

"If we ever get home," Jack says, grabbing a cookie.

"We will. You'll see." I sip my tea, recalling huge piles of snow lingering at Priest Lake when we started work in the spring. Priest Lake is isolated, though not as isolated as we are here. Hardly anyone stays over the winter in the Hill's uninsulated cabins. Most cabins have the water heaters drained, antifreeze poured in the toilets, and the windows boarded up. But a few people live year-round at the lake, driving to Priest River to work or working as linemen to restore power after a huge windstorm or a heavy snowfall breaks trees over power lines.

A friend of ours once told us about the regulars drinking at the corner tavern during the winter. I imagined the bar lights sparkling off partially filled liquor bottles, the smell of spilt beer, the smattering of regulars. He said he'd climbed onto a barstool and ordered a beer. The lit jukebox played Willy Nelson. The pool tables sat empty, and someone down the bar sat with her forehead resting on her arms, weeping. *Bummer*, I thought.

Idaho's drinking age is nineteen. I became a legal drinker in Idaho after we married, but not the first summer we stayed at the campground. That summer when I was only eighteen, we snuck into the bars. They never checked my ID, not that I recall, anyway. After we finished up at the resort last season, we readied our truck for a road trip around the US. People warned us that taking off in the fall was a bad idea. We would surely run into bad weather. We shrugged off their concerns, assuring them that all would be fine.

And it was, though we almost immediately drove into a howling blizzard while driving through the mountains of Montana. I recall Jack clutching the big steering wheel of the old Ford bread truck as we navigated the snowy pass. I was terrified, biting my fingernails as we pushed through the driving snow, the tanned bear skin we'd nailed to a sheet of plywood tied to the top of the truck flapping in the wind. The truck did fine, but a big wind gusted at one point, breaking the plywood ties and sailing the plywood off the top of the truck and over the mountainside.

It was a bummer, those high winds and blowing snow, but even worse, what if our sailing sheet of plywood had hit the car behind us? When I think back, it seems I knew at a deep level that any of us could bite the dust at any time. And then, this tough life would be over.

By the time we started downhill, the snow had retreated from its furious assault. We breathed more easily as the truck careened smoothly through the black of night, headlights reflecting off winter flakes and plowed berms piled high at the edge of the highway.

We traveled down, down, down into Montana, pulling into a KOA where we parked for the night. We heated soup and ate saltines and drank shots of Southern Comfort before turning in, exhausted but exhilarated. Far out: we were off on our honeymoon road trip.

I look up from my daydream and turn to the forest. "Oh man, it's snowing."

Jack looks outside. "Shit, yes!"

I feel cozy in my gray sweater. And our cabin atop Corral Hill is staying warm enough with the propane heater, but just barely. "We should call Arizona," I say. "Tell him it's snowing."

"He probably already knows. Look at Camas Prairie."

I look past him. "I can't see anything."

"Shit, that's what I mean. It's coming down hard out there."

"Bummer," I say, moving toward the radio.

"Thought you were scared of the radio!"

"Oh, brother," I say. "I'm a seasoned lookout now." I pick up the radio to call and return the mic immediately to its holder. "I'll call tomorrow," I say. "There's nothing we can do now. Besides, *Green Acres* is on in a minute. Don't want to miss it."

The snow falls steadily while the cast of *Green Acres* tries to get Arnold the pig to predict the weather. The flakes are tiny, barely visible until you look beyond the catwalk into the distance. Then the white of the falling snow looks similar to fog or smoke. Or just a misty cloud, like the one that has been sitting over us for the past couple days.

And then it stops, the sun comes out, the trees drip, and the catwalk turns slushy. When *Green Acres* is over, Jack goes down to the outhouse. He returns with a couple of boxes from the truck. Soon, I have our stores packed away. Our clothes are all dirty in the heaped-up laundry basket, minus a few items still in the drawers beneath the bed.

"Really, when Arizona does call us down, it won't take us long to move out." My heart leaps when I look around. It's funny, the feeling of longing arising in me. Both for the tower in the Clearwater National Forest and for my home in Spokane.

epilogue

We are accustomed to dense woods, mountain streams, wind, rain, heat, lightning, isolation, and the smell of piss and outhouse mixed with dry, browning undergrowth. And, of course, fog! And now, just like that, we live on Magnolia Street in Jack's childhood neighborhood with its bare magnolia trees, raked lawns, tidy paint jobs, washed and waxed cars, and tall pines carpeting the ground with a thick blanket of needles.

It is mid-October and already the first frost has flattened Spokane's vegetable gardens and the last of the fall flowers. After the drive down from Corral Hill in the Clearwater National Forest, we left the Scout on a consignment lot and headed for Spokane. The bread truck is now parked outside in the driveway while we set up in Jack's old bedroom.

It all seems too convenient, the ease of living with electricity, running water, and modern plumbing. Luxuries everyone appears to take for granted. I reach around people to turn off lights and switch off faucets left running too long, receiving rude looks from family members and friends in return. It is, however, cool to not have to haul drinking water uphill from the stream, and even better not to descend three stories to use the outhouse in the middle of the night.

Squeak asked Jack to sweep up every pine needle in the front yard, including those completely covering the shake roof. Jack Sr. said to bag them and stack the bags by the driveway, readying the needles for the dump. A neighbor has a truck. He has offered to load the bags along with everyone's yard waste and drive them to the dump sometime next week. Several bulging black plastic bags already line the curb beyond our parked bread truck. They look like giant black jack-o-lanterns in need of scary orange faces.

Jack's father scurries around the corner of the garage with a handful of additional black plastic bags. He'll help Jack fill them with the sharp brown needles swept into piles along the driveway. Jack doesn't like climbing on roofs. Pine needles are slippery, rolling stiffly together like tiny straws. Once he refused to sweep leaves off a cabin roof at Hill's Resort. Our boss demanded that Jack do as he was told. But Jack shook his head and walked away. His boss grew furious and ordered someone else to climb the ladder to the roof. That guy promptly slid off, falling to the ground and breaking his arm. But these pine needles aren't wet, just a rolling brown carpet, slick as rain-soaked tower stairs.

Jack bends to pick pine nuts off the needle-littered driveway. He cracks one between his teeth, extracting the tiny nutmeat and spitting out the shell.

His father says, "Time's a-wastin'. Go on, now." He holds the ladder steady against the eaves.

Jack steps onto the first rung, then the second. Obviously, neither of us fear heights—I mean, we've been living at forty-five feet for nearly six months now. I stand back, shivering in the chilly fall air, watching the two of them spar. Squeak's in charge and Jack resists his authority so he can be in charge too.

Jack takes his time sweeping needles off the roof with the push broom. Brown spears rain down like straw in a windstorm. He stops and spits a shell in an arc from eave to driveway. I know how much he relishes the piney white meat the size of a grain of barley.

Like everything, size eventually gets compared. My new doctor says the mass in my abdomen is the size of a chicken egg. The first doctor compared it to a lemon. Whatever size they imagine, it will eventually shrink to the size of an apricot, then cherry, then pea, and to a grain of rice, and finally, *prest-o change-o—gone, kaput, finis.*

There is a protocol, of course. The doctor says the medicine is expensive and I'll need both shots and pills that will stop my periods for a year. Without the medicine, the cysts won't dry up. Apparently, there isn't just one mass, but many globs of errant tissue hanging out here and there in my abdomen. The doctor calls the cysts "endometriosis." Once the year has passed, I'll take hormones that will encourage ovulation. And then, a pregnancy and live birth.

We have a little money saved from the summer on the tower, but probably not enough to cover all the doctor's visits and expensive medicine. I express my concern about the cost of the medicine. The doctor says to ask my father for help. I imagine calling my stepdad but decide we are officially estranged, since he never wrote back to me.

Not speaking with each other seems right, but it also makes me feel sad. I'm sure it will drive a wedge between my sister and me. I've decided to ask my mother about my real father. I hope I can meet him some day. Maybe that will fill the ache in my heart for a father's love. But, for the time being, I have my mother, my father-in-law, and my sister and her husband. And of course, I have Jack.

THE END

afterword

Many adventure stories have the hero or heroine off exploring, expending physical energy, fighting the elements and dangerous situations, and eventually reaching their goal. An adventure could be as minor as taking a walk on a winding trail through an old-growth forest, rafting a summer swift river, walking from quaint village to village in Ireland, or manning an isolated lookout tower for a season. For some people, reading stories about others' adventures is enough. For others, including me, doing something different and physically demanding has enlivened my life more than once.

Jack and I camped and worked at Priest Lake in Idaho, we drove the bread truck around the United States, we climbed mountains including the 7,350' Gunsight Peak in the Selkirks. We had run-ins with black bears, broke down on motorcycle trips deep in the mountains, attended huge rock concerts (though smaller than Woodstock), and bought a mini farm, becoming first-time farmers for a few years in the late '70s. All of these events culminated with our ultimate adventure, having a child in our mid-twenties.

Now, in my seventh decade, I'm pretty happy walking three miles a day with our new dog, Lucy. Still I dream of living on a tower again. There are still towers that are manned for fire season! On many you can get reservations and stay a few nights, much like an Airbnb, only you have to carry in your own food and water (which weighs a lot) and use an outhouse. It wouldn't be cushy, but it would be fantastic!

Part of this daydream includes the desire to spend time in nature . . . another part is this weird calling I feel to live in isolation, at least for a short while, which seems both terrifying and life-changing to me. I'm not entirely sure why I desire such an experience—something about surpassing fear and settling into a mindset of delight in each moment of living here on our beautiful earth.

I did learn a lot about myself the night a lightning storm built on the horizon while staying overnight at Park Butte Lookout— a seven-mile hike to a historic lookout that sits on a rocky butte at 5,450' overlooking a glorious view of the Mt. Baker Wilderness and a closeup of Koma Kulshan and Easton Glacier. When I saw the storm clouds building to the southeast and witnessed the first flash of lightning on the horizon, I grew terribly frightened. Park Butte Lookout, built in 1932, was held together with cables and turnbuckles. It also had a metal bed with springs and a mattress, metal desk, and a metal table with plastic containers for drinking water collected from melted snow. There was no longer a fire-finder in the center of the room; still, the room didn't have any lightning-safe areas to sit. And the woman whom I spoke to at *Friends of Park Butte* said, "You don't want to be in the tower during a lightning storm."

I decided that if the storm came close, I could run into the night and huddle in the alpine forest. Even that seemed dangerous to me—maybe safer than inside, but the storm never came close enough for me to abandon the lookout. I spent a sleepless night, and on the way down the mountain, I talked to campers who said the thunder was loud and the storm came close, and "yes," they were frightened. Still, the adventure proved something to me . . . I was much braver when I was twenty-one than I was in my fifties.

Something good came from that overnight stay. I felt a soul satisfaction that is hard to achieve otherwise. An adventure not only gives a person a physical accomplishment to be proud of, but it also leaves a person with a story to tell their grandkids and possibly great grandkids. "Did I ever tell you about my big adventure living on a fire lookout tower with your Grandfather Jack back in the '70s?"

I hope you've enjoyed *Struck*, and that you continue to find deep satisfaction from the little and big adventures in your life.

Carpe Diem,
Nancy Canyon

acknowledgments

STRUCK: A Season on a Fire Lookout, would not exist without those who supported my many attempts at shaping this story into a book. Thanks to Robert Ray and Jack Remick for teaching me to write scenes and plot them with Aristotle's Incline. Thanks to Cheryl Strayed, whose memoir, *Wild*, helped me realize the shape of my story. Special thanks to all my writing-practice friends who wrote and edited with me through the years. Because of you, these pages came to life, first in my journal and now in a published memoir: Brenda Miller, Katie Humes, Lorinda Boyer, Gerri Luginbill, Deb Brosten, C.J. Prince, Susan Erickson, Carla Shafer, Rae Ellen Lee, JS Nahani, Courtney Putman, Eileen Gribble, and many more. And to my early readers: Anneliese Kamola, Barbara Clarke, Linda Suther, Jenni Cottrel, Anita Boyle, Loretta Etchison, Kay Little, Kristen Van Bodegraven, Katie Dexter, and Ron Pattern—much appreciation for your invaluable feedback. Thanks to my editor, Dana Tye Rally, and to those who championed this story: Cami Ostman, Laura Kalpakian, and Laurel Leigh (RIP). Thank you to my publisher, Lisa Dailey, for her creativity, astuteness, and patience. Thank you to Andrea Gabriel for spinning her cover design magic using my collage of Corral Hill, the newspaper article, and old photographs. Thanks to my friends who worked as fire fighters, forest rangers, and lookout attendants during the same era, and who regaled me with lively stories, bringing the times back to life. And to my sister who said, "This is your book and your story, write freely." To my husband, who read different versions of *STRUCK*, ad nauseum, as the memoir evolved—thank you for loving this book as much as I do. And for loving me.

about the author

Nancy Canyon is the award-winning author of *Celia's Heaven* (novel), *Saltwater* (poetry), *Dark Forest* (short stories) and publisher of *Women's Bodies, Women's Words* (anthology). Her writing has appeared in numerous publications, including *Writing the Land: Channels*, *I Sing the Salmon Home: Poems from Washington State*, *True Stories*, *Raven Chronicles*, and *Water~Stone Review*. She holds an MFA in Creative Writing from Pacific Lutheran University and a Certificate in Fiction from the University of Washington. She launched her writing career in '97 while studying with Natalie Goldberg in Taos, New Mexico.

Ms. Canyon works as a writing coach for The Narrative Project, an instructor for Chuckanut Writers, and as a fine artist affiliated with Women's Painters of Washington. She is a Writing the Land poet and a member of the Forest Fire Lookout Association. She lives near Lake Whatcom in Bellingham, Washington, with her husband Ron Pattern and their dog Lucy. For more about Ms. Canyon, see www.nancycanyon.com.